THE ENGLISH

Short Story

1880 - 1945

A CRITICAL HISTORY

TWAYNE'S CRITICAL HISTORY
OF THE SHORT STORY

William Peden, General Editor
University of Missouri-Columbia

The American Short Story, 1850–1900
> Donald Crowley, University of Missouri-Columbia

The American Short Story, 1900–1945
> Philip Stevick, Temple University

The American Short Story, 1945–1980
> Gordon Weaver, Oklahoma State University

The English Short Story, 1945–1980
> Dennis Vannatta, University of Arkansas-Little Rock

The Irish Short Story
> James F. Kilroy, Vanderbilt University

The Latin American Short Story
> Margaret Sayers Peden, University of Missouri-Columbia

The Russian Short Story
> Charles Moser, George Washington University

THE ENGLISH
Short Story

1880 - 1945

A CRITICAL HISTORY

Joseph M. Flora, Editor

University of North Carolina at Chapel Hill

Twayne Publishers

The English Short Story
1880–1945:
A Critical History

Copyright © 1985 by G. K. Hall & Company

All Rights Reserved
Published in 1985 by Twayne Publishers
A Division of G. K. Hall & Company

70 Lincoln Street, Boston, Massachusetts 02111

Printed on permanent/durable
acid-free paper and bound in
the United States of America

Book production by Marne Sultz
Book design by Barbara Anderson

Typeset in 11 pt. Perpetua
by Compset, Inc. of Beverly, MA

Library of Congress Cataloging in Publication Data

Main entry under title:

The English short story, 1880–1945.

(Twayne's critical history of the short story)
Bibliography: p. 165
Includes index.
Contents: Introduction / Joseph M. Flora—
The exotic short story : Kipling and others
Robert Gish—D.H. Lawrence / Weldon Thornton—[etc.]
1. Short stories, English—History and criticism.
2. English fiction—19th century—History and criticism.
3. English fiction—20th century—History and criticism.
I. Flora, Joseph M.   II. Series.
PR829.E53   1985   823'.01'09   84-22450
ISBN 0-8057-9357-7

Contents

Acknowledgments

I am grateful to William Peden for his work as General Editor of this series and for his long-time dedication to the short story. I wish also to thank Alan Baragona, Christine Lape Flora, Alan Spearman, and Anne Zahlan for their suggestions and help with bibliographic detail. Diana Dwyer and Jo Gibson have been of immense assistance in typing chores. Most of all, I thank Robert Gish, Weldon Thornton, Joanne Trautmann Banks, Richard Harter Fogle, James Gindin, and William Peden for their efforts to refocus attention on some major achievements in a rich period of the English short story.

Chronology

1850	Robert Louis Stevenson born, 13 November.
1857	Joseph Conrad born, 3 December.
1865	Rudyard Kipling born, 30 January.
1870	H. H. Munro born, 18 December.
1874	W. Somerset Maugham born, 25 January. Walter de la Mare born, 25 April.
1878	A. E. Coppard born, 4 January.
1879	E. M. Forster born, 1 January.
1881	P. G. Wodehouse born, 15 October.
1882	Stevenson, *New Arabian Nights*. Virginia Woolf born, 25 January.
1885	Stevenson, *The Dynamiter: More New Arabian Nights*. D. H. Lawrence born, 11 September.
1887	Stevenson, *The Merry Men and Other Tales and Fables*.
1888	Kipling, *Plain Tales from the Hills, Soldiers Three: A Collection of Stories*, and *Wee Willie Winkie and Other Child Stories*. Katherine Mansfield born, 14 October.
1891	Kipling, *Life's Handicap*.
1893	Stevenson, *The Bottle Imp* and *Island Nights' Entertainments*. Kipling, *Many Inventions*.
1894	Stevenson, *The Ebb Tide: A Trio and Quartette*. Jean Rhys (Ella Gwendolyn Rees Williams) born, 24 August. Stevenson dies, 3 December.
1895	Kipling, *The Jungle Books*. Stevenson, *The Amateur Emigrant from the Clyde to Sandy Hook* and *The Body Snatcher*.
1896	Stevenson, *Fables, The Strange Case of Dr. Jekyll and Mr. Hyde, with Other Fables*, and *The Suicide Club*.

1898   Conrad, *Tales of Unrest*. Kipling, *The Day's Work*.

1899   Maugham, *Orientations*.

1902   Conrad, *Youth: A Narrative, with Two Other Stories*. Kipling, *Just So Stories*.

1903   Conrad, *Typhoon and Other Stories*. Wodehouse, *Tales of St. Austin's*.

1904   Kipling, *Traffics and Discoveries*. H. H. Munro, *Reginald*. Graham Greene born, 2 October.

1905   H. E. Bates born, 16 May.

1906   Kipling, *Puck of Pook's Hill*.

1908   Conrad, *A Set of Six*.

1909   Kipling, *Actions and Reactions*.

1910   Kipling, *Rewards and Fairies*. Munro, *Reginald in Russia and Other Sketches*.

1911   Forster, *The Celestial Omnibus*. Mansfield, *In a German Pension*. Munro, *The Chronicle of Clovis*.

1912   Conrad, *'Twixt Land and Sea*. William Sansom born, 18 January.

1914   Lawrence, *The Prussian Officer and Other Stories*. Munro, *Beasts and Super-Beasts*. Wodehouse, *The Man Upstairs*.

1915   Conrad, *Within the Tides: Tales*.

1916   Stevenson, *The Waif Woman*. Munro dies, 14 November.

1917   Kipling, *A Diversity of Creatures*. Wodehouse, *The Man with Two Left Feet*. Woolf, *Two Stories* (with Leonard Woolf).

1919   Munro, *The Toys of Peace and Other Papers*. Wodehouse, *My Man Jeeves*. Woolf, "Kew Gardens."

1920   Mansfield, *Bliss and Other Stories*.

1921   Coppard, *Adam and Eve and Pinch Me: Tales*. De la Mare, *Story and Rhyme*. Maugham, *The Trembling Leaf*. Stevenson, *When the Devil Was Well*. Woolf, *Monday and Tuesday*.

1922   Coppard, *Clorinda Walks in Heaven: Tales*. Lawrence, *England My England and Other Pieces*. Mansfield, *The Garden Party and Other Stories*. Wodehouse, *The Clicking of Cuthbert*.

1923   Coppard, *The Black Dog and Other Stories*. Mansfield, *The Dove's Nest and Other Stories*. Wodehouse, *The Inimitable Jeeves*. Mansfield dies, 9 January.

1924   De la Mare, *Ding Dong Bell*. Mansfield, *Something Childish and Other Stories*. Munro, *The Square Egg and Other Sketches, with Three Plays*. Wodehouse, *Ukridge*. Conrad dies, 3 August.

1925 Coppard, *Fishmonger's Fiddle: Tales*. De la Mare, *Broomsticks and Other Tales*. Wodehouse, *Carry On, Jeeves*.

1926 Bates, *The Seekers*. Coppard, *The Field of Mustard: Tales*. De la Mare, *The Connoisseur and Other Stories*. Kipling, *Debits and Credits*. Maugham, *The Casuarina Tree*. Wodehouse, *The Heart of a Goof*.

1927 Bates, *The Spring Song and In View of the Fact That . . . : Two Stories*. De la Mare, *Told Again: Traditional Tales*. Rhys, *The Left Bank*. Wodehouse, *Meet Mr. Mulliner*.

1928 Bates, *Day's End and Other Stories*. Coppard, *Silver Circus: Tales*. Forster, *The Eternal Moment*. Lawrence, "Rawdon's Roof" and *The Woman Who Rode Away and Other Stories*. Maugham, *Ashenden*.

1929 Bates, *Seven Tales and Alexander*. Wodehouse, *Mr. Mulliner Speaking*.

1930 Bates, *Pink Furniture*. De la Mare, *On the Edge*. Lawrence, *Love Among the Haystacks*. Mansfield, *The Aloe*. Munro, *The Short Stories of Saki*. Pritchett, *The Spanish Virgin and Other Stories*. Wodehouse, *Very Good, Jeeves*. Lawrence dies, 2 March.

1931 Coppard, *Nixey's Harlequin: Tales*. Maugham, *Six Stories Written in the First Person Singular*. Wodehouse, *The Jeeves Omnibus*.

1932 Bates, *The Black Boxer*. Coppard, *Fares Please*. Kipling, *Limits and Renewals*. Lawrence, *The Lovely Lady*.

1933 Bates, *The House with the Apricot and Two Other Tales*. Conrad, *Complete Short Stories*. Coppard, *Dunky Fitlow: Tales*. De la Mare, *The Lord Fish*. Maugham, *Ah King: Six Stories*. Wodehouse, *Mulliner Nights*.

1934 Bates, *The Woman Who Had Imagination and Other Stories* and *Thirty Tales*. Lawrence, *A Modern Lover* and *The Tales of D. H. Lawrence*.

1935 Bates, *Cut and Come Again*. Coppard, *Polly Oliver: Tales*. Greene, *The Basement Room and Other Stories*. Wodehouse, *Mulliner Omnibus* and *Blanding's Castle*.

1936 De la Mare, *The Wind Blows Over*. Maugham, *Cosmopolitans: Very Short Stories*. Wodehouse, *Young Men in Spats*. Kipling dies, 18 January.

1937 Bates, *Something Short and Sweet: Stories*. Coppard, *The Ninepenny Flute: Twenty-One Tales*. *The Short Stories of Katherine Mansfield*; Wodehouse, *Lord Emsworth and Others*.

1938 Bates, *Country Tales: Collected Short Stories*. Pritchett, *You Make Your Own Life*.

1939   Bates, *The Flying Goat: Stories* and *My Uncle Silas: Stories*. Coppard, *You Never Know, Do You? and Other Tales*. Greene, *Twenty-Four Stories*. Lawrence, *Stories, Essays and Poems*. Weekend Wodehouse.

1940   Bates, *The Beauty of the Dead and Other Stories*. Maugham, *The Mixture as Before*. Wodehouse, *Eggs, Beans, and Crumpets*.

1941   Woolf dies, 28 March.

1942   Bates, *The Greatest People in the World and Other Stories by Flying Officer "X."* De la Mare, *Best Stories*.

1943   Bates, *How Sleep the Brave and Other Stories by Flying Officer "X."* De la Mare, *The Magic Jacket and Other Stories*. Woolf, *A Haunted House and Other Stories*.

1944   Bates, *Something in the Air*. Coppard, *Ugly Anna and Other Tales*. Sansom, *Fireman Flower, and Other Stories*.

1945   De la Mare, *The Scarecrow and Other Stories*. Mansfield, *Collected Stories*. Pritchett, *It May Never Happen and Other Stories*.

1946   Coppard, *Selected Tales*. De la Mare, *The Dutch Cheese and Other Stories*.

1947   Bates, *Thirty-One Selected Tales*. Coppard, *Dark-eyed Lady*. Forster, *The Collected Tales*. Maugham, *Creatures of Circumstance*.

1948   Coppard, *Collected Tales*.

1951   Coppard, *Fearful Pleasures*. Maugham, *The Complete Short Stories*.

1952   Maugham, *The Complete Stories*.

1954   Coppard, *Lucy in her Pink Jacket*. Greene, *Twenty-One Stories*.

1956   De la Mare dies, 22 June.

1957   Coppard dies, 13 January.

1963   Bates, *Seven by Five: Stories 1926–1961*. Greene, *A Sense of Reality*.

1965   Maugham dies, 16 December.

1967   Greene, *May We Borrow Your Husband*.

1968   Rhys, *Tigers Are Better Looking*.

1969   Maugham, *Seventeen Lost Stories*.

1970   Forster dies, 7 June.

1971   Lawrence, *The Princess and Other Stories*.

1972   Forster, *The Life to Come and Other Stories*.

1973 Greene, *Collected Stories*. Woolf, *Mrs. Dalloway's Party: A Short Story Sequence*.

1974 Mansfield, *Undiscovered Country: The New Zealand Stories*. Bates dies, 29 January.

1975 Wodehouse dies, 14 February.

1976 Rhys, *Sleep it Off, Lady*. Sansom dies, 20 April.

1979 Rhys dies, 14 May.

Introduction

The English Short Story, 1880–1945 celebrates both the birth of the short story in England and its richest period there. Whereas the years 1880–1920, described by Helmut E. Gerber as "not only the kindergarten of the short story but its university,"[1] may have witnessed the international flowering of short fiction, the genre took a somewhat independent course in Great Britain. The year 1920 did not, as Gerber recognizes, mark any end of British achievement in the form: many of those who discovered its potential in the early years of the century had much of their best work ahead of them in 1920, and there were others who in that year had yet to begin. Virginia Woolf argued that human nature had changed in 1910 and with it British literature. As she heralded the arrival of the modern period, she was certainly aware that the writers who were making the English literary scene marvelously vibrant were often master short-story tellers. She learned from them, made her own contribution to the genre, and welcomed others who helped make it a major British form, at least through 1945.

The British, it is true, had been somewhat tardy in recognizing the potential of the short story, a genre sharply defined in theory by Edgar Allan Poe and natural to the practice of the great American prose writers of the nineteenth century. At about the time that the British were just learning the lessons of Poe and Maupassant, William Dean Howells observed: "I am not sure that the Americans have not brought the short story nearer perfection in the all-around sense than almost any other people."[2] Howells suggested that the form is "peculiarly adapted to the American temperament" because of the national tendencies to speed and impatience. But he also offered a theoretical explanation for the development of the genre in his native land, citing the phenomenal success of American magazines. Howells was, of course, writing as an editor of *Harper's*, one of the most prestigious of such magazines, but his vision was broad. He saw American magazines creating a climate for short stories almost to the exclusion of the serials that characterized British and continental magazines and newspapers. He declared that because of the operation of supply and demand, the art of writing short stories had become in America "so disciplined and diffused" that periodicals suffered no lack of them.

Increased demand prompted by a new proliferation of periodicals (and perhaps too by the transatlantic migration of the haste and impatience Howells had earlier noted in America) also operated in Great Britain. Interest in the newer fiction also altered the traditional English periodical with its preference for the serialized novel. When Victorian high seriousness was countered by the "art for art's sake" movement of the last two decades of the nineteenth century, English writers abandoned expansiveness and turned for models to the Continent. To be sure, many of the Victorian prose giants had written "shorter" tales. One thinks of Dickens's *A Christmas Carol* (1843) or George Eliot's *Scenes of Clerical Life* (1858). But narrative economy was not natural to Dickens and Eliot, and they— like their peers—preferred a broad canvas. Even Thomas Hardy, who may lay strong claims to being a modern poet, belongs essentially to the Victorian tradition in his novels and in his three collections of short tales: *Wessex Tales* (1888), *Life's Little Ironies* (1894), and *A Group of Noble Dames* (1891).

The Victorians, concerned as they were with the social order, found the broader canvas of the novel particularly congenial. In America, on the other hand, there was a dearth of established forms and institutions that, Nathaniel Hawthorne had argued, impoverished the national experience. Perhaps in part because of the paucity of the subject matter that inspired the English realists, much of nineteenth-century American fiction was romantic, and American writers turned to the tale as a fitting vehicle for the fantasy, the romantic, and the grotesque that gripped their imaginations. These elements, hardly congenial to Victorian England, are often the essence of the modern short story, which strives—like romantic poetry—for unity of atmosphere and effect. Thus, as the nineteenth century and its literary traditions receded, younger writers in England (like James Joyce in Ireland) found that they had much to learn, not only from such European masters of short fiction as Anton Chekhov and those French writers who had learned their Poe, but from the Americans and especially Poe himself. His critical tenets, exalting art over nature, had seeped into Victorian England and were at last embraced in the "Decadent" reaction against Victorianism at the end of the nineteenth century: if art be superior to nature, the short story is an ideal form for attaining Walter Pater's desired quality of the "gem-like flame."

While the "art-for-art's sake" school was accompanied by a certain amount of foolishness, it brought to England many attitudes that fostered the development of the modern short story. The omniscient narrator, compelled to describe and explain, plays a diminished role in a form given to beauty and to implication of meaning through structure. Appropriately *The Yellow Book*, that prototypical creation of the fin de siècle, looked very different from the established periodicals of the nineteenth century. Its color and book format and its Beardsleyan art work were the more obvious signs of the change in direction manifested in the nature of its fiction. The fiction published in *The Yellow Book* was not particularly shocking in subject matter; it was, however, decidedly short—even the stories by Henry James. And much of it was by writers—like James—who can now be seen to have had a hand in shaping the modern English short story: Ella D'arcy, Hubert Crackanthorpe, George Gissing, John Buchan, Arnold Bennett, and H. G. Wells.

For several reasons, *The Yellow Book* was short-lived, lasting only from 1894 through 1897. So was its offshoot, *The Savoy*, founded after Beardsley was forced to leave his position with *The Yellow Book* in the aftermath of the Oscar Wilde scandal of 1895; it lasted only one year, 1896. (Even though Wilde had been purposely excluded from *The Yellow Book* and even though he and Beardsley were not friends, in the public mind they were both linked with the unusual periodical.) But *The Yellow Book* and *The Savoy* helped to make a point, and the birth of other periodicals after World War I created new outlets for the short story. Among these were the *Criterion*, edited by T. S. Eliot, the *London Mercury*, edited first by J. C. Squire, then by Middleton Murray, and later by Max Plowman and Richard Rees. The little magazines were, of course, legion, and many did not endure. But their importance to the rise of the modern short story in England is considerable in that they provided many outlets for writers. By publishing short fiction, the more secure periodicals helped writers to support themselves while they also labored on novels. But for many of these writers, the short story was not just a source of income but a vehicle attractive in itself, a challenge worthy of strenuous effort. It is apparent in the 1980s, when the market for short stories is very limited, how fortunate these writers were in finding a publishing climate right for their experimentation.

If the British short story triumphed during the period surveyed in this book, many devotees of the genre have decried a steady decline in the genre in England since World War II, and some have concluded that the current state of the art is moribund. No single fact can account so decisively for the waning of British achievement in the genre as the decline of publishing opportunities after World War II. Since then, writers have tended to look to the universities and to television for support. Most commentators agree that the climate for the cultivation of the short story is not now nearly so healthy as it was in the first half of the century. Lovers of the form will, understandably, look at the period covered by the essays in this book with some nostalgia.

As many critics have observed, the first major writer in the British Isles to specialize in the short story was Robert Louis Stevenson. His "A Lodging for the Night," first published in the October 1877 *Temple Bar*, is generally recognized as the first modern British short story. "Markheim" (1884), Stevenson's most famous short story, suggests something of Poe; however, Stevenson's emphasis on strong moral conflicts could as easily remind readers of Nathaniel Hawthorne. "Thrawn Janet" (1881) removes the reader to seventeenth-century Scotland where belief in witches and the Evil One was as vivid to the community as ever it was to Hawthorne's New England Puritans. Even Stevenson's longer works show that he saw the value of a limited scope. He was—again like Hawthorne—attracted to the suggestiveness of romance rather than to the expansiveness of the traditional novel. His *Dr. Jekyll and Mr. Hyde* (1886) and *The Beach of Falesá* (1882) are works of the middle range. Even his *Master of Ballantrae* (1889), a fine example of romance, is not a lengthy work. But Stevenson was not, ultimately, as morally earnest as was Hawthorne, and he did not pursue ambiguity as consistently as Hawthorne did. He attracts most powerfully through the lure of the remote, the strange, the exotic, and so helped inaugurate one of the major traditions of the modern British short story, a tradition that Robert Gish in the first essay of this collection calls the exotic short story.

As Gish's essay reveals, a major portion of the exotic tradition was the story of empire and later of expatriation. The British Empire, on which the sun never set, included climates and conditions and peoples that could intrigue readers in England by their very strangeness. Short fiction, sometimes as splendid journalism, lent itself easily to portrayal of and reflection on the unusual. The British were, understandably, eager for reports on the vivid forms of life "out there."

There were, of course, changes in emphasis as the exotic short story developed. A large part of Kipling's appeal was journalistic. Although Kipling's narrators may sometimes tease readers with suggestions of their deeper unrest, his characters are mainly men of action—heroic and colorful, but not reflective. Readers seldom experience the nerves of these characters. Those writers who followed Kipling increasingly saw possibilities for revealing deeper secrets of the psyche. Joseph Conrad's "The Secret Sharer" (1912) is surely a tale of suspense and high adventure, but it is also a memorable portrayal of the double self—a self divided against itself. Conrad's finest portrayal of the double self is his *Heart of Darkness* (1902), a work beyond the short story, but nevertheless short fiction—and indispensable to twentieth-century literature. As Gish charts the history of the exotic short story in England, we see that by mid-century the journalistic origins of the theme of the divided self have been largely submerged by an emphasis on the personal. Expatriation or foreignness had become less and less literal and more and more metaphorical.

In the final reckoning, the most intriguing of the British short-story writers in the period before World War II may be D. H. Lawrence. Although Gish does not explore Lawrence among his company of exotics, Lawrence's appeal often touched on the strange and bizarre, and he was literally an expatriate and a wanderer who could never find home. Many of his works, especially his later works, attract in part for the same exotic reasons that Kipling's tales attracted. Lawrence's "The Princess" (1924) (set in the mountains of New Mexico) bears noticeable kinship to Kipling's masterpiece "The Man Who Would be King" (1888). Lawrence's later stories (again like Kipling's) sometimes deal with the mythic or occult or preternatural. The most famous example is "The Rocking Horse Winner" (1926), but there are others: "The Border Line" (1924), "The Woman Who Rode Away" (1924), and—perhaps his strangest story—the novella "The Man Who Died" (1929).

Of course, Lawrence was often powerfully exact and precise about the England he knew best. (Ernest Hemingway claimed that it was Lawrence who had taught him how to "do" country.) Certainly a story like the famous "Odour of Chrysanthemums" (1909, revised 1911) evokes the world around Nottingham with the kind of particularity that we find in *Sons and Lovers* (1913). The event of that story is, of course, all too commonplace in the mining communities of Lawrence's day and our own. But Lawrence managed to take his readers quite unforgettably into the mind of the wife whose husband dies in a mining accident. That story, like many of Lawrence's, stays lodged in the reader's memory.

The place of D. H. Lawrence in the history of the modern British short story is, then, both multidimensional and major. Many would argue that he and James Joyce have been the most important practitioners of the short story from the British Isles. Probably Joyce's influence has been greater, even though after Joyce learned from the genre what he wanted, he set it aside. The art of short fiction was useful to Lawrence throughout his life. For the most part, our questions about Joyce's *Dubliners* (1914) and their place in his progress have been answered. For Lawrence, as Weldon Thornton persuasively argues in his essay, the matter is otherwise. Thornton both defines the issues of the current state of criticism on Lawrence as a writer of short fiction (and in part as writer of fiction) and insists that the hard work of reading Lawrence's short fiction has just begun. Thornton faults the critics for not recognizing that Lawrence's approach to character is very different from that of Henry James or James Joyce (Lawrence is, for example, frequently compared with Joyce and criticized for not following a Joycean model). Calling for more attention to contextuality in a Lawrence story, for less confusing of the levels of characters' consciousness with their author's views, Thornton makes his case with pointed references to "An Odour of Chrysanthemums," "The Prussian Officer" (1914), "The Blind Man"

(1920), and especially "England, My England" (1915, 1921). Although he warns against letting preconceptions about Lawrence's ideas or philosophy take over the analysis of a story, he recognizes that there is a moment when the reader should seek congruences between the needs and motives of the characters and Lawrence's ideas.

Lawrence, as is well known, had little use for James Joyce, finding him a dirty mind and a pernicious influence. But no account of the modern English short story could fail to pay tribute to the profound impact of the Irishman's work on the genre in England. Chief among those who learned from Joyce was Virginia Woolf, who—though she also had reservations about some aspects of Joyce—paid him memorable homage. It is difficult to imagine Woolf's work without taking into account Joyce's achievement. And, as Joanne Trautmann Banks reminds us in her essay, Woolf saw Joyce as a writer who could "take a slight situation and read in it the profundities of life." Although Woolf looked increasingly to the novel to sustain her (Banks suggests that Woolf's need for a unifying element accounts, at least in part, for that preference), and although the volume of Woolf's production in the short story is not great, the short story was especially appropriate to her vision precisely because Woolf found her greatest skill in portraying moments of illumination.

Katherine Mansfield's name is frequently paired with that of Virginia Woolf, and Banks acknowledges that for both the Joycean example is major. From the start, readers compared Woolf and Mansfield, and the comparison is apt for a number of reasons that Banks assembles with great deftness. Unlike Woolf, however, Mansfield was exclusively dedicated to the shorter form, and in her brief life she produced a sizeable and important body of short fiction. Charting the development of Mansfield's career, Banks substantiates her claim that among writers of the short story Mansfield is "arguably her generation's best practitioner in English."

But best practitioner of a kind of short story, some readers would insist to Banks. While Woolf and Mansfield, influenced as they were by Joyce, must be counted as avant-garde writers, there were other writers little concerned with new directions, who harkened back to the very English tradition of the comedy of manners, especially as polished by the Edwardians. For Americans, it could be argued, the work of Saki (H. H. Munro) and P. G. Wodehouse represents a special strand of British exoticism that has managed to stay exotic, that appeals by its remaining the same. The popularity with television audiences of *Wodehouse Playhouse* or a series like *To the Manor Born* testifies to the continuing viability of a comedy of polished wit. The British were noticeably resistant to the pull of naturalism, preferring presentation of the eccentric to the "slice of life." It is not surprising that the well-made comedy of manners would turn up in the guise of the short story. This hardy British variety was superbly cultivated by Saki and Wodehouse, to the delight first of the British public, and then of other English-speaking peoples as well. In the fourth essay of this book, Richard Harter Fogle analyzes the achievement of these two prolific writers, charting some interesting parallels between them, but defining as well the particular quality of each, and convincing us that their short stories were "concocted with an art that conceals art."

The penultimate essay of this collection, James Gindin's study of the short fiction of A. E. Coppard and H. E. Bates, also accents the solidly English, a conservative strain. Both Coppard and Bates put an emphasis on the plain and ordinary that has persisted in British fiction at least since Defoe. Indeed, like Defoe, Coppard and Bates were men of ordinary background. Like him, they were intent on avoiding the pretentious, the inflated—it seems appropriate to say, the exotic. With a marked preference for "country matters," they did not rely on symbolism or metaphor, but preferred the anecdote or direct representation of event and character. The flavor of the English countryside and the folk tale permeates most of Coppard's fiction, and although Bates's experiences in the Royal Air Force during World War II broadened his range, he too is probably best remembered for his scenes of the English countryside. In any case, Coppard and Bates—whose lives coincide with the period covered by this book—are not "modernists" in the sense that Woolf or Mansfield or Lawrence are. Neither do they write with the polished wit of Saki or Wodehouse, but they are masters of their kind, a kind significant in the history of the short story in England.

The final essay in this collection focuses on the important short fiction of V. S. Pritchett that was published before 1945. Since the first of these, *The Spanish Virgin and Other Stories*, had been published as early as 1930, Pritchett is solidly a part of the history of the short story before the post–World War II years. He continued to write short stories after the war, and in large part because of his work in fiction and criticism, he is considered by many one of the most able writers in English at the present time. He has no more fervent admirer than William Peden, whose essay here charts the course of Pritchett's early work—work that holds up very well even against Pritchett's later successes. A bridge to the postwar years, Pritchett's work may be our best evidence that it is too soon to announce the end of British success with the short story. Pritchett is, by any serious reckoning, an important figure in the history of the British short story.

There are several ways to approach that history. Readers wishing a running commentary on British and American short fiction of the period (as well as accounts of the short fiction of other nationalities) are well advised to consult the seven-volume *Critical Survey of Short Fiction* (1981), edited by Frank N. Magill. Two volumes discuss elements of short fiction and give historical overviews; five volumes survey individual authors. The approach of this new book is less encyclopedic than that of Magill's volumes, and the writers of these essays have been given a less prescribed format.

It goes without saying that this collection does not attempt to close discussion of the English short story. There are other ways of grouping short stories; there are other writers in the genre who deserve critical attention, and the bibliographies that follow the essays point to the achievement of some of these. If much work remains to be done before a fair assessment of the short fiction of D. H. Lawrence is finally achieved, the challenge to work on other short fiction is also real. The case of Sylvia Townsend Warner (1893–1979) is a case in point. Warner is hardly known in the United States, and her reputation is based chiefly on her novels. She has demonstrated range and power in the genre of the short story; she has had success in the realistic mode as well as the fantastic mode. Admitting that the achievement of Warner—and of others of her British contemporaries—is also deserving of study, the six essayists who wrote for this book have, nevertheless, suggested some of the currents of change in short fiction, accented a range of traditions within the genre, and celebrated some masters. The present collection is an invitation to fuller exploration, a challenge to closer scrutiny of the English short story, 1880–1945. It is, above all, a celebration.

Joseph M. Flora

University of North Carolina
at Chapel Hill

THE EXOTIC SHORT STORY:
KIPLING AND OTHERS

Exoticism is only one theme, one concern of the British short story in the first half of the twentieth century, but it is an important one. Much of the fiction by major writers of this period reflected a new interest in travel, tourism, and settlement in faraway places. Usually writers who turned to distant and exotic settings achieved their greatest distinction in the novel. Nevertheless, the short stories of such writers, aside from reinforcing their "companion" longer fiction—novellas and novels—are of considerable importance on their own terms. Colonialism, with all its complexity of motive and result, underlies all such interest in so-called "exotic" fiction. E. M. Forster's account of the British experience in India, *A Passage to India* (1927), regarded by some as, like Joyce's *Ulysses*, one of the greatest novels of the twentieth century, is probably the most obvious example in novel form of the biographical and artistic passages associated with British colonialism and exoticism.

Forster's novel, however, and the travels that brought it into being, is one of many instances of exoticism and the larger forces behind it. Forster himself wrote several short stories that can be classified as exotic. But he is part of a larger tradition which in Britain includes, most notably, Robert Louis Stevenson (1850–94); Joseph Conrad (1857–1924); Rudyard Kipling (1865–1936); W. Somerset Maugham (1874–1965); and Graham Greene (b. 1904). Others also bear mentioning in this context, among them: Walter de la Mare (1874–1956), Jean Rhys (Ella Gwendolyn Rees Williams, 1890–1979), and William Sansom (1912–76). And still other masters of the short story form—like D. H. Lawrence (1885–1930) and Theodore Francis Powys (1875–1953)—qualify, at least tangentially, as explorers of the exotic—Lawrence in such stories as "The Princess" and "The Woman Who Rode Away" set in the American Southwest and Mexico—and Powys in the strange fables of a Dorsetshire made alien and known under such aliases as Dodder, Madder, and Folly Down. Assuredly, not all of these authors are interested in exotic themes in identical or exclusive ways. For one thing, not all of them write about the same places. However, whether their stories are set in India, Malaya, Africa, Mexico, the Caribbean, Paris, or even rural England, they dramatize the conflicts of personality and culture experienced by travelers in lands which—whether distant or near—are indisputably strange.

The reactions of these authors to remote places and their native peoples are by and large the reactions of wanderers, expatriates, or even refugees who find themselves in realms of exile and estrangement, of threatening "adventure." In spite of their common ground, however, there are striking differences in style. Even so, each is preoccupied with the interactions of the British interloper and the indigenous native in a locale which to the one is familiar and to the other is strange. Such interactions go far in identifying exoticism in a modern British short story. Analysis of such interrelationships of character and setting will make possible a truer definition and a better understanding of exoticism both as impulse and as a major literary mode of modernism.

Exoticism has not developed in the modern British short story only. As both theme and as literary mode, it is part of the much larger Western tradition of romantic adventure narrative, extending from Homer's *Odyssey* and Dante's *Divine Comedy* through the beginning of the novel's picaresque tradition in *Don Quixote*, continuing through the eighteenth century with accounts of encounters with odd and foreign sights such as Swift's *Gulliver's Travels* and in the nineteenth with the eponymic escapades in canto form of Byron's *Don Juan*, and finally emerging in the exotic narratives of such present-day writers as V. S. Naipaul and Paul Theroux.

Much of American literature, moreover, is by its very nature an exotic enterprise—from early colonists' diaries of settlement in the New World to assessments by both residents and visitors, like Alexis de Tocqueville's *Democracy in America*. Certainly, the frontier forays of Irving's Captain Bonneville and Cooper's Natty Bumppo suggest the continuing exoticism of the recording and imagining of the American West, a land characterized by sublime topography, strange flora and fauna, and, most exotic of all, the American Indian, known variously as "savage" and friend. The journals, diaries, and "reports" of famous explorers like Lewis and Clark, and later, Captain John Charles Fremont, of writers like Mark Twain and more or less anonymous Westerners such as prospectors in the California gold rush—all bespeak the exoticism of the American West.[1]

In addition, as old frontiers have disappeared and new ones opened up, the adventure narrative has evolved into science fiction—yet another strain of literary exoticism. All literature is not, of course, reducible to exotic themes and modes, but it is true and should be emphasized that the exotic aspect of modern British short fiction is but the shadow of a magnitude, a characteristic common to a large body of national and narrative literatures.

Ian Watt attributes the fact that the exotic became a major mode of later nineteenth-century European literature to the fashion earlier set by Chateau-briand (1768–1848) and by Byron (1788–1824) and suggests that the formulae for such popular romances—at least those which involved a love story and a happy ending—were current in the literary marketplace as Conrad found it when his first novel, *Almayer's Folly*, was published in 1895 and when his earliest short stories came out in 1896.[2] In France, Watt reminds us, the novel about foreign lands became immensely popular at the dawning of the twentieth cen-tury with the writings of Pierre Loti (1850–1923). And in England, Kipling and Stevenson, and then at a lower literary level Rider Haggard (1856–1925), were the pioneers in the exotic story. As for Conrad, Watt believes, "there is no reason to suppose that [he] was particularly indebted either to Stevenson or Kipling beyond their part in creating an audience for exotic narrative."[3]

Even so, there are elements of plotting and characterization, of setting and atmosphere—shared by Kipling and Conrad, and by Maugham, Forster, Greene, de la Mare, and Sansom. Lines of influence, even tradition, can be clearly estab-lished. Whatever the degrees of influence, each of several modern British story-tellers, each with his own individual adaptations, helped establish the exotic short story as a major literary genre in English.

In his definition of the exotic short story, W. Somerset Maugham credits its British beginnings to Kipling:

[The exotic story] is the story, the scene of which is set in some country little known to the majority of readers, and which deals with the reactions upon the white man of his sojourn in an alien land and the effect which contact with peoples of another race has upon him. Subsequent writers have treated this subject in their different ways, but Rudyard Kipling was the first to blaze the trail through this new-found country, and no one has invested it with a more romantic glamour, no one has made it more exciting and no one has presented it so vividly and with such a wealth of colour. He wrote many stories of other kinds, but none in my opinion which sur-passed these. He had, like every writer that ever lived, his shortcomings, but remains . . . the best short-story writer that England can boast of.[4]

Details of Kipling's role in the development of exoticism in the modern British short story temporarily aside, Maugham's definition is inseparable from consid-erations of British colonialism in all of its political and racial, philosophical and psychological, complexity—and beyond that it is similarly inseparable from both the causes and the results of the *angst* and alienation associated with mo-dernity. Furthermore, the importance of geography, or as it is usually termed, of setting, is of major significance. One notion that connects exoticism as Kipling developed it with those authors who, like Maugham, if not directly influenced by him, found him exemplary, is this: in varying degrees Kipling and the others were, in different generations and in different places, expatriates, travelers separated from their homeland by their own volition—individuals who in the process of coming to terms with their own brand of self-imposed exile among strangers, incorporated elements of the exotic worlds they knew firsthand into the artistry of their stories.

Such geographical and aesthetic tourism is an integral part of one of the most comprehensive and self-defining modern ideas, the idea of alienation, the puzzlement of belonging or not belonging to a landscape, of knowing one's home. In this respect, the very act of writing for others who share the author's original home and, as Maugham suggests, know little of the new and alien country being written about, has important rhetorical implications, implications about isolation in relation to community.

Maugham's definition of the exotic short story is decidedly ethnocentric: the "reactions" he is concerned with are those of the white man; the "effect" of "strange lands and peoples" which to him is significant is the effect on the white man. The varieties of point of view and tone possible from such an authorial stance are nevertheless much wider than Maugham may seem to have suggested. Alien lands and peoples—the "otherness" of it all—can, after all, be rejected or accepted, idealized or ridiculed. Thus the leeway for irony or satire in all their guises is immense in exotic short fiction.

Although he does not cite Maugham and is not discussing either exoticism or the short story as such, Jeffrey Meyers in his study of the colonial novel in effect amplifies Maugham's definition. Meyers sees colonial fiction as forming two large streams, "one of them in the tradition of Kipling's early stories, the other deriving from *Kim*, Conrad and Forster."[5] The first stream Meyers sees as composed of pure romantic-adventure novels that operate primarily in terms of stereotypes and melodrama. About this kind of colonial novel Meyers observes:

[T]here is no real involvement with the stereotyped native, who is important not as an individual but as an example of what the Englishman must overcome and suppress; nor with the traditional culture or the tropical setting, which merely serves as an exotic background. And the white men are overwhelmingly triumphant against the treacherous and greedy natives, usually with the help of their loyal and self-sacrificing counterparts. The heroes . . . are physically strong but shallow and uninteresting, and they generally do not learn anything from their adventures. There is a clear distinction . . . between good and evil, and all moral issues are seen from only one point of view. Everyone who disagrees with the hero is either foolish or evil, and the villain is clearly delineated.[6]

Meyers sees the other kind of colonial novel as of a much better quality, the work of novelists who "find in the tropics a great lure and attraction, a great temptation to atavism, a universal fascination with the savage and the incomprehensible."[7] (The colonial novel may very well be restricted to tropical locales as Maugham and Meyers suggest, but it should be understood that exoticism in fiction is not necessarily limited to the tropics—for deserts, mountains, many "sublime" climatic zones can provide exotic settings.) The novelists Meyers analyzes are Kipling, Forster, Conrad, Cary, and Greene. Characterizing their colonial novels further, Meyers asserts that these novelists,

by taking the archetypal night journey, by returning to pure nature uninhabited by man, . . . can also return to a free unconscious state and liberate the repressed primitive element in themselves. They feel that the acquisition of technological civilization has caused serious damage to the human spirit, which can perhaps be redeemed by a temporary return to a more primitive and prelapsarian element. [These writers] understand the vast potentialities for portraying the dramatic contrasts and tensions of men caught between two civilizations. Their novels evaluate their own civilization and moral standards, and consider two important questions: what happens to the "civilized" white colonist when he is confronted with an alien culture? And what happens to the natives and their culture under colonialism?[8]

Meyers profiles the protagonists of the colonial fiction of Forster, Conrad, Cary, and Greene as typically modern antiheroes; "quiet, defensive, undistinguished, yet sympathetic . . . , they are somewhat disappointing and limited, for they are victims of circumstances they cannot master. They are seriously compromised by the colonial situation, and have an awareness of their own guilt and complicity in it."[9]

Such generalizations must be adjusted somewhat to fit the attitudes and the overall character and conflicts of the protagonists found in the stories of the many English writers who lived and traveled in exotic places and transformed their experiences into short-story form. Although exoticism in literature is a more comprehensive category than colonialism, much of what Meyers says of the colonial novel complements Maugham's initial outlining of the boundaries of exoticism as found in the short fiction of Kipling and of those who, like Maugham himself, came afterwards and were either directly or indirectly affected by him.

Whatever the other qualities that contribute to exoticism, it is far from static and is by definition concerned with interrelationships among white "stranger," indigenous "native," and (as observed by oftentimes empathetic but nevertheless ethnocentric British writers) alien landscapes. It is against the background of this definition that the exoticism of several modern British short stories can now be examined.

There is general agreement that the nature of the short story, whether exotic or otherwise, began to change during the last quarter of the nineteenth century. In England this change in short fiction was completed by the time of the transition from late Victorian to Edwardian-Georgian, a transition to modern times and temperaments. Like Maugham, most observers of literary history single out Kipling's short fiction as marking the watershed in the development of the modern British short story, noting that, among other devices such as his unique use of irony, his economical, reportorial openings "launched the true short story in England."[10] Notwithstanding the American influence of Edgar Allan Poe (1809–49) and the nineteenth-century continental influences of Guy de Maupassant (1850–93) and of Anton Pavlovich Chekhov (1860–1904), Kipling is still the modern figure who most influenced the direction in which the short story developed in England.

With his first volume of short stories, *Plain Tales from the Hills*, published in 1888, Kipling simultaneously advanced and synthesized the techniques and concerns of Poe (the supernatural and fantastic); of Maupassant (anecdotal focus, economy, and realism); and of Chekhov (devotion to atmosphere and an intimate feeling for place). Thus he is not, as he is typically considered, just the dominant late nineteenth-century spokesman for British imperialism and industrialism, but also a prominent practitioner of the modern exotic story.[11]

Kipling, like Maupassant, is concerned with anecdote and plot for their own sake; he is also, like Chekhov, adept at the creation of atmosphere and setting. In the many biographical and critical studies of Kipling, repeated mention is made of the importance of place—be it England, India, Africa, America, or elsewhere—to his life and art and for the source material that his wanderings provided. Angus Wilson cites Kipling's "persistent evasion of introspection" and his reluctance to question the source of his characters' anxiety as the failing that keeps him from attaining the rank of Chekhov.[12] On the other hand, Wilson contends, Kipling's greatest strength was perhaps the imaginative world he created out of the real world, a place of artifice but "always [with] its own powerful and exact geography of place and colour and smell and touch."[13]

It can be argued that Kipling's evocation of place, so memorable to his readers, is for him—as it is for the other authors in the exotic tradition analyzed here—at once the external and internal source of the alienation of his characters. It should be observed, too, that exotic, otherworldly places described in realistic detail make for a blurring of the boundary between fantasy and fact and make Kipling, as Bonamy Dobrée contends, both realist and fabulist.[14] Certainly Forster took a different, more liberal and scolding attitude toward imperialism than did Kipling; however, Forster's "fantasies," as he called them in the intro-

duction to *The Collected Tales* (1947), place him squarely in the tradition of exoticism inaugurated by Kipling.

In taking the title of *The Strange Ride of Rudyard Kipling* (punning on "The
Strange Ride of Morrowbie Jukes"), Angus Wilson's biography of Kipling points
up not just Kipling's journey through life but the fact that many of his characters
are also travelers and tourists in alien lands, observers and reporters of strange
convergences of life in one place to audiences who live in another. In this sense,
Kipling's own voice, though variously disguised, seems (like Byron's) invariably
identical with the voice of his narrators. What Randall Jarrell says of Kipling can
thus also be said of his characters: "Kipling was no Citizen of the World, but,
like the Wandering Jew, he had lived in many places and known many peoples,
an uncomfortable stranger repeating to himself the comforts of earth, all its
immemorial contradictory ways of being at home."[15]

As in the closely autobiographical story "Baa Baa, Blacksheep" (1888), the
account of a tormented child's separation from his parents and his forced alienation as a "black sheep," Kipling's own voice is very much present in *Plain Tales
from the Hills*. As a journalist and recorder of colonial happenings for vicariously
enthusiastic readers "home" in England, Kipling the traveler-reporter editorially
intrudes to judge personages and events—so that although primarily an observer he is a participant as well. There is recognizably much of the author in his
narrators, his personae, and in the composite characters whose lives he
dramatizes.

In "Thrown Away," for example, the point to Kipling's story (clearly his
"moral") is that "There was a Boy once who had been brought up under the
'sheltered life' theory; and the theory killed him dead."[16] Since his story ends in
suicide, Kipling's protagonist, known only as the Boy, affords the life-lesson that
"coming out" to India in all of its strangeness and for all of its luster of romantic
exoticism is serious business—so serious that naive and cloistered virtue is of
little use in such a different and lonely world. In India the Boy and all Englishmen who come there—unless they adapt and toughen up, as do the narrator
and the British major, who take an empathetic interest in the Boy and cover up
for his suicide—are left to their own devices and are easily "thrown away"—
like the Boy's life and the letters of grief and guilt found with his body. Essentially what the Boy fails to realize, after he takes his work, his gambling, and his
women "too seriously" for some months, is the all too obvious fact that India is
not England.

A more supernatural tale of alienation, guilt, and death in a remote land is
"The Phantom 'Rickshaw" (1885), in which the complexities and confusions of
frame narrative as Kipling uses it add to the "dark and disturbing" mood estab-

lished, even before the story begins, in the epigraph. This is a tale about the mental and emotional dissolution and consequent death of Theobald Jack Pansay, a Bengal civilian whose shocking experiences we learn both from his own letters and through the reminiscing of a primary narrator who knew both Pansay and Doctor Heatherlegh, the physician who attempted to rid him of his hallucinations and the guilt which presumably prompted them. In "The Phantom 'Rickshaw," which exemplifies Kipling's use of "frame" narrative and multiple points of view, it is the first-person account of the secondary narrator, Pansay, which holds the attention of the reader. The effect of the story within the story, told by a speaker racked by fever and agitated by "blood-and-thunder magazine diction" (*BRK*, 71), as of the more abbreviated epistolary accounts in "Thrown Away" (in many ways a draft version of this story), is to reinforce the isolation of the protagonist as a stranger in a strange land.

Doctor Heatherlegh fails to appreciate fully the darkness of Pansay's mind and the "realities" of his exotic experiences, preferring to counsel (much like the narrator and major in "Thrown Away") that in India (Simla) one should at all costs avoid becoming distraught. His motto is "lie low, go slow, and keep cool" (*BRK*, 70). But if ever there were a tormented soul incapable of following advice under circumstances so fatuous, it is Pansay. Having first taken Mrs. Agnes Wessington as his mistress, then tiring of her, and finally hating her, Pansay ceases all attention to her and ruthlessly ends the affair. His engagement to Kitty Mannering, however, provokes Mrs. Wessington's death. It is her reappearing ghost, always seen in the rickshaw where she had learned of Pansay's and Kitty's engagement, which relentlessly follows Pansay—accompanied by the "Powers of Darkness"—to his grave.

Ironically, Pansay is both pursued and left alone. His sightings of Mrs. Wessington, her phantom yellow rickshaw, and his ever more disturbed and shaken reaction to such horrors, alienate him from Kitty and the Anglo-Indian society of Simla. Pansay's exotic aberrations become both the cause and the effect of his madness. Mrs. Wessington's ghostly encounters with Pansay are all the more spine-chilling for their civility. The obsessed Pansay is completely lost in the "numbing wonder that the seen and the unseen should mingle so strangely on this earth to hound one poor soul to its grave" (*BRK*, 85).

"Thrown Away" and "The Phantom 'Rickshaw," then, both point to the life-threatening psychological dangers inherent in Britain's imperialistic occupation of India—a place not only of exotic beauty but, as Kipling presents it, of sinister disorientation, a place that calls for a special toughness of mind and psychological and spiritual adaptations.

If India is a place of potential madness for those visitors who cannot adapt, it is also portrayed by Kipling as a world where adherence to certain laws and duties, where loyalty and responsibility to friends, can lessen the exotic dangers. Few readers of *The Jungle Books*—whether children or adults—can forget the courage in the face of threats to survival that marks the Mowgli fables. Clearly, Kipling's jungle world is one of his most beautiful and most alien. Mowgli, however, does adapt and learn his lessons about the "Law," and in "Kaa's Hunting," a story of initiation, Kipling illustrates the crucial importance of complying responsibly with new ways when instructed in them. Mowgli learns with some trauma the negative results of the anarchy that the Bandar-log (the Monkey People) represent.

As part of the Jungle People, those on the ground and not in the trees, Mowgli is told by his assigned mentor, Baloo, the Brown Bear, that any dealing with monkeys is taboo, for they are dirty and shameless and crave the attention of the Jungle People who must, out of their own sense of dignity, refuse to notice them. (Parallels with Swift's Yahoos in the final book of *Gulliver's Travels* come to mind—including the element of misanthropy in the irony of the inferiority of the humanly shaped Bandar-log.) Mowgli's antics especially interest the Bandar-log because he, in his human, physical outlines, resembles them. Thus they think him a potential leader and kidnap him while he sleeps between the protective Baloo and Bagheera the Panther. As prisoner, Mowgli is whisked away through the trees, his trail marked only by Chil the Kite, who reconnoiters for the Seeonee Wolf Pack and Mowgli's jungle brothers.

Since Kaa the Rock Python is the mortal enemy of the Bandar-log, his assistance in rescuing Mowgli is essential. If Baloo and Bagheera want Mowgli returned out of love and pride, Kaa's motive is more cunning, for he loathes the Monkey-People who have dared call him "earthworm" and "speckled frog." Besides, he is hungry.

If ever protagonist faced an unknown and exotic surrounding, it is Mowgli at Cold Lairs, the Lost City where he is taken and kept, hidden away in a rotting summerhouse while Bagheera and Baloo, and finally Kaa, storm the ruins to save him. Captive in the lost city (not wholly unlike the American inventor held prisoner in Africa in Kipling's story "The Captive"), Mowgli is nonetheless not impervious to the exotic splendor around him:

Mowgli had never seen an Indian city before, and though this was almost a heap of ru'ns it seemed very wonderful and splendid. Some king had built it long ago on a little hill. You could still trace the stone causeways that led up to the ruined gates where the last splinters of wood hung to the worn, rusted hinges. Trees had grown into and out of the walls; the battlements were tumbled down and decayed, and wild creepers hung out of the windows of the towers on the walls in bushy hanging clumps. (*BRK*, 312)

Although Bagheera and Baloo wage a noble war against the monkeys, it is Kaa who saves Mowgli, the Panther, and the Bear. Kaa's satisfaction comes in the meal of Bandar-log that his victory secures him. Bagheera and Baloo are happy for their lives and for Mowgli's deliverance. Mowgli's satisfaction is in accepting the punishment meted out to him by Bagheera and the Law, which requires that "Sorrow never stays punishment" (*BRK*, 319). Mowgli's temporary separation from his animal brothers and his forced journey to the Lost City has steeled him for further tests of maturation and knowledge. In the Mowgli stories, then, exotic places and circumstances serve constructive rather than destructive purposes; they can affirm the victory of life and growth over the death that vanquishes the Boy in "Thrown Away" and Jack Pansay in "The Phantom 'Rickshaw."

Perhaps the most famous example of Kipling's exoticism is "The Man Who Would Be King," which, though written in the late 1880s, early in Kipling's career as a writer of short stories, remained unsurpassed. Both for its realistic and romantic assumptions and techniques, it represents the epitome of Kipling's early exoticism. Here place and event are twice removed in the telling—again creating a double-framed narrative distance. Certainly the journalist who relates his exotic meeting and dealings with the two soldiers of fortune and "gentlemen at large," Peachy Carnehan and Daniel Dravot, relates a strange tale, and he relates it from a remote spot in India. Moreover, he is, in a significant sense, a vagabond colleague of Carnehan and Dravot and an actor in their drama. However, it is Carnehan's tale, which he tells to the journalist three years after having left with Dravot to become kings of Kafiristan, that carries the exotic elements of the story to their climax.

This is not just a tale of India, Afghanistan, and ambition. It is a tale of extremes—the remotest of locales in India and Afghanistan—of heat and cold, of light and darkness, of refined and rough character, of striving for the highest of prizes at the greatest of risks. Thus, the humor of the story is more than outweighed by its horrors—for both the journalist narrator who hears and tells of these two loafers who would be kings and for the reader who becomes an accomplice in the grand scheme.

The various extremes of setting and action and the shifts in point of view contribute significantly to the story's exotic effect. It begins with the journalist-narrator on a train in transit to Mhow from Ajmir heading into the central Indian desert, into Jodhpur territory. In this no-man's land, the narrator first meets Carnehan and undertakes to deliver a cryptic message to Dravot, described as a big red-bearded man, at the Marwar Junction. The encounter, the message, the parties involved—all are bizarre. Identities, blurred by mysterious impersonations and curious roles, change as swiftly as the train moves through

India. It is not only the narrator's chance meeting with Carnehan, his curious message, and its delivery that are odd; his own purpose for travel and his destination, though presented somewhat matter-of-factly, are also decidedly strange.

Leading a double life himself, the narrator-journalist, both friend and traitor, reports Carnehan and Dravot to authorities who intercept the two schemers and turn them back from the Degumbar borders. It is later as he writes obituaries of colonists and muses about the more exalted happenings on the other side of the world in England that a second strange meeting takes place with Carnehan and Dravot. In the dark and heat of a late Saturday night the two travelers make a surprise appearance before the journalist. At this meeting Carnehan and Dravot announce their plans to go to the remote corner of Afghanistan to a mountainous province called Kafiristan, there to rule as kings. Although he aids the two adventurers again, this time with maps and information, the journalist tells them that if they attempt such a mission they will be "cut to pieces" and warns them about the place—"It's one mass of mountains and peaks and glaciers, and no Englishman has been through it. The people are utter brutes, and even if you reached them you couldn't do anything" (*BRK*, 135). Appropriately, they leave from the most chaotic of locations within the city, the Kumharsen Serai, the one disguised as a ragged priest, and the other as his servant. Claiming to be heading to Kabul through the Khyber Pass to sell toys to the Amir, they are outlandish even for the Serai.

The last encounter with Carnehan, two years after his departure with Dravot, is, however, the most bizarre. Again the night is hot in the pressroom, the hour is late, and the journalist's nerves are taut. A "rag-wrapped, whining cripple," Carnehan enters, a scarred and twisted semblance of his former self: "He was bent into a circle, his head was sunk between his shoulders, and he moved his feet one over the other like a bear" (*BRK*, 139). Reduced to the circumstance of a beggar, he tells his adventurous tale of Dravot's rise to king of Kafiristan— and offers his friend's severed (but gold and turquoise-crowned) skull as grisly evidence of their joint fall. Carnehan's tale, and Kipling's, of the journey, the stay, and the flight from Kafiristan provide the climax of the story, but the ironic juxtapositions of points of view and the graduated degrees of remoteness from England all contribute to the powerful exotic effect of "The Man Who Would Be King."

Evidence that Kipling's exoticism extends into his twentieth-century stories and is of a whole with them, allowing him to utilize the themes and devices refined in so many of his early narratives, is provided by two stories set in Africa: "The Captive" (1902) and "Little Foxes" (1909)—two narratives that ambivalently reveal the at once idealizing and disillusioned attitudes he held toward British colonialism in the new century.

"The Captive" reflects Kipling's firsthand knowledge of South Africa and the Boer War. One of the most intriguing aspects of this story, however, is that it is neither the British nor the Dutch who provide the perspective from which the story is told. It is, rather, an American weapons and munitions inventor, capitalist, and soldier of fortune, Laughton O. Zigler, who narrates the motives and events leading up to his fighting for the Boers and his capture by the British. Significantly, too, for what it seems to reflect of both Kipling's attitude and that of the British and Dutch, black Africans are ironically on the periphery of things—alluded to merely as casualities.

Certainly the voice of the narrator, as well as that of Zigler himself, is ironically humorous, even glib, in the face of the human deaths and destruction wrought by the new artillery weaponry being put to the test (for economic as well as scientific reasons) in the war. Amid the civility shown him after the extended artillery exchange between conventional British guns and his newly conceived and built "Laughton-Zigler automatic two-inch field gun, with self-feeding hopper, single oil-cylinder recoil, and ball-bearing gear throughout," Zigler (stereotyped as the mercenary American) shields himself from the realities of death with the evasions made possible by racial blindness and the exigencies of advertising: "I was pleased right through that I hadn't killed any of these cheerful kids; but none the less I couldn't help thinking that a few more Kaffirs would have served me just as well for advertising purposes as white men. No, Sir. Anywhichway you regard the proposition, twenty-one casualties after months of close friendship like ours was—paltry."[17]

Although Kipling is notorious for his assumptions of the superiority of any white over the dark "infidel," he does not identify with Zigler, a man who commends his Dutch commander because he "didn't lose niggers." Here, Kipling's condescension, intended in good fun, is rather directed against Zigler and his zeal for the technology of war. In part, too, "The Captive" can be read as evidence of Kipling's equating both Americans (Zigler is described ambiguously as a "ginger-coloured," "native-born American") and Kaffirs as—in their respective ways—inferior colonials. Although Zigler is a good sport and does act out of principle in his insistence on remaining a captive along with his adopted Boer compatriots, and though Kipling does seem to admire his scientific ingenuity, neither Kipling nor the reader cares deeply about his fate. And this despite the lengths to which Kipling goes to depict Zigler as a talkative, red-blooded boy from Ohio, to show us his alienation behind a barbed-wire fence yearning to see, of all things, the ads at the back of *Harpers* or to read *Scientific American* "yet once more" (*RKS*, 31). Kipling satirically displays Zigler as superficial, as a loner doomed in his smug self-reliance, ironically confronting social and historical forces far larger than he.

In "Little Foxes" the native Ethiopians are more at the center of things than are the unfortunate Kaffirs of "The Captive." In this fable reminiscent of *The Jungle Books*, not only the native peoples but the Great River Gihon and the fox, "Abu Hussein," assume the magnitude of characters representative of abstract qualities of endurance and cunning. Irony, satire, and humor come into play again in this story, which attempts to ridicule what Kipling presents as the well-meaning but naive reform efforts of "New Era," anticolonial Britishers back home, persons like the indignant, crusading member of the House of Commons, Mr. Lethabie Groombride.

Having been told in exaggerated jest of the cruel policies of beating and mutilation implemented by the governor of the Gihon province of Ethiopia to expedite his fox hunts, Groombride organizes a committee and travels from England to the province to inquire into the reported inhuman excesses of the British colonists. Ironically, however, thanks to his uncooperative and mischievous interpreter who provides him with just the wrong word for his speech to the allegedly persecuted people of the Gihon valley, Groombride achieves nothing more than his own total embarrassment.

Subtitled "A Tale of the Gihon Hunt," Kipling's story had its source in an anecdote told him by an original "Master" of the Gihon Hunt, and the entire story functions mostly as a practical joke to demonstrate that the ways worked out by colonial administrators (be they ever so inane and selfish), when accepted by those governed, should not be changed—proving, in effect, that when it comes to the ways of empire as to those of Mowgli's jungle, the end justifies the means. The scheme the governor institutes to further his fox hunting and please himself and his hounds is a new law—a law of the hunt and not of British courts and judges. It requires that a dollar be given to every man on whose land Abu Hussein is sighted and another dollar to anyone on whose land Abu Hussein is killed. Those on whose land are found holes into which the fox can run, on the other hand, will earn only a beating. This precedent is observed over several generations of fox hounds and through the administrations of two governors.

The incidents, the "glories" of the Gihon Hunt, are described in terms of exotic violence and strange travelers: the time of "the kill in the market-place, when the Governor bade the assembled Sheikhs and warriors observe how the hounds would instantly devour the body of Abu Hussein; but how, when he had scientifically broken it up, the weary pack turned from it in loathing"; the time "when Abu Hussein forsook the cultivation, and made a six-mile point to earth in a desolate khor—when strange armed riders on camels swooped out of a ravine, and, instead of giving battle, offered to take the tired hounds home on their beasts" (*RKS*, 179). Relying on the log book of the Gihon Hunt, Kipling describes just enough of the feats of hounds and men to fabricate a "chronicle" of exotic and epic proportions. The hunt is the stuff of legends, exaggerated by non-Ethiopians in the interest of the "honour of Ethiopia." And for the sake of that "honour," too, reports the governor's emissary, ugly torture, exotic torture, is meted out to any who refuse to comply with the laws of the hunt.

To this tall tale Mr. Groombride listens in gullible horror: how men are beaten on the feet with a strip of old hippo-hide soaked in copperas and as sharp as a boar's tusk, a "chastisement" that often results in gangrene and a whole caste of amputees called "Mudir's Cranes" because "they are left with only one foot." With a disregard for natives similar to Zigler's in "The Captive," the inspector explains with playful irony the benevolence of the governor and his fox hunters:

We've a Hunt fund for hot tar. Tar's a splendid dressing if the toe-nails aren't beaten off. But huntin' as large a country as we do, we mayn't be back at that village for a month, and if the dressings ain't renewed, and gangrene sets in, often as not you find your man pegging about on his stumps. . . . We call 'em the Mudir's Cranes. You see, I persuaded the Governor to bastinado only on one foot. (*RKS*, 181)

Though the actual punishment amounted to no more than a few taps on the offender's shoulder, the inspector's "put-on" of Mr. Groombride seems to be rather perversely relished, as indeed, is Mary Postgate's killing of the young German aviator in another and even more disturbing of Kipling's war tales. Conrad, Maugham, Forster (in his own typically ironic way), and Greene, in their short fiction, make the horrors of atavism yet more frightening. But ironic treatments of the civilized retreat to savagery, of imperialism stripped of the varnish of salvation and progress, pervade the works of both the early and late phases of Kipling's exoticism.

Aldous Huxley in his classic essay "Wordworth in the Tropics" (1929) offers a theory of man's ambivalence toward nature that goes far to explain aspects of primitivism at once attractive and repulsive: "Our direct intuitions of Nature tell us that the world is bottomlessly strange: alien, even when it is kind and beautiful; having innumerable modes of being that are not our modes; always mysteriously not personal, not conscious, not moral; often hostile and sinister; sometimes even unimaginably, because inhumanly, evil."[18] Although Joseph Conrad's talents go beyond Kipling's, his early short stories, those of *Tales of Unrest* (1898), clearly point toward the continuation of the kind of exoticism Kipling introduced into the modern British short story. On their own terms and as important experiments in the genre, these early stories anticipate Conrad's novella masterpiece *Heart of Darkness* and significantly complement Kipling to the point that it is possible to say that Conrad must share with Kipling recognition for charting the early course of exoticism in the modern British short story.

Lawrence Graver, suggesting that Conrad in his early short stories owes Kipling more than a small debt,[19] is interested less in the "adventure-tale" exoticism of the two writers as in shared narrative techniques (insofar as such shared techniques can be separated from the subsuming literary mode)—especially point of view and tone, the mixing of "the jaunty and the macabre."[20] Despite his disapproval of Kipling's politics, Conrad did regard him as among the "first" of "people in literature who deserve attention" and wrote an essay (now lost) defending both himself and Kipling from the attacks of those who considered *Captains Courageous* and *The Nigger of the "Narcissus"* vacuous.[21]

Speaking of Kipling's "The Man Who Would Be King" and Conrad's "An Outpost of Progress," Graver sees similarities too close to be accidental: "Aside from the occasional tonal likeness, both stories describe the breakdown of two European egoists who had hoped to get rich quickly in a primitive society, and both end with scenes of slaughter and crucifixion."[22] In terms of both endings and exoticism, such comparisons can be drawn as well with several stories by Maugham, Forster, and Greene. (Although they are much less Kiplingesque, Conrad's "The Lagoon," and to a lesser extent "Karain: A Memory," also in *Tales of Unrest*, provide other classic examples of Conrad's exoticism.)

The irony in Conrad's title "The Outpost of Progress" is apparent from the story's beginning. As the director of ivory trading stations makes known on the visit that opens the tale, this particular outpost in the center of Africa is the most useless, and the two agents—Kayerts, the chief, and Carlier, the assistant—are the most stupid and unresourceful employees he had yet seen. This verdict is confirmed, too, by the other man on the staff of the outpost, Henry Price, a "Leone nigger" known by the natives as Makola. He despises the two white men and runs the affairs of ivory trading more or less in spite of his "superiors." Another presence, the cross-marked grave of the first chief and builder of the outpost, offers an ironic commentary on just how unprogressive, how regressive, the place, its purpose, and its chief and assistant really are. The first chief had died of fever just as he had completed his house, leaving things to Makola and his god—and the antagonistic spirit of place.

Left alone, with the inspector's promise to return in six months to check on their "progress," the two white men begin to see, insensitive as they are, the exotic and sinister forces they are up against:

They had been in this vast and dark country only a very short time, and as yet always in the midst of other white men, under the eye and guidance of their superiors. And now, dull as they were to the subtle influences of surroundings, they felt themselves very much alone, when suddenly left unassisted to face the wilderness; a wilderness rendered more strange, more incomprehensible by the mysterious glimpses of the vigorous life it contained.[23]

But it is not so much the incomprehensible wilderness around them that does them in—not the natives, not physical dangers imposed from the outside. It is the effect of isolation on their own inherent greed, their own jealousy, their own psychological inadequacy, that leads to their undoing. The theme of civilization's fragility, its veneers easily peeled away, which Conrad so masterfully develops in *Heart of Darkness*, clearly gets an early trial in the exoticism of this story as seen in this editorializing by the narrator:

The contact with pure unmitigated savagery, with primitive nature and primitive man, brings sudden and profound trouble into the heart. To the sentiment of being alone of one's kind, to the clear perception of the loneliness of one's thoughts, of one's sensations—to the negation of the habitual, which is safe, there is added the affirmation of the unusual, which is dangerous; a suggestion of things vague, uncontrollable, and repulsive, whose discomposing intrusion excites the imagination and tries the civilized nerves of the foolish and wise alike. (*TU*, 86)

For days into months the two white men languish in their solitude, reading a little, looking out on the mysterious life that surrounds them. Conrad's rendering of exotic atmosphere is effective in building the psychological tension that eventually will pit the two white men against each other. Their fate is as inexorable as the river and the forest which they see daily but ironically never understand: "On the sands in the middle of the stream, hippos and alligators sunned themselves side by side. And stretching away in all directions, surrounding the insignificant cleared spot of the trading post, immense forests, hiding fateful complications of fantastic life, lay in the eloquent silence of mute greatness" (*TU*, 90–91).

The natives, as Conrad characterizes them—Makola, the "civilized" assistant, old Gobila, chief of the neighboring village, the small group of dangerous men from coastal Loanda who come out of the forest with guns and ivory—offer no help to those whom civilization abandons. It is Makola who beguiles Gobila's people into getting drunk so that ten of them can be traded as slaves to the Loanda tribesmen in exchange for ivory. Old Gobila compounds the moral confusion by offering extra human sacrifices to placate "all the Evil Spirits that had taken possession of his white friends" (*TU*, 101).

At first condemning Makola's intrigues as inhuman, then swayed by the high quality of the ivory to applaud them, Kayerts and Carlier come to regard "oppression, cruelty, crime, devotion, self-sacrifice, virtue" (a whole litany of abstractions that the narrator intrusively comments on) as but empty words. The ideals of civilization are easily compromised in such remoteness. The white men become so disoriented that just at the end of their six-months stay, at the very moment the director in his steamer rounds the river to the post, they become mortal enemies over a lump of sugar for coffee—and who is in command of it. The magnitude of their moral compromises in accepting Makola's trade of men for ivory is equated with absurd trifles of authority and courtesy. In an ending as reminiscent of Maugham's stories "Mackintosh" and "The Outstation" as of Kipling's "The Man Who Would Be King," Kayerts shoots Carlier and then hangs himself on the cross that marks the grave of the first chief. When the director finds Kayerts, he looks at a swollen tongue, mockingly pointed at him—in the direction of progress and its "Great Civilizing Company."

If "An Outpost of Progress" can be viewed as a shorter, earlier, less successful version of *Heart of Darkness*, it is a more significant story on its own terms than many critics allow. Bernard C. Meyer, however, goes so far as to say that the story "stands above the rest of the short stories" written during Conrad's early period because of its "power and atmosphere."[24] In part at least, that power and atmosphere are attributable to exoticism, of which "An Output of Progress" is an early instance, a bridge from Kipling to Maugham and other later masters of the exotic tradition in the modern British short story.

W. Somerset Maugham, who, thanks only in part to William R. Benét and Desmond MacCarthy, came to be known as "the English Maupassant,"[25] began in earnest to write short fiction in the 1920s. He attributed much of his success to *Cosmopolitan Magazine* and its American editor, Ray Long (*SM*, 1: xiv), and he credited much of his conception of the genre to his experience as a dramatist: "I like a story that fits. I did not take to writing stories seriously till I had had much experience as a dramatist, and this experience taught me to leave out everything that did not serve the dramatic value of my story. It taught me to make incident follow incident in such a manner as to lead up to the climax I had in mind" (*SM*, 1: xx). Important also to Maugham's artistry as an author of short fiction was the fact that he had traveled several times around the world and in his travels found the materials for his stories.

From Maugham's first book of stories, *Orientations* (1899), to a posthumous edition of *Seventeen Lost Stories* in 1969, a dozen volumes of his stories have been published. He believed the best writers were prolific, what he called "copious." Urbane, precise, ironic, witty, competent—he has been labeled all of these things. His cynicism has been called cheerful, and his major theme has been generalized as that of "the world well lost."[26] Graham Greene observes that for most readers the name Maugham conjures up "adultery in China, murder in Malaya, suicide in the South Seas, the coloured violent stories which have so appreciably raised the level of the popular magazine."[27] Others agree that it is as a writer of "popular fiction" in magazines—and in adaptations for radio, film, and television—that Somerset Maugham is most widely known.[28]

It is fitting, then, to analyze briefly what is behind Maugham's "exotic" inclinations by a look at two of his most popular stories. They illustrate how important travel was in finding material for his stories, in his "search for emotion."[29] As with Kipling's and Conrad's exotic tales, one sees in Maugham just what geographical and human alienation and "exile" can mean.

Maugham's first gathering of exotic short fiction, *The Trembling of a Leaf* (1921), was subtitled "Little Stories of the South Sea Islands" and included such now-familiar tales as "Rain" and "Mackintosh." They are hardly "little" stories at all except in the sense of Thomas Hardy's versions of "life's little ironies." Characteristically, they are not stories about ordinary, "good" people on a pleasure-filled outing; rather they are tragic stories about peripheral men and women, people "on the edge," who find themselves in life and death situations. Although death and tragedy are universal, Maugham's rendering of character is his own. As Maugham explains it, "I write stories about people who have some singularity of character which suggests to me that they may be capable of behaving in such a way as to give me an idea that I can make use of, or about people who by some accident or another, accident of temperament, accident of environment, have been involved in unusual contingencies."[30]

On a sea voyage to Apia, Dr. Macphail, the compassionate survivor of events in "Rain" and himself a wanderer, encounters two Christian missionaries to the South Seas, Mr. and Mrs. Davidson, and the disreputable Sadie Thompson. When the ship is delayed at Pago-Pago, even the Davidsons, stationed in a district north of Samoa, find the island—volcanic rather than coral like theirs— alien; in Mrs. Davidson's judgment the place is more corrupt: "The steamers' touching makes the people unsettled; and then there's the naval station; that's bad for the natives. In our district we don't have difficulties like that to contend with" (*SM*, 1: 3). Dr. Macphail, Maugham, and the reader are all offended by the Davidsons' condescension toward the natives and their pagan customs, by the Davidsons' ironic alienation from the Christian assumptions of their work as missionaries. Maugham establishes the sanctimoniousness of the Davidsons, their puritanical aversion to any kind of carnality on the part of the natives (notably "marriage customs," dancing, free-flowing clothing such as the lava-lava), and prepares the reader for their pious labeling of the prostitute, Sadie Thompson (one of their own race), as a sinner and damned.

Symbolically, as the ship enters the harbor of Pago-Pago, rain begins to fall— a gentle rain at first and then, for the duration of their stay and the story, persistent, oppressive—as oppressive as the distorted Christianizing morality of the missionaries. A ten-day delay occasioned by an outbreak of measles on their schooner sets the stage for Mr. Davidson's attempted conversion of Miss Thompson and for his own disastrous succumbing to the temptations of the flesh.

As harlot, hussy, criminal, and repentant sinner, Sadie Thompson is an exotic character in her own right. Sadie, having come most recently from Iwelei, the red light district of Honolulu (described in detail by Maugham), her clothes and boisterousness go far in stereotyping her, especially for the missionaries and for Mrs. Macphail, who pronounces her tasteless and common, dressed in her showy "white frock" and "shiny white boots with their high heels, her fat legs bulging over the tops of them" (*SM*, 14). Never able to find a really "good" girl in any of the islands, the Davidsons find Sadie Thompson's looks and behavior utterly "sinful." Also stranded on Pago-Pago and made to board in a trader's house, along with the Davidsons and the Macphails, Sadie Thompson, actually a fugitive from a prison sentence imposed upon her in California, is forced into a kind of ostracism even beyond what she has known up to that time. Mr. Davidson in his soulless, cold Christianity reports to the island governor her dancing and partying with sailors and extracts from him an order for her deportation on the first ship for San Francisco. Davidson's self-imposed duty is to impress people with a sense of sin, and, as relentless as the rain, he sets forth to perform this duty with Miss Thompson just as he had with the island natives. Boastful of his record of breaking those who, like the Danish trader Fred Ohlson, flout him, Davidson wages a fearsome campaign to teach Sadie that when he says to turn off her gramophone and stop dancing she had better obey.

Dr. Macphail, although well-intentioned in his compassion, can no more convince Davidson to abate his efforts to persuade Miss Thompson that she is a sinner than he can stop the nerve-wracking rain. The effect of the situation and the place tells on Dr. Macphail, who is brought to damn the bay that somehow attracts rain from all over the Pacific:

When the rain stopped and the sun shone, it was like a hothouse, seething, humid, sultry, breathless, and you had a strange feeling that everything was growing with a savage violence. The natives, blithe and childlike by reputation, seemed then, with their tatooing and their dyed hair, to have something sinister in their appearance; and when they pattered along at your heels with their naked feet you looked back instinctively. You felt they might at any moment come behind you swiftly and thrust a long knife between your shoulder blades. You could not tell what dark thoughts lurked behind their wide-set eyes. They had a little the look of ancient Egyptians painted on the temple wall, and there was about them the terror of what is immeasurably old. (*SM*, 23)

But the violence in the story does not come from the natives. It is Davidson who, praying every night with the broken Miss Thompson as she awaits deportation, yields to his own carnality and commits a sin that, in his eyes, damns him so completely he can only, in despair, slit his own throat. Miss Thompson is left behind to tax Macphail with the weakness of men and thus to bear witness to the motive for Davidson's violent end: "You men! You filthy, dirty pigs! You're all the same, all of you. Pigs! Pigs!" (*SM*, 39).

"Mackintosh" is another of Maugham's Samoan stories—exotic in locale, character, and theme. In this story the attention is not on the missionaries but on the governors. Like the equally famous "The Outstation," and Conrad's "An Outpost of Progress," "Mackintosh" concerns a conflict between two government officials: Walker, who over his twenty years as administrator of the island of Talua has become a legend, and his Scottish subordinate, Mackintosh. Different in every aspect of temperament and interest, Walker and Mackintosh are increasingly alienated from each other and from the natives they rule. Mackintosh perceives Walker, though not without a mitigating ambivalence, as a gross and sensual old man whose ways elicit his contempt. Walker, in turn, despises the fastidious Mackintosh as a prig but tolerates him as a "queer fish." Although he suppresses the resentment bred in him by Walker's jokes and bullying, Mackintosh broods on ways to get even with his boss. Hatred takes complete possession of him.

Central to their conflict is their attitude toward the island and its Kanaka natives. Walker loves the island, thinking it "like the garden of Eden" (*SM*, 79) and cherishes for the natives a rough tenderness: "He loved them because they were in his power, as a selfish man loves his dog, and his mentality was on a level with theirs" (*SM*, 79). Mackintosh, on the other hand, has no real understanding of the island or the natives. Ironically, Walker's troubles and eventual demise come at him from all quarters—from Mackintosh and from the natives. His authority is challenged by young Manuma, the son of Chief Tangatu of the village of Matautu, who demands a hundred pounds for his people to complete the island road that Walker has ordered built. Walker refuses to accede to this demand, and by importing natives from another village at twenty pounds and demanding that the Matautu villagers reimburse him for these salaries as well as face the ruin imposed by the laws of island hospitality, which force him to allow the outsiders, literally, to eat them out of house and home, he outwits the natives and humiliates Manuma, who then attempts to kill him with a knife thrown from ambush. Mackintosh loathes Walker's bullying of the natives (and of himself) so much that he also plots vengeance. Mackintosh's agony—from life on the island, from Walker's dominance—builds to drastic proportions: "Here he was a prisoner, imprisoned not only by that placid sea, but by his hatred for that horrible old man. He pressed his hands to his aching head. He would like to kill him" (*SM*, 89). Conveniently for Mackintosh, Manuma takes the revolver planted for his use and shoots Walker who, before he dies, forgives his killer and all his native "children," leaving Mackintosh to govern the island.

In a paradoxical reversal similar to that of the ending of "Rain," Mackintosh is so devastated by the way Walker accepts his death and is so fearful of the thought that the island is his to manage, that he takes the same revolver which killed his chief, walks out to the lagoon, and puts a bullet through his head: "An hour later half a dozen slim brown sharks were splashing and struggling at the spot where he fell" (*SM*, 103). Like the missionary Davidson, the bureaucrat Mackintosh is forced to see his true self in the ironic virtue of his antagonist. In both their cases, exile becomes eternal.

Thus in terms of plot, characterization, setting, atmosphere, and tone, Kipling, Conrad, and Maugham display many shared aspects of exoticism in their short stories. The tradition continues, but with unique modifications, in the short fiction of E. M. Forster. Most obviously, Forster's early stories evince a preoccupation with the fabulous and the fantastic that puts him closer to Kipling than to Conrad and Maugham. In the pairings of isolated male companions that turn up repeatedly in exotic stories by Kipling, Conrad, and Maugham, there are hints of a homosexual theme which Forster also suggested—even perhaps in *A Passage to India*. In many of Forster's short stories, however, notably those published posthumously, this theme becomes explicit, and in some of the exotic stories, white travelers are involved in relationships that are doubly taboo—erotic relationships not only between males but between males of different races.

More celebrated as a novelist, Forster nevertheless began his career as a writer of short stories. During his lifetime he published two volumes of short fiction: *The Celestial Omnibus* (1911) and *The Eternal Moment* (1928). The tales in these relatively slight volumes were combined, in 1947, into one volume of twelve stories, and Forster is by and large remembered (in terms of the modern short story) for three tales, all frequently anthologized fantasies from *The Collected Tales*: "The Celestial Omnibus," "The Road from Colonus," and "The Machine Stops." Most of Forster's early tales have as their setting either Italy or Greece and are based in part on his experiences as a tourist in those places. Although Forster's protagonists are often displaced tourists, these tales, according at least to Maugham's definition, are not "exotic."

Another fourteen or so stories, though written much earlier, were published posthumously as *The Life to Come and Other Stories* (1972). These stories are more exotic than fantastic (although the two modes are related insofar as Forster defined fantasy as at least in part involving the device of introducing "ordinary men into no-man's-land, the future, the past, the interior of the earth, the fourth dimension").[31] Like Forster's posthumous novel *Maurice* (1971), most of them deal with homosexual themes. These stories, only two of which were previously published, were written within the large span of years from 1903 to

1962.[32] Forster's bibliographer and incisive commentator, Frederick P. W. McDowell, rightly insists that Forster's finest tales illustrate a "skilled fusion of realism and fantasy."[33] Identifying the center of such a fusion even more specifically, George H. Thomson argues that the short stories not only expose "the bare bones of Forster's art," they "are early proof that he was fascinated by mythic perspective."[34] Agreeing that Forster was indeed fascinated by myth and fantasy in his short fiction, Lionel Trilling very early held that Forster's short fiction was inferior to his novels precisely because his mythology seems "academic and arch, and . . . generates a tone which is at war with the robust intention of the stories."[35] It is against such a critical background that Forster's short fiction should be placed when considering it as "exotic fantasy" in Maugham's sense of exotic and in Forster's sense of fantasy.

"The Life to Come" and "The Other Boat"[36] are, by consensus, among the best of Forster's posthumous stories (although because of their erotic nature they do not have the universal appeal of his masterpieces, "Celestial Omnibus" and "Road to Colonus").[37] Both stories end tragically for their homosexual protagonists and dramatize an isolated and despairing union of two different races and cultures, futilely attracted to each other in faraway places. In both stories, love gives way to vengeance.

"The Life to Come" (written in 1922) is a four-part story structured around literal and figurative phases of day and night, light and dark. In the allusiveness of the title and in the themes of benevolence and sacrifice, Forster (as in *A Passage to India*) ironically and satirically undercuts the Christian notion that "God is Love." In so doing he seeks to indict, much as Maugham does in "Rain," the hypocritical proselytizing of the heathen by a Christian missionary, Paul Pinmay. Sent to a never-named primitive locale to attempt the conversion of a resisting young inland chief, Vithobai, Pinmay returns to his fellow missionaries on the coast and reports that he, like those before him, has failed to bring the Christian message to the chief and his people. What he neglects to tell, for he is guilt-stricken almost to the point of suicide, is that Vithobai had understood Pinmay's sermonizing on God's love to mean physical love and that Pinmay yielded to it one "midnight" in the "dark," "vast," forest in an enchanted hut: "A remote, a romantic spot . . . lovely, lovable . . ." (*LC*, 65). Exotically and erotically rendered in their union of "pagan limbs" and "golden ruffled hair," amid contrasting ornaments of Vithobai's "scarlet flowers" and Pinmay's "Holy Bible," the missionary's sin and defilement is the boy chief's glory and cause for devotion. Ironically, and in Forster's treatment, humorously, out of clandestine sin has come success, news naively greeted by Pinmay's superiors with the words, "Here we have the triumph of youth, oh it puts us to shame" (*LC*, 69).

In the ten years that he is to administer to Vithobai's people, however, Pinmay proves no "brother in Christ," insisting that the chief be christened "Barnabas," that he dress more decently in European clothes, and that he never mention that secret night liaison. In a word, Pinmay's character is altered—"He was no longer an openhearted Christian knight but a hypocrite whom a false step would destroy" (LC, 71). He keeps his hold over Barnabas by damning him for the church's sake and teasing the maturing chief with the promise, "Not yet."

At the five-year mark of his official term, Pinmay plans to marry a medical missionary, a lady of high Christian ideals. A crisis develops when Barnabas gives his "beloved brother" a horse and cart as a wedding present. While taking Pinmay for a drive, Barnabas again confesses his love, causing Pinmay to change his reply of "Not yet" to "Never." The final five years of his ministry see Barnabas recede from leadership as Christianity secures its hold.

Finally, dying from consumption and a broken heart, Barnabas is visited by Pinmay who explains to him the nature of their past sin together. Barnabas responds to Pinmay's pleas for repentance with a dagger to the heart. Pinmay's promises of a life to come spent together in eternity are fulfilled in a way never expected. In what Forster describes as the "dark spirited" passion of their mutual death and the ghastly reenactment of their flower-strewn, night union of ten years previously, Vithobai, a reinstated chief, subdues his conqueror and dies: "Mounting on the corpse, he climbed higher, raised his arms over his head, sunlit, naked, victorious, leaving all disease and humiliation behind him, and he swooped like a falcon from the parapet in pursuit of the terrified shade" (LC, 82). Pinmay will forever be an outcast, not just as missionary to dusky pagans in an exotic forest, but as a man estranged from both his honest and his dishonest selves.

"The Other Boat" (begun in 1913) is an even longer attempt by Forster to explore the estrangements of hidden homosexual love between a respectable Britisher named Lionel March, a contemporary "Nordic warrior" who has risen in army rank for fighting African natives in the Boer War, and a non-European, mixed-caste native, called rather too playfully by Forster "Cocoanut" because of his dark, round face and peculiarly shaped head. Making his own obvious moralistic comment on both racial prejudice and conventional sexual mores, Forster again in this story uses the title on numerous imagistic and thematic levels to drive home his lesson: "otherness" is a relative term, and hypocrisy in love and life will not do.

There are two main story lines, one past and one present, both dealing with boats perceived and designated as "other." Both boats are in transit and exemplify the voyager's remembrances and promises, departures and arrivals—"passages" from and to new and startling discovery and awareness. The primary boat to which the title refers, and the one that gives motive and meaning to the entire story, is the boat in the Suez Canal where Lionel March and Cocoanut met as children, thrown together by happenstance and childhood. Lionel was a passenger with his mother in her disillusioned home flight to England from India and a husband, Major Corrie March (like his son, large, muscular and "a hundred percent Aryan"), who while on duty in the East "went native" and deserted his wife and five children. Lionel, in the course of that passage and a later one on another boat, this time in the Red Sea where he again meets Cocoanut, proves very much his father's son (and worse in his mother's social sphere), for he begins a homosexual affair with a "native."

On the second boat, the S. S. *Normannia*, ironically en route back to India ten years later, Lionel and Cocoanut take passage together, and from Gibralter to Sicily to Port Said combat all the cultural conventions that prohibit such a relationship. In some rather silly sexually explicit scenes, Cocoanut makes love to his "Lion of the Night." If Lionel is the lion, Cocoanut is the monkey: "Monkey's got to come along to tell a Lion he's alive" (*LC*, 181). Lionel finds himself between two worlds, socially as well as geographically, as he tries to convince his fellow Britishers Colonel and Mrs. Arbuthnot (and even by letter his mother), that he very much resents being forced by the crowded conditions to share a berth with a "wog" like Cocoanut. Like Pinmay in "The Life to Come," Lionel March agonizes in his hypocrisy. His guilt is heightened by his ambivalent enjoyments, including the gifts that Cocoanut, rich, mysteriously criminal, and influential in shipping circles, lavishes on him—"A Viking at a Byzantine court, spoiled, adored and not yet bored" (*LC*, 180). Mrs. March is again robbed of her own by a native lover, and Lionel's fiancée, Isabel, is too.

Cocoanut, shameless in his love for Lionel, deliberately leaves the door to the cabin unlocked in the expectation that March will be found out and thus forced to remain with him as an outcast. But the plan fails when March discovers the door unlocked and, realizing Cocoanut's attempted exposure, heads for the deck and his own class of people. He is shocked into the recognition that "if he forfeited their companionship he would become nobody and nothing" (*LC*, 192). He had risked losing his profession in the army, and Isabel's regard as well as his mother's. But in returning to his cabin to sleep, he seals his fate. Cocoanut bites March's arm, and, in an act of brutal revenge and passion, the Nordic warrior is once again back killing savages. He murders Cocoanut and then commits suicide "naked and with the seeds of love on him," by diving into the sea. Devoured by sharks like Maugham's Mackintosh, he leaves a legacy of scandal and disgrace.

David Shusterman suggests that what Forster's short stories reveal most is potential; "that he might have become one of the masters of this type of fiction."[38] Although Shusterman is not talking about Forster's posthumous short stories, the evaluation still holds. Currently Forster's short stories are viewed as tentative and mainly as a means to fuller understanding of his novels. For whatever the reason, and it was probably his growing interest in homosexual themes, Forster did not succeed in the short story form as consistently as Kipling and Maugham. But, as a man and writer between two worlds and two kinds of morality, he was assuredly exotic.

Two of the most modern of the writers in the exotic tradition of the British short story—but not all that far removed from the Edwardian-Georgian worlds of Forster and Maugham—are Jean Rhys and Graham Greene. Like Conrad, Maugham, and Forster, known more as novelists than for their short stories, they too are interested in the traveler to strange lands—real and imagined. And like Kipling, Conrad, Maugham, and Forster, they sought and found much of their material on their world travels and in their remote residences. Their worldviews, like those of the other authors considered, go far beyond the exotic, but it is nevertheless possible to identify their literary kinship without taking anything away from other aspects of their works.

Jean Rhys's last published book, *Smile Please: An Unfinished Autobiography* (1979), confirms just how truly autobiographical are the vignettes of her earlier volumes of short fiction: *The Left Bank* (1927), *Tigers Are Better Looking* (1968), and *Sleep It Off, Lady* (1976).[39] As autobiographies go, *Smile Please* is fragmented not only in that it is "unfinished." The "chapters" within the two major parts of the book are brief and self-contained. Even though Rhys, just before her death, proclaimed the first part of the autobiography "finished," whereas the second part is a posthumous joining together of drafts and notes by Rhys's editor and friend, Diana Athill, about the same degree of thematic, chronological, and geographical unity obtains in the two. Her autobiography is, however, not shapeless, but its effect—like that of her short fiction—is restrained and anecdotal. Furthermore, just as her autobiography focuses first on her childhood in Dominica and then on her early and later adulthood in London and Paris, so does her short fiction fall into two distinct groups, stories with Antillian and Parisian settings and the proportionately fewer stories about England. "All her writing, she used to say, started out from something that had happened, and her first concern was to get it down as accurately as possible."[40]

In a transparent way Rhys's art was her life (though she lived through much more than she wrote about), and the voice in her fiction is seemingly identical with the voice in her autobiography. What V. S. Pritchett observed in his review of *Smile Please* is to the point: "Her position as a displaced person was that there was no position. That was what caught the attention of the later generation who came to see her point. Displacement had become a norm."[41] As a woman and as a writer, she lived and wrote exotically. Because of the gap of almost half a century between her first short stories in *The Left Bank* and her later pieces in *Tigers Are Better Looking* and *Sleep It Off, Lady*, Rhys's stories fall into two groupings, but they are not mutually exclusive, for even her stories about life in the London, Vienna, Montmartre, and Montparnasse of the 1920s allude to the turn-of-the-century days in the Antilles. Early and late, Rhys wrote about the various places she had lived.

Any consideration of the critical response to Rhys's early short fiction should begin with Ford Madox Ford's preface to *The Left Bank* (1927). Ford, whose 1925 affair with Rhys is recounted in her *Postures* (1928), paid tribute to her writing ability and, from his position as editor of the *Transatlantic Review*, was an early champion of her work. According to Stella Bowen, another of Ford's loves, Rhys came into her and Ford's life from "an underworld of darkness and disorder, where officialdom, the bourgeoisie and the police were the eternal enemies and the fugitive the only hero."[1] Ford saw a connection between Rhys's life in the West Indies and in Paris: "Coming from the Antilles, with a terrifying insight and a terrific—almost lurid!—passion for stating the case of the underdog, she has let her pen loose on the Left Banks of the Old World—on its gaols, its studios, its salons, its cafés, its criminals, its midinettes—with a bias of admiration for its midinettes and of sympathy for its lawbreakers" (*LB*, 24). Saying this much about the influence of place on theme, Ford nevertheless believes Rhys's concern to be more with hardship and emotion than with locality in her accounts of European life: "So she hands you the Antilles with its sea and sky— 'the loveliest, deepest sea in the world—the Caribbean!'—the effect of landscape on the emotions and passions of a child being so penetrative, but lets Montparnasse, or London, or Vienna go" (*LB*, 26). But if specific topographical reference is missing in some of her stories, identifying atmosphere is not.

"Tea With An Artist" is mapped out meticulously as set first in a café in the Montparnasse district and then north in "the real Latin Quarter" in the flat of a Flemish painter, Verhausen, on the *quatrième à droite*. The story is filled with wondrously brief but lucid strokes of character and setting, and even more minimal strokes of quaintly suspenseful plot. The narrator, a persona readily identifiable with Rhys, while at a café with a friend sees an interesting old man. The man is an artist, Verhausen, who, though quite prolific and at one time successful, is now judged "really dotty," "a rum old bird," "a bit of a back number" because he hides his paintings, refusing to exhibit or sell them. With the help of her companion, the narrator arranges to visit the artist and see some of his work. Graciously offered tea, the narrator is viewing the paintings, one of which is of startling beauty, great and golden art in the manner of the Dutch school, when the female subject herself enters the room, hardly as impressive in reality s in Verhausen's idealizing vision. The narrator then goes into the late-after-
oon street with her thoughts.

What is so effective in Rhys's telling is her rendering of human perceptions and the textures of place and moment—of the artist and his subject, of the street, of objects. For example, the artist: "It was obvious that this was not an Anglo-Saxon: he was too gay, too dirty, too unreserved and in his little eyes was such a mellow comprehension of all the sins and the delights of life" (*LB*, 73); the street in the Latin Quarter: "It was an ancient, narrow street of uneven houses, a dirty, beautiful street, full of mauve shadows. A policeman stood limply near the house, his expression that of contemplative stupefaction: a yellow dog lay stretched philosophically on the cobblestones of the roadway" (*LB*, 75–76). As she leaves Verhausen's dwelling, the narrator ponders her impressions of the visit: "It was astonishing how the figure of the girl on the sofa stayed in my mind: it blended with the coming night, the scent of Paris and the hard blare of the gramophone" (*LB*, 81). In this same way, the reader leaves Rhys's story, her word-picture, with a lingering sense of city and citizen, of people's pasts hidden away among the obvious daylight and more obscure shadows of living.

Other vignettes in *The Left Bank*, especially "Hunger" and "A Night," take the reader into the even darker intimacies and exotic displacements of starvation, loneliness, and contemplated suicide: "No money: rotten. And ill and frightened to death. . . . Worse!" (*LB*, 109). In "A Night" one sees Rhys wanting to get out not only of Paris but of her life. In despairing night thoughts, she melodramatically constructs a way of death—a purchased revolver from the pawn shop, the barrel against the roof of her mouth, the trigger pulled. She prays for a friend, imagines the man she could love, says the Litany to the Blessed Virgin which she learned as a girl. "Ripping words," "A devil of a business" she calls it— alone, at night, down and out in Paris.

Like her autobiography, Rhys's stories concern the nostalgic aching heart of a lost childhood in the Caribbean, of the smile mustered for a portrait at age six, at once fixed and long vanished. In that early picture she had moved. A pity. It was a symbolic portrait of a life on the move, a life photographed again in her stories. Sad. Smiling. Such is the womanhood that faced Rhys in fiction and Rhys in life. She was her own best estranged and exotic heroine.

Thomas F. Staley suggests that the fictive world, the ambience, of Jean Rhys's stories is more like that of Chekhov than of Maupassant and is unique in English short fiction after World War I: "The special tone and feel of the stories seem to bear little similarity to short fiction that was written in England at the time, and certainly the condition and fate of their heroines would have seemed exotic if not remote when compared with those of English contemporary writers."[43] Another way of seeing Rhys's short fiction is as evidence that the exotic tradition in the British short story extended far beyond Kipling, beyond the Great War.

The short stories of Graham Greene, like his novels, are very much related to his travels. They are populated by numerous travelers who travel far and wide. But his critics have been most concerned with that country of the mind known as "Greeneland": "A buzzard flaps across a dusty Mexican square and settles heavily on a tin roof . . . in West Africa the laterite roads turn a fragile pink at sundown, then are swallowed by darkness."[44] Greene, in his autobiography, has likened the motive for his travels (and for his exotic settings and character involvements) to the reasons underlying the Russian roulette he literally used to play to escape boredom:

A kind of Russian roulette remained too a factor in my later life, so that without previous experience of Africa I went on an absurd and reckless trek through Liberia; it was the fear of boredom which took me to Tabasco during the religious persecution, to a *léproserie* in the Congo, to the Kikuyu reserve during the Mau-Mau insurrection, to the emergency in Malaya and to the French war in Vietnam.[45]

And as in Russian roulette, violence and death await Greene's travelers.

Relatively little has been written about Greene's short stories—at least in comparison with the generous and growing critical reaction to his novels. Greene's first volume of short fiction was published as *The Basement Room* in 1936—taking its title from one of his now most famous stories. Other volumes are: *Twenty-one Stories* (1954; published in Great Britain as *Nineteen Stories* in 1947); *A Sense of Reality* (1963); and *May We Borrow Your Husband* (1967), the last three of which were published as *Collected Stories* in 1973. Over a span of five decades, from 1929 into the 1980s, Greene's publication record is impressive; in addition to nearly twenty novels, miscellaneous essays, travelogues, plays, and an autobiography, he saw published about fifty short stories, roughly one third of them written before 1945. Fully aware that the short story form has been a part of his life as a writer from the beginning, Greene does contend, however, that he has remained "a novelist who has happened to write short stories"—a distinction between what he sees as "two different ways of life."[46]

Two of Greene's most characteristic pre–World War II exotic stories are found in *Twenty-One Stories*, "A Chance For Mr. Lever" (1936) and "Across the Bridge" (1938). Often anthologized but seldom written about, individually and together they take the reader to the heart of "Greeneland" and what Greene discusses metaphorically as Russian roulette.

In his frequently quoted essay "The Lost Childhood" (1947), Greene establishes the importance that novels like those of Rider Haggard and Stanley Weyman had for him as a child. Travel, adventure, deeds of daring—all focused, for the young author-to-be, around a key crisis, "the moment when life took a new slant in its journey towards death" (*GCE*, 13). Had he not read *King Solomon's Mines*, Greene says, he most probably would not have almost joined the Nigerian

Navy or later, in 1935, found himself "sick with fever on a camp bed in a Liberian native's hut with a candle going out in an empty whiskey bottle and a rat moving in the shadows" (*GCE*, 15). And had Greene not experienced fever in Liberia, he most probably would not have projected that darkness into "A Chance For Mr. Lever." After he had read Marjorie Bowen's *The Viper of Milan*, Greene says, his future as a writer and his grand "pattern" were fixed: "perfect evil walking the world where perfect good can never walk again" (*GCE*, 18).

The Mexico in which Joseph Calloway finds himself in "Across the Bridge," as well as the Africa where Mr. Lever takes his last chance, do indeed exemplify a world devoid of any perfect good. Five weeks away from his comfortable London home and his wife, Emily, and ten days into the forests of the Republic of Liberia, Lever, an aging heavy machinery salesman, seeks a Mr. Davidson whose endorsement for a machine useful in the mining of gold will assure him a prosperous retirement. When he finds Davidson dying from yellow fever, he ineptly forges the machinery approval, thinking he has made his fortune. But, the narrator tells us, Lever's chance is also his doom, for Davidson's illness had been transferred to Lever by one barely perceived mosquito bite on the ankle. Lever's Africa, like that of Conrad's Kurtz, is a world of horrors beyond his reckoning: "cockroaches the size of black-beetles flattened against the mud wall [of his hut]"; "narrow, steep, lost paths, the snakes sizzling away like flames, the rats, the dust, the naked diseased bodies."[47] He can only write letters full of platitudes to Emily as he penetrates ever deeper into the bush where he soon finds evidence of pervasive death, coming first upon a bloated native corpse stuck in one of Davidson's trial mine shafts and then upon Davidson's own "lemon-yellow" visage and the "black vomit which stained his shirt and khaki shorts" (*TOS*, 154).

By means of frame narration in which Greene's knowing narrator directly addresses the reader, the outcome of Mr. Lever's short-lived scheme to capitalize on Davidson's death is ironically doomed: Mr. Lever will never again reach England, Emily, and home. In three days' time his forging of Davidson's signature will be rendered meaningless by his own parallel, anguished death—two men lost to their own hopes. The disturbing question is whether or not Mr. Lever's ignorance of his coming death is the work of a kindly god. The narrator, enlightened by his own travels, knows better: "The story might very will have encouraged my faith in that loving omniscience if it had not been shaken by personal knowledge of the drab forest through which Mr. Lever now went so merrily, where it is impossible to believe in any spiritual life, in anything outside the nature dying round you, the shrivelling of the weeds" (*TOS*, 157). Davidson, Mr. Lever—and to some extent the reader—wind up crushed and abandoned on a distant continent.

Another of Greene's stranded victims is the antiheroic millionaire criminal, Mr. Joseph Calloway, in "Across the Bridge." Mexico rather than Liberia is the setting for this story about a fugitive and his pursuit. Calloway's tale is told by an observer-participant, a fellow Britisher living on the cheap side of a Rio Grande border town and waiting for a fortnight, really not much caring, for a twenty dollar ride to Yucatan. In befriending Calloway for a time, the narrator comes to know his story, how he had left Guatemala and come north to avoid extradition for absconding with funds from the Halling Investment Trust. With his companion of a few days, Lucia (another wanderer), the narrator is witness to the tragicomic efforts of two detectives who cross the bridge to find Calloway and extradite him. Before that can happen, however, Calloway crosses the bridge to the American side of the border to find his dog—an English setter mix—and is killed by the detectives' car as they swerve to avoid hitting the dog. As in Mr. Lever's case, death comes to Calloway as part of life's irony.

The story is filled with ambivalences. Calloway is rich but a criminal, just how much of a criminal depending on whether he is in Europe or Mexico or which side of the border he is on; his dog is "very nearly an English setter," which his master needs but kicks and hates in the "intimacy" of caring enough to be an enemy; Lucia comes into the narrator's life only to leave in a car headed across the border—she is nothing in particular, but beautiful; the detectives find Calloway and talk to him but do not recognize him at first; Calloway wins out in that the government officials do not give the detectives their extradition orders—but he loses his life. Nearly everyone on both sides of the border speaks English, but Calloway believes everyone speaks only Spanish, and this adds to his isolation. The narrator is both involved and uninvolved, apathetic and interested, entertained by the spectacle he sees unfolding but also disturbed by it. And the two towns, Mexican and American, are inverted images of each other: "There was no interest in the place for anyone; it was just damp and dust and poverty, a kind of shabby replica of the town across the river. Both had squares in the same spots; both had the same number of cinemas. One was cleaner than the other, that was all, and more expensive, much more expensive" (*TOS*, 85). And there is the bridge—a symbol of the transition that faces all of the characters in the story. The narrator looks upon Mr. Calloway and his predicament, his end, rather cynically realizing—as he says—the human being's "capacity for self-deception, our baseless optimism that is so much more appalling than our despair" (*TOS*, 94).

Two other writers of short stories belong solidly in the exotic tradition, although neither is as widely read as the likes of a Kipling or a Conrad, a Maugham or a Forster, a Rhys or a Greene. Walter de la Mare, the first of the two, was writing stories throughout much of the period in which the exotic mode was developed. William Sansom's work, coming later, indicates that the tradition had not run its course as the British went into the post–World War II years.

Walter de la Mare, over his long and prolific career, published sixteen volumes of short stories.[48] An esteemed author in his lifetime, he has, since his death, held surprisingly little fascination for either readers or critics. Although interest in de la Mare has been largely confined to attention to the more frequently anthologized pieces such as the poem "The Listeners" (1912), he has in fact contributed significantly to the tradition of the exotic short story.

Critics who have turned their attention to de la Mare's short fiction have invariably been extravagant in their praise. One of the staunchest of his admirers is Edward Wagenknecht, editor of the collected tales, who compares de la Mare's descriptions favorably to those of Dickens. Wagenknecht describes de la Mare's "inward eye" as one that fixes best for only "a moment or two," and suggests that this may explain why he has worked so extensively in the short story form.[49] Another partisan commentator on de la Mare's stature as a writer of short stories is Doris Ross McCrosson, who concludes: "His preoccupation with good and evil puts him on a level with Hawthorne and Conrad; his mastery of suspense and terror is equal to Poe's; the subtlety of his characterizations occasionally rivals James'."[50]

Favorable as they are, the few assessments of de la Mare's short stories only hint at the deep and pronounced exoticism that marks them. Not so much concerned with British imperialism as, for example, Maugham, de la Mare most often sets his stories in the familiar environs of England—rural or urban, present or past. But as in the stories of Kipling, Forster, and especially T. F. Powys, the familiar and the seemingly ordinary (whether of character or of setting) often prove strange and most bizarre. Thus, de la Mare's stories tend to have the kind of ambivalently realistic and at once romantic atmosphere that pervades the *Lyrical Ballads* of Wordsworth and Coleridge. De la Mare begins in the world of the commonplace, the recognizable (as does Coleridge in the "conversation" poems), only to throw over it a coloring of fancy and imagination. The result, as in Hawthorne's tales and romances, is a "natural supernaturalism" that encompasses conventions at once believable and fantastic, in time and out of time. His short stories also partake of an oneiric atavism, that arcs back to the autochthonous "folk" tale.[51]

Indeed, both Coleridge and Blake are often mentioned when critics attempt to describe the "visionary" atmosphere and themes, and the eerie effects of de la Mare. Dreams and the dreamer figure prominently in his work—as do adaptations of frame narration, audience entrapment, the compulsive tale-telling of "speakers" who have been beyond the pale, and numerous allusions to the archetypal character of the Ancient Mariner. Neither the distortions of high romanticism nor those of sheer fantasy, however, account for de la Mare's atmosphere of fabulated otherworldliness (somehow at once of and beyond this place and time). Plots are discernible in de la Mare's stories; events do build to an identifiable climax and resolution. All the same, the telling, the creation of the story-world, supercedes motive and action. And, as in Hawthorne's tales, any "horror" that exists is not blatant but rather symbolic and enigmatic—and so all the more disturbing and awesome.

De la Mare assuredly conveys that sense of "oblivion and the abyss" that modern man so keenly feels in relation to loneliness, alienation, madness, and death. At the same time—and this is his triumph and ultimately that of exoticism in literature—he suggests that in the story and in its telling may reside sanity and community and perhaps salvation. Many of his stories illustrate his sense of the exotic, but none so well as "The Vats" (from "*The Riddle" and Other Stories*, 1923), and "Cape Race" (from *The Wind Blows Over*, 1936). Both are the work of an author at the top of his craft, skillfully merging form and subject.

"The Vats" utilizes one of de la Mare's favorite conventions: a traveler recounting his travels to listeners who share the teller's awe and are thus held spellbound by the yarn and the "yarning." The discovery of the vats—large pools or cisterns of water—takes place in a locale discoverable on no map other than that of the mind and at an unidentifiable time in the recent past. In a "long ago and far away" kind of opening, the narrator stresses the fairy-tale point: "Many years ago now—in that once upon a time which is the memory of the imagination rather than of the workaday mind, I went walking with a friend" (*CTM*, 434). That walk is the tale. "The Vats" simply tells of the amazing discovery of a special phenomenon in a place exuding a strange spirit, the spirit of ancient times, of Stonehenge—and of Eden itself. Even more than in a Conrad tale, atmosphere is all—the sight and sense of the vats, their setting and discovery, their description: it is the perceptions of the narrator that fascinate. Allegorically, the story reflects man's journey through life and recounts a recognition of the majesty and mystery of sublime beauty and the ability to perceive it, if only momentarily, in the vast convergence of personality, time, and space. The vats, called by a name that ironically suggests "vast," are primeval on the landscape. Staring inexpressibly at them, the narrator retrospectively rallies himself out of initial silence to offer a prose-picture, filled with richly exotic, almost Keatsian, imagery of man attempting to comprehend marvel: "They lay slumbering in a grave, crystal light, which lapped, deep as the Tuscarora Trough, above and around their prodigious stone plates, or slats, or slabs, or laminae; their steep slopes washed by the rarefied atmosphere of their site, and in hue of a hoary green" (*CTM*, 437). Paragraph after paragraph of enchanting description follows, amounting to the portrayal of a mere glimpse into "the shadow of a magnitude" of the biological and geological forces intuited on that one walk.

There are many romantic precedents for such exquisite confrontation with the inexpressible. The waters in the vats are described in terms of the exotic geography of world travel:

Waters, imaginably so clear as to be dense, as if of melted metal more translucent even than crystal; of such a tenuous purity that not even the moonlit branches of a dream would spell their reflex in them; so costly, so far beyond price, that this whole stony world's rubies and sapphires and amethysts of Mandalay and Guadalajara and Solikamsk, all the treasure-houses of Cambalech and the booty of King Tamburlane would suffice to purchase not one drop. (*CTM*, 439)

It is a moment of memory, an epiphany retold against a background of silence—and as refreshing as that elixir of life that the narrator believes to fill the vats.

Another at once real and sublime confrontation with "oblivion" occurs in "Cape Race." In this tale of travel a young woman, Lettie, sails the open sea, the North Atlantic off the Newfoundland coast, on her way to New York and a new life as wife of a balding and somewhat boring career man complete with pampering mother. When Lettie sees Cape Race and Mistaken Point (the name suggestive of her own marital decision) off the ship's bow, she is entranced. Even to sight land is unusual, since, on this voyage, the land has usually been fog-bound (figuratively, again, representative of Lettie's clouded state of mind until the moment when she "sees" both Cape Race and her own situation). The happenstance of the sighting proves a revelation for Lettie; Cape Race (suggestive of the "race" of Lettie's life) is suddenly endowed with "newfound" significance: "How romantic and how amazing! Newfoundland indeed. And that it should have been there for centuries upon centuries continually in sound of its perpetual breakers beneath its low mounded hill, and that she had never seen it before! What completely commonplace things could sometimes almost suffocate you, not of course with any novelty, but with some hidden meaning" (*CTM*, 367).

The ordinary, even paltry, condition of Lettie's life is contrasted with the significance of Newfoundland and with the presence of the ship itself so wondrously positioned in the middle of the ocean. The contrast is heightened by the arrival on board of a bird disoriented from having flown into the glass-walled saloon, which Lettie retrieves—unlike the Ancient Mariner—in order to release it. De la Mare continually reinforces the identification of Lettie herself with the fragility and captivity of the bird. Lettie, as she readies the bird for release and ponders its fate, herself yearns for flight back to Cape Race and finds the anonymity it holds out more appealing than the safe monotony that life with George promises. She too is supremely forlorn, a captive.

The exoticism of William Sansom is a much more violent brand than that of not only de la Mare, but other writers in the tradition whose stories involve destruction. Many of Sansom's stories are based on his experience in the National Fire Service in London during World War II. They offer compelling evidence that the consciousness of modern man is inextricably associated with a kind of extended twentieth-century angst and paranoia—becoming almost an exoticism of the future, both psychological and physical in its boundaries, at once dreaded and traumatic. As surrealistic and Kafkaesque as his stories are, the perceptions of his narrators and the mind-mappings of his characters are recognizable and authentic—they ring true in a kind of exotic yet familiar universality of doom. There is little of utopia and much of the apocalypse (both individual and social) in Sansom's writings. And yet, chilling as they are, they are also beautiful.

In terms of the history of the modern British short story, *Fireman Flower* (1944) assuredly approaches classic status as part of Sansom's canon; but it also needs singling out as a classic on its own terms.[52] In its dozen stories, the last of which is "Fireman Flower," exoticism mingles with the ironic and the grotesque in a music of words so orchestrated as to be simultaneously thundering and exquisitely soft. Sansom's lyrical and imagistic "performance" is devastating in its control, an artistry that finds itself altogether at odds with the chaos and destruction, the mutilations and aberrations that, if never quite explained, are nevertheless described in hair-raising detail. Thus his "prose pictures," his "prose poems" are so soothing and painful, so contradictory in effect as to be exasperating—dream become nightmare.

Destruction—ironically naive and calculated—surrounds his characters and the times and places in which they confront the almost naturalistic fate that is their undoing. In "Through the Quinquina Glass" a would-be teller of tales invents the name and a life for an anonymous man in a "severe black coat" as he sits across the room at a café table. Colored by the green gloom of the quinquina glass and the fatuous quips of his companion, the narrator imagines a story of deceit, of love betrayed, of the black-coated customer's mania to revenge his wife's infidelity, a mania that takes the strangest of convolutions—but none so shocking as the man's actual suicide in the café, the hardly imagined ending for the invented story—a betrayal and a confirmation of the narrator's guesses. It is an ending all the more powerful because of its showing, unfiltered by the quinquina glass, not its telling. Reader and narrator are left with little to say, only to stare.

In "Difficulty with a Bouquet," dramatic irony prevails less catastrophically as this time a more legitimately omniscient narrator (accompanied by an equally voyeuristic reader) watches a love-stricken man pick some flowers and start to take them to "Miss D.," the rather plain but attractive "elderly girl of about twenty who had come to live in the flats opposite his garden" (*FF*, 83). Anticipating rejection, the man drops the flowers in the gutter rather than carry through his Prufrockian "grand" notion, as Miss D. watches from her window and wishes that the flower from such a neighbor could somehow be intended for her.

"Saturation Point" is a more horribly ironic version (doubly ironic in its surprise ending) of a wartime "cinema of the mind." As is typically the case with Sansom's ways of involving the reader as an accomplice in the experiencing of the scene and events, both the characters and the reader soon know the full revulsion of the story's sadomasochistic "saturation point." The reader is led to expect that the seductive "Gaustette" will use the silver carving knife she conceals to stab the torturer "commandant" who kills old men by kicking in their brains and burns the flesh of young girls with a cigar stub, but it is the military monster who finally is saturated with his own sadism and Gaustette who is mutilated. In the climactic scene, she lifts the hem of her gown for an unexpected purpose: "A brillant arc of silver as the knife descends through its wild parabola! Gaustette slices—a long cut of meat from her own leg! . . . Drugging herself at the loin, Gaustette has had her leg roasted for the commandant's table" (*FF*, 182–83)! No horror the sadist could devise could "better" such an act; in Sansom's words, the commandant's "decay of fulfillment has begun" (*FF*, 183).

Such destruction and insane violence as this (not to mention in any detail the phobia and madness found in such stories as "Pansovic and the Spiders," or the anguishing absurdities of captivity and punishment in "The Long Sheet") make the author's accounts of destruction by fire all the more otherworldly and hellish. With awesome clarity and verisimilitude—because, no doubt, of Sansom's own wartime hazards as a firefighter during the bombing of London—stories such as "The Wall" and the centerpiece "Fireman Flower" draw the reader into the vortex of exoticism where death is a given and deliverance a surprise, even something of an anticlimax, for there is little cheer if one is resurrected to a wasteland. As Sansom says simply but with allegorical implications, "A wall will fall in many ways." Beyond the understatement is the certainty that walls of many kinds will indeed fall. The fireman narrator in "The Wall" describes the inevitable: "It may sway over to the one side or the other. It may crumble at the very beginning of its fall. It may remain intact and fall flat. This wall fell as flat as a pancake. It clung to its shape through ninety degrees to the horizontal. Then it detached itself from the pivot and slammed down on top of us" (*FF*, 161). The bricks and mortar come tearing into the fireman's flesh, but miraculously he is dug out, for in one of those unbelievable ironies, when the wall falls he is accidentally framed by a window space.

In "Fireman Flower" the reader follows a fireman named Flower (a name of tender ironies against the harshness of the flames and smoke) from the call and truck ride to the "seat of the fire." In the mode of Robert Browning's "Childe Roland to the Dark Tower Came" and all the throng of "quest" literature behind that, "Fireman Flower" is a surrealistic, symbolic search for the source—filled with false turns, distortions of time and space, objects and ideas. On one level it is the story of firefighting told from the point of view of a fireman who prides himself in his task and his readiness—the preparation of his colleagues and their equipment, and their resolve to put out fires regardless of the effort or cost. On a more allegorical level, it is a recounting of both an archetypal (as well as literal) descent into hell, a long night of the soul, a trial of faith versus doubt that must be met, ostensibly with others but ultimately alone.

A warehouse engulfed by flames becomes the stage for everyman's battle with meaning and madness, substance and nothingness, illusion and reality, memory and the future, good and evil. In some ways the story is World War II in microcosm. In his obsessive motivation to arrive at the "seat of the fire" and confront it for what it is, Flower fights his way into a world, almost blossoms his way, into a world of mirrored doppelgängers and old friends calmly awaiting his arrival amid the flames and smoke, the acrid smells, and the nerve-shattering sounds and shapes of a building, of shape and function, breaking asunder. Flower's is a frenzied search for the center—and after numerous smaller victories and realizations about himself and his cause, he ascends to the roof of the building and an ecstatic fondness for the night, his wet sleeve, and a catalog of dismal and wonderful things: "of distant beauties and the comfortably ugly, of all human affairs by different standards good and bad—so that he loved a single rusted nail as he loved the Giaconda smile, the factory's time clock as he loved the mold of autumn leaves, a mausoleum as he loved the crèche, a cat's head in the gutter as he loved the breasts of Joan" (*FF*, 236).

Such disparate things juxtaposed this way afford an oblique commentary on the effects of Sansom's talents and exoticism. Richard Church places Sansom with that special kind of writer who is "more, and of a nobler heredity, than the mere recorder of births, deaths, and marriages; that . . . is concerned with the mystery of words and their music, and with events as representing something larger than our social comprehension can envisage."[53] For some readers, Sansom's stories may amount to little more than mannered verbiage, perhaps nothing but affectation—the rendering of a world of words as empty at the core as a fire-gutted warehouse. For others, Sansom's stories reinforce the notion that faced with the darkness of the void it is the storyteller's words that hold forth a promise.

Thus Sansom's vision may easily take us back to earlier writers in the exotic tradition, but especially to Greene. Having witnessed two great wars and other monumental horrors, Greene has shown little propensity for optimism. But even in the works of his later Victorian precursor, Kipling, there is already the shadow of disillusionment to come. As did those who came after him in the practice of exotic fiction, Kipling shows white men in alien lands confronting absurd choices and facing failure. Kipling was merely one of the first to utilize his travels, his sense of displacement at being a tourist, only purportedly a "superior" in distant places among darker skins, an Englishman among diverse cultures and peoples where even Great Britain's far-reaching colonizing influences finally faded.

Not only did Kipling and his heirs—each in his own way—extend the subject and theme of exoticism and thus the scope of the modern short story; they also enhanced our understanding of the alienation common to those who live in the twentieth century, early and late. In speaking of Conrad in particular, George Steiner notes that "he had, with merciful stoicism, focussed the romantic motif of aloneness, as it had originally been developed on the high Byronic plane, on the twilight of common survival."[54] And this is precisely the contribution of exoticism to the short-story tradition. The modern British short story is often the product of "refugees" in exotic places and situations, exiles of culture, of class, of sexuality, or—the ultimate exoticism—of death.

Robert Gish

University of Northern Iowa

D. H. LAWRENCE

This essay, while not polemical, assumes that the short stories of D. H. Lawrence have not yet been fully appreciated for their psychological and artistic subtlety, and that distinctive aims and devices recurrent in the stories have yet to be adequately understood. This lack of understanding persists because Lawrence conforms so poorly to the twentieth-century's post-Flaubertian, post-Jamesian image of the artistic craftsman. At the same time Lawrence is—especially in the psychological presentation of his characters—more individual and more radically experimental than practitioners of the "received experimentalism" to which we have become accustomed in the work of artists such as Joyce.[1]

Lawrence's work calls into play psychological perceptions and aesthetic sensibilities not fully exercised by most avant-garde literature. It requires also a willingness to go to the works as free as possible from preconceptions about what constitutes "good art" and from expectations of finding illustrated in the stories the ideas expressed in Lawrence's essays or letters. The fervor and frequency of Lawrence's own expository comments have encouraged the ideational approach, and the very subtlety of the stories has made the crutch it offers a temptation to critics. Even critics favorably disposed toward Lawrence are sometimes surprised to discover that a story does not simply illustrate some doctrine; they seldom show an inclination, however, to go on to analyze the methods by which Lawrence achieves this subtlety.[2] Mark Schorer, for instance, in his influential essay "Technique as Discovery," presumes that the mode of authorial presence espoused by Henry James, Conrad, and Joyce is the only defensible one and that Lawrence's departure from it in *Sons and Lovers* and other works is a mark of his technical failure. Such misapplication of modernist theory, no less than criticism overly concerned with biography or "doctrine," can interfere with a full appreciation of the technical and psychological skill and the thematic subtlety of Lawrence's work.

While D. H. Lawrence is regarded as a first-rate writer of short stories and is represented in every collection of modern short stories, his stories bear few similarities to those of other short-story writers before him or after. Although

Lawrence read and admired those writers prominent in what has come to be regarded as the high line of descent of the modern short story—Poe, Flaubert, Maupassant, Joyce, Chekhov, Mansfield, Hemingway—they had no great influence on him, nor he on them. These writers emphasize economy, careful selection of the "epiphanic" moment and the supporting detail, skillful contrivance of some single effect. They aspire to refine their own presence out of any existence in the story and abjure telling in favor of showing. Their stories are psychological in the sense that they focus upon a crucial turning point, some clear realization, in the life of a character. Frank O'Connor quotes a line from Gogol's "The Overcoat" to epitomize such dramatic turns: "and from that day forth, everything was as it were changed and appeared in a different light to him."[1] Lawrence's psychological presentation, on the other hand, admits of few such sharply cognitive epiphanies, his narrative voice may assume a palpable presence, and his presentation is relatively diffuse.

Although the modernist line of descent in short fiction has been held in the highest critical esteem, there is nevertheless another important species of story, indigenous to Britain and represented in the works of Stevenson, Hardy, Kipling, and, more recently, A. E. Coppard and H. E. Bates. Stories of this tradition, perhaps better called tales, are characteristically of broader scope and more diffuse presentation, often running far longer than the length sanctioned by Maupassant's paradigm (for example, Stevenson's "The Beach at Falesá," Hardy's "The Distracted Preacher," Kipling's "The Man Who Would Be King," Coppard's "My Hundredth Tale," and many of Bates's works). Stories of this tradition are more likely to involve a narrator, either playing some role in events or, at least, as story-teller. The events recounted may cover several years; plot is elaborately embellished. Characters on the other hand are less sharply focused upon, tending to assume their places in some larger scheme of action and setting. And within this counter-tradition there are variations—from Stevenson's penchant for the violent and *outré* to Coppard's more subdued realism. Lawrence has more in common with the storytellers of this latter school (especially if Hardy is included) than he does with the mainline modernists, but there are significant differences. In a story by Lawrence, plot is never the primary interest, and the narrator rarely appears in his own person or speaks in his own voice. The interest is more intensely psychological, the conception of character more complex, the style more imagistic than in most tales.

Critical studies of the short story have done little to place Lawrence in reference to either school or to examine the literary influences upon him. Whereas some critics have suggested affinities with George Eliot or Thomas Hardy, they have made no case for influence on Lawrence's practice specifically of the short story. Walter Allen's *The Short Story in English*, for instance, consistently praises

Lawrence's technique and insight and ranks him "second only to Kipling in English writing."[4] But other than briefly comparing "The White Stocking" with Chekhov's "The Darling" (which was not in fact translated into English until after *The Prussian Officer* had been published), Allen makes little effort to trace the ancestry of Lawrence's short stories or to assign him a place in the history of the form. Similarly, T. O. Beachcroft praises Lawrence's stories and the "remarkable contribution" the stories of *The Prussian Officer* volume made "to the form as well as the substance of short stories," yet fails either to discuss Lawrence's predecessors or his disciples in the genre, or indeed to analyze his contribution to it, remarking that at times "one feels he is simply not interested in the form of the story."[5] Lawrence scholars too have neglected influences on Lawrence as a writer of short stories, despite the clear record both in his letters and in Jessie Chambers's *D. H. Lawrence: A Personal Record*, of his attentive reading of works by Balzac, Maupassant, Zola, Gorky, Hardy, as well as of those writers appearing in the *English Review*.[6]

Only Keith Cushman in "The Young D. H. Lawrence and the Short Story" explores Lawrence's origins as a writer of short fiction and documents what Lawrence had to say about the short story as a genre. Cushman designates Gorky and Maupassant as "the most important early influences on Lawrence, the short-story writer," and claims that, at least for a time, Lawrence espoused realism and "saw himself as belonging to this 'school' "—though Cushman weakens the integrity of his position when he counts Hardy a realist simply on the basis of his desire to make "fiction speak directly to the reality of human experience." Cushman's claim for Lawrence as realist rests on some ambiguous statements by Jessie Chambers to the effect that Lawrence was thrilled by Maupassant's technique, and most of all on a letter from Lawrence to Louie Burrows in which Lawrence recommends a reading of the *English Review* as "the best possible way to get into touch with the new young school of realism." Cushman assumes that the realism Lawrence refers to is that of Maupassant and Gorky.[7]

A closer look at the context of Lawrence's remark and at the *English Review* shows that in fact Lawrence means by realism something much broader than the practice of those writers. In the letter to Burrow, Lawrence describes the *English Review*:

It is very fine, and very "new." There you will meet the new spirit at its best. . . . It is the best possible way to get into touch with the new young school of realism, to take the *English Review*. In this month's issue [i.e., October 1909], there is a particularly fine story, [Anne Douglas Sedgwick's] "The Nest"—such a one as you would find nowhere but in the *English*, and a magnificent story. . . . I return you the "Goose Fair"—you may as well keep it entirely. If I had it I should write it out again, and vivify in places: but you will use your own discretion. . . . But pray do not write *too* romantically: write as near to life as possible. You needn't be pessimistic or cynical, but it is always best to be true. The *English Review* is finely truthful, on the whole.[8]

This letter provides sufficient context to clarify that what Lawrence means by realism is at a far remove from the school of Maupassant. Cushman himself puzzles over Lawrence's admiration for Sedgwick's "The Nest" and acknowledges that it "is certainly radically unlike the short stories of Gorky [and] Maupassant."[9] Furthermore, although Lawrence does advise Louie Burrows not to write "*too* romantically" in "Goose Fair," he then goes on to warn against pessimism or cynicism—frequent elements in Maupassant—in favor simply of being true to life. In light of Lawrence's specific reference to the October 1909 issue of the *English Review* and his persistent association of that magazine with the "new" mode, it is revealing to examine J. A. Hobson's "The Task of Realism" in that issue.[10] Using the term in neither a strictly literary nor philosophical sense, Hobson calls for a new and more comprehensive approach to experience; the "fuller" realism he advocates takes into account "creative or interpretive hypotheses," and can thus be distinguished from "the cruder realism whose only facts were hard and dead." Hobson sees "that realism which to-day is struggling for positive expression" as moving a step beyond its "early inroads" into the fictional, poetic and dramatic works of "Tolstoy, Zola, Ibsen, Shaw, Brieux," and while he acknowledges that "At first sight realism may appear an extremely inadequate word to express that striving of head and heart which is replacing the dissipation and distraction of the earlier rationalism," he can find no other adequate term. In a closing statement, perhaps echoed in Lawrence's praise of the *Review*, Hobson calls on the magazine to champion this new realism, hoping that "those who accept the view that experiments in collective self-consciousness, as a means of accelerating and directing the 'urge of the world' towards human enlightenment and well-being, are likely to yield great results, will recognize that a rendering of realism in many fields of thought and art is the most profitable use for such a *Review*."

Even while presenting his arguments for Lawrence as realist, Cushman notes aspects of his work, notably the "rare emotive power," that separate him from the mode of Maupassant and Gorky, and finally can only admit that "the question of Lawrence's relation to the tradition of the short story remains curiously elusive."[11] This elusiveness is in part due to the very nature of the short story itself; of all modern literary forms, it is the least determined by literary convention, the most likely to be all things to all people. The link of the short story with the perennial human inclination to present experience in brief narrative accounts is borne out by A. E. Coppard who, in the foreword to his *Collected Tales*, contrasts the novel, an art form with a clear distinct pedigree, with the short story, "an ancient art originating in the folk tale." "Cut a person off from all contact with tales," Coppard observes, "and he will assuredly begin to invent some."[12] So while some theoreticians may present one or two types of the story as paradigmatic (e.g., those of Maupassant or Chekhov), such modes by no means exhaust the possibilities.

An even more important reason for the resistance Lawrence's stories oppose to all attempts to label them lies in the author's distinctive mind and talent, and especially in his attitudes toward and his uses of art. Lawrence, more than other writers, used his writings to explore experience, to try out tentative ideas and feelings. He seems to have been able to empathize so thoroughly with his characters and their situations as to emerge from the experience of writing having learned something. Most people can develop no alternative to trial and error for coming to terms with experience; most writers, even, are too concerned with the place of their work in the literary tradition or its acceptability to the reading public, to write in a fashion truly exploratory. But for D. H. Lawrence, even early in his career, the act of writing was an act of exploration, of working through feelings and problems.[13] The author's well-known statement in a 26 October 1913 letter to Arthur McCleod bears this out: "one sheds ones sicknesses in books—repeats and presents again ones emotions, to be master of them."[14]

The exploratory quality in Lawrence's work does not indicate lack of authorial control; rather, it suggests that the control is intuitive and wholistic rather than narrowly cognitive. Lawrence judges the rightness of an evolving creation not by the degree of its conformity to some preconceived notion he intended to illustrate, but by his informed intuition about whether the work is on the right track. This is, of course, the gist of many of Lawrence's comments to correspondents about his works in progress, especially during 1913 and 1914 when his talent was evolving so quickly. In a 23 April 1913 letter to Arthur McCleod, for instance, he says of *The Sisters* (later *Women in Love*): "I am doing a novel which I have never grasped. Damn its eyes, there I am at page 145, and I've no notion what it's about. I hate it. F[rieda] says it is good. But it's like a novel in a foreign language I don't know very well—I can only just make out what it is about."[15] The exploratory emphasis of his writing is reflected too in his comment in "Morality and the Novel," that when "the novelist puts his thumb in the scale, to pull down the balance to his own predilection,"[16] he violates the integrity of his purpose. For Lawrence, art can give experience form, a distinctive ordering at once affective and cognitive and so more subtle and comprehensive than any form based upon sheer conceptualization. This capacity of art as a tool for exploring the always fearful steps into the future is frustrated if it is misused mere-ly to illustrate some preconceived idea.

The exploratory use of art suggests one reason that Lawrence's works exist in so wide an array of forms—not his indifference to form or genre, but his needing different lengths and modes to explore problems of different scope or depth. And while the novel can by its nature deal with issues of larger scope and greater depth—which is why for Lawrence it is the "one bright book of life"[17]—his various short stories are the appropriate mode for their subjects.

Lawrence's attitude toward literary form is a concomitant of his view of art as exploratory. Often in his letters—especially during 1913 and 1914—he com-ments on the form of some work he is reading or writing: he distinguishes between form as received aesthetic convention, and form as the appropriate and effective manifestation of the writer's subject and purposes. In his essay on Thomas Mann (written in May 1913), he faults both contemporary German literature and the school of Flaubert for craving a logical aesthetic form that attempts to fix "the definite line of the book." "But, can the human mind," Lawrence asks, "fix absolutely the definite line of a book, any more than it can fix absolutely any definite line of action for a living being?"[18] Although he rejects any too great attention to form as aesthetic convention, he is interested in form in the sense of the most appropriate mode of expression, and this concern runs through his letters during this period. In a letter of 24 December 1912 to Ernest Collings, Lawrence makes the distinction, speaking first of the difficulty of find-ing "exactly the form one's passion . . . wants to take," and later in the same letter defying the demands of convention: "They want me to have form: that means they want me to have their pernicious ossiferous skin-and-grief form, and I won't."[19]

Even before Lawrence came into his own voice fully and confidently (during the rewriting of The Prussian Officer stories and of The Sisters into Women in Love),[20] his writings did not easily fit the schools and conventions and forms of the writers he was reading. From early on, Lawrence showed an impressive inde-pendence of artistic imagination, which expressed itself most persistently in the distinctiveness of his techniques. His technique of psychological presentation in The Rainbow, Women in Love, and many of the stories is particularly distinctive and remains, even for present-day readers, more difficult than the "received," Joyc-ean mode of stream of consciousness, which conforms better to our image of ourselves as minds in bodies.

What, then, can be said about Lawrence's place in the short story? First, he did read widely in the genre, as is shown by his various references during his early years to Balzac, Gorky, George Eliot, Gissing, Anatole France, Maupassant, Hardy, Chekhov, Gertrude Bone, H. G. Wells, W. W. Jacobs, Anne Douglas Sedgwick, Alphonse Daudet, Zola, and others. But Lawrence expressed interest in or admiration toward very different types of writers, reflecting his wide-ranging curiosity and sympathy rather than any intention slavishly to imitate. That Lawrence had little theoretical interest in the short story as a genre has been noted by several critics and is reflected in the paucity of his commentary on the genre brought to light by Cushman's concerted search for it in his essay discussed above. And it seems clear that the writers who were most influential on his stories were the same as those who influenced him in other genres.[21] Foremost among these was Hardy, from whom Lawrence learned much about natural settings (the "spirit of place"), about the relationships between human personality and the circumambient universe, and about the subtlety and complexity of the forces working subliminally within human beings, and who served Lawrence as sounding board for his own emerging view of life.[22]

Lawrence's influence on subsequent writers is also problematic and has been scantily discussed. H. E. Bates, in his *The Modern Short Story*, has a chapter entitled "Lawrence and the Writers of Today," in which he argues that "Lawrence, being true to his own vision, will always be closer to life than either Kipling or Wells, and in that respect alone he set an example . . . which a new decade of writers eagerly followed."[23] Philip Hobsbaum, more specific, points to Lawrence's heightening of demotic speech through metaphor and alliteration "until it almost reaches the level of poetry" as the "aspect of his work that has had so much influence on later writers such as Len Doherty, Alan Sillitoe, Stan Barstow, Stanley Middleton, Bill Naughton, Keith Waterhouse, Philip Callow, among others."[24] Lawrence's influence seems most palpable in the stories of Coppard and Bates (and perhaps T. F. Powys), largely because of similarities of setting and of subject matter. Obviously lacking in even the best stories of these writers, however, are the intensity and the complex psychology that distinguish Lawrence's works.[25]

Whereas for several decades now critics of Joyce have distinguished James Joyce and Stephen Dedalus, even the most recent Lawrence criticism is infected by tangential biographical questions. Philip Hobsbaum, for example, opens his discussion of Lawrence's late stories with the pronouncement that they "share . . . the expression of the author's hatred for certain former friends, notably John Middleton Murry."[26] Thus Hobsbaum turns away from the stories themselves to make the critically debilitating assumption that they are flawed by unassimilated animus and rancor.

Much of the challenge and complexity of Lawrence's works arises out of their narrative point of view, the very aspect of Lawrence's technique (or lack of it) that Mark Schorer dwells upon in "Technique As Discovery."[27] In that essay Schorer brings to bear upon Lawrence several assumptions about point of view and literary form that stem from the practice of James, Conrad, and Joyce. The essence of Schorer's objection is that Lawrence does not remain "objective" in his presentation—that, on the contrary, in *Sons and Lovers* "Morel and Lawrence are never separated, which is a way of saying that Lawrence maintains for himself in this book the confused attitude of his character." The result, Schorer says, is "a psychological tension which disrupts the form of the novel and obscures its meaning."[28]

Lawrence's technique is not, however, a flawed version of the Jamesian method, but an alternative method, in some respects even more subtle and demanding, that arises from different assumptions about the relation of author to character. Ironically, in illustrating his contention that Lawrence's point of view is muddled, Schorer suggests (only to denigrate) the subtlety Lawrence achieves. "At the same time that *Sons and Lovers* condemns the mother," Schorer writes, "it justifies her." Surely that is no fault: surely Mrs. Morel is so complex a character that she should evoke both condemnation and justification. But since Lawrence does not achieve his complexity of tone through recognizable techniques sanctioned by other writers, Schorer presumes there is no technique involved. Instead of concluding that the point of view is subtle and complex, he concludes that it "is never adequately objectified and sustained."[29]

Lawrence simply did not turn as readily to the literary establishment for his paradigms and standards as did many of his contemporaries. Whether this expressed independence or merely idiosyncrasy, suffice it to say that Lawrence very largely went his own way. One manifestation of his independence is a view of authorial presence significantly different from that being touted by others. The "received" view during the 1920s was the ideal of objectivity described by Stephen Dedalus in *A Portrait of the Artist as a Young Man*. According to this view, "the artist, like the God of the creation, remains within or behind or beyond or above his handiwork, invisible, refined out of existence, indifferent, paring his fingernails."[30] Lawrence, however, intended not to withdraw himself from his characters, but rather to dwell in each of them as fully as possible. Thus, while writing from the perspective of a given character, Lawrence strives to put himself fully into the situation of that character, to empathize with the character sufficiently so as to present vividly and convincingly his feelings, wishes, thoughts—even his confusions. When he shifts to the perspective of another character, however, Lawrence does the same for him or her. Lawrence would, then, accept the principle that good writing aims at balance and fairness in the presentation of character, but whether such balance is best achieved by distancing oneself from the characters or by regarding each with as much empathy as possible, is, Lawrence would say, debatable.

Such a strategy of characterization does have tangible effects. For one, it renders the tenor of Lawrence's stories utterly different from that of Flaubert's or Joyce's, so that instead of austerity and dispassion, there is in every line of Lawrence's prose a quality of energy and intensity. Especially pronounced in such early stories as "Odour of Chrysanthemums" and "The Prussian Officer," this quality inheres as well in such later stories as "The Rocking-Horse Winner" and "Sun." For another, it leaves critics floundering in strange objections. Schorer objects that in *Sons and Lovers* Lawrence "maintains for himself the confused attitude of the character," thus generating "a psychological tension which disrupts the form of the novel and obscures its meaning." Ironically, the psychological tension that Schorer complains of is an effect that Lawrence must have intended. It could, in fact, be said that Lawrence "presents with wonderful fidelity and complexity the confused attitude of his character," and so generates a "psychological energy that stretches the form of the novel"—and the short story.

The kind of psychological energy generated by the subtleties of Lawrence's characterization in *Sons and Lovers* also marks the short story "England, My England." The heart of the story is Egbert's carefully chronicled decline from carefree joy, to irresponsibility, to self-denigration, and then to despair and "fatalism." Through seven years of marriage to Winifred, Egbert's heart has gradually become "hard with disillusion: a continual gnawing and resistance,"[31] a state of mind totally alien to the earlier Egbert who had brought the self-justifying beauty of the rose to the more materially productive stock of his wife's family. Yet, it is difficult to see Egbert affirmatively, even in the early parts of the story. He is described, for instance, as having "plenty of friends, of the same ineffectual sort as himself, tampering with the arts, literature, painting, sculpture, music" (*CSS*, 2: 308). Clearly this statement does not represent Egbert's self-evaluation; neither, however, does it represent an "authorial" last word. Though not static or simple, the narrative voice in "England, My England" speaks mainly from the perspective of the Marshalls; the ambivalence that Egbert elicits is produced by the subtleties of Lawrence's use of point of view. Although Lawrence might be expected to favor Egbert's more aesthetic view of life in the rivalry between him and the "strong-limbed, thick-bodied" Marshalls, the underlying attitude is not so easily established. And the strength of the story derives, at least in part, from the fine balance of attitude that it maintains.

The complexity in Lawrence's works of the authorial relationship to the characters is then due not only to the various dimensions of personality he is dramatizing, but also to a handling of point of view very different from that of many of his contemporaries. While Lawrence's presentation is often omniscient, some of what appears omniscient is not. Often passages that appear omniscient actually reflect a character's limited or even mistaken perspective, presented with such fullness and conviction as to sound "authorial." Such a comment is indeed authorial in that it may represent a thought or a feeling so fleeting or so subliminal that the character has no clear awareness of it and could not himself give it articulation. Thus the words printed on the page may represent something so vaguely formed that the character would deny it to be his thought. Or the text may present with fervor a feeling that is intense but fleeting, that does not represent the character's typical or considered thinking. Or, what is set down on the page may represent a conscious, articulated thought, but one that the character himself does not believe—a rationalization that allows his true motives or feelings to run on unmolested beneath the surface. And Lawrence may present all such thoughts, feelings, and rationalizations with a directness and vividness that confers apparent authorial sanction. He strives to do justice to a whole array of psychological subtleties that are not often caught in literature and that challenge modern conceptions of the mind's "integrity."

If what a character says may indeed by atypical or mistaken, if comments made by the narrative voice may only appear authorial, the burden upon the reader is considerable: how can he know where to stand, how does he know how to respond to any given passage? He must, of course, judge by the larger context, and in reading a D. H. Lawrence short story, the reader is obliged to remain tentative in accepting any passage, evaluating any character. Only after he has begun to grasp the psychological context of the story and the basic life-stances of the characters, can he judge the precise point of view behind any description or reflection. Reading a Lawrence story involves movement from part to whole and back to part.

The presentation of Isabel's psychology in "The Blind Man" illustrates some of the complexities of Lawrence's use of point of view. Technically, "The Blind Man" is omniscient; the author moves about in time and space and carries us into the minds of the characters. The story opens with Isabel Pervin waiting for the arrival of her friend Bertie and for the return of her husband. Of her anticipation of Bertie, the reader is told: "Her dearest and oldest friend, a man who seemed almost indispensable to her living, would drive up in the rainy dusk of the closing November day" (CSS, 2: 347). Isabel's reverie suggests that Bertie is important to her in a way that simply is not borne out by subsequent events, and it is likely that if Isabel could be challenged as to why she regards Bertie as "indispensable to her living," she would quite honestly deny any such feeling. But Lawrence is not misrepresenting Isabel. In her state of tension and anticipation—rooted deeply in concern for her husband and in her pregnancy, and, more shallowly, in looking forward to both Bertie and Maurice—she truly does have a flicker of feeling validly represented by the phrase quoted. In some way, on some level, she does feel that she could hardly stand it if Bertie were not to appear. But this impulse lies beneath thought and feeling, in some almost physical dimension not sanctioned by articulation. A level of Isabel's psyche is thus reflected that could not have been penetrated by first-person interior monologue: Isabel would not have said to herself, "My dearest and oldest friend, a man almost indispensable to my living, shall soon drive up." But the use of third-person indirect presentation enables Lawrence to represent states beneath any the character can express, or even feel very coherently.[32] Such a presentation does venture into psychological terrain almost uncharted.

An earlier story, "New Eve and Old Adam," shows a less technically proficient Lawrence struggling to find ways to dramatize his complex psychological interests. Lawrence devotes two long paragraphs to describing the husband's feelings, only to add, "He was not aware of this." He then resorts to explicit description of the husband's state of being: "But, again, the reasonable being in him knew it was ridiculous, and he remained staring at the dark, having the horrible sensation of a roof low down over him; whilst that dark, unknown being which lived below all his consciousness in the eternal gloom of his blood, heaved and raged blindly against him" (*CSS*, 1: 82). Later in this story, three levels of psychology are at work in Lawrence's rendering of the wife's charges against the husband: "the unpardonable thing was that you told me you loved me.—Your *feelings* have hated me these three months, which did not prevent you from taking my love and every breath from me.—Underneath you undermined me, in some subtle, corrupt way that I did not see because I believed you, when you told me you loved me" (*CSS*, 1: 93). But the husband is not the villain the wife's statement makes him out, largely because he understands no better than she the forces they are struggling with. He *tells* her he loves her, which is true. But on the level just beneath this articulation, his *feelings* (italicized in the story) resent and resist the torture he endures, and he doubtless has been trying to free himself. On a deeper level still than that of coherent feeling, he is committed to his wife in a way that deserves to be called love. And while the story only imperfectly dramatizes these psychological states in husband and wife, it does convey their mutual misunderstanding, their confused mixture of need and fear.

In "*A Propos* of *Lady Chatterley's Lover*," Lawrence observes that everyone has shallow needs and wishes and profound needs and wishes, but that it may be extremely hard at any given time to discriminate between them.[33] Lawrence allows his characters to reflect both sorts of needs and wishes, and the reader cannot easily disentangle them. In "Two Blue Birds," for example, it almost certainly requires a second reading to sense that Mrs. Gee's "gallant affairs" mean nothing to her and that she is using them in hopes of stinging her husband into some response. And in the early masterpiece "The White Stocking," young

Elsie does not know precisely what she is after in her flirtation with Sam Adams, but surely it lies in the direction of a fuller relationship with her husband rather than any real involvement with the blustery Adams.

Another distinctive feature of Lawrence's work is his ability to represent the psychological states of his characters and their milieu with unparalleled fullness. Among the several essays attempting to do justice to this quality, one of the most interesting is Donald Ross's discussion of Lawrence's use of third-person attributed narration. Quoting a paragraph of description-reflection from the wife's point of view in "The Shadow in the Rose Garden," Ross comments, "These images, the Edenic 'gate,' the confusion, are not necessarily available to the character's conscious mind. Lawrence does not suggest that she could say in words that these things are her thoughts; in fact, the wife's spoken words are utilitarian and not at all lyrical. In her sparse dialogue, her most expressive words are 'strange,' 'fond,' and the cumbersome 'not-straightforward.' Lawrence uses attributed narration to depict a rich mental life for a virtually inarticulate character."[34] The only questionable feature of Ross's analysis is the word "mental" in the last sentence, which implies that what Lawrence articulates is present in the wife's *mind*, whereas it is better described as a *state of being*.

These psychological dimensions of Lawrence's work remain elusive, however, partly because they involve a conception of the self unfamiliar to the modern reader. Lawrence goes beyond the idea of an "individual mind" to view personality as involving much more than the ego can conceive, as resting upon a continuum with the body and with the circumambient situation. It involves an affective penumbra around the person that seems to come out of that region where the field of consciousness shades off into everything surrounding it.[35] Lawrence's approach to personality recalls Virginia Woolf's description of life as "a luminous halo, a semi-transparent envelope surrounding us from the beginning of consciousness to the end," and in his novels and stories Lawrence tried to convey "this unknown and uncircumscribed spirit."[36] Lawrence himself, in his 5 June 1914 letter to Edward Garnett, gave a famous defense of the conception of personality he was attempting to capture in *The Wedding Ring* (later *The Rainbow*):

I don't agree with you about the Wedding Ring. You will find that in a while you will like the book as a whole. I don't think the psychology is wrong: it is only that I have a different attitude to my characters, and that necessitates a different attitude in you, which you are not as yet prepared to give. . . . [S]omehow—that which is physic—non-human, in humanity, is more interesting to me than the old-fashioned human element—which causes one to conceive a character in a certain moral scheme and make him consistent. The certain moral scheme is what I object to. In Turguenev, and in

Tolstoi, and in Dostoievski, the moral scheme into which all the characters fit—and it is nearly the same scheme—is, whatever the extraordinariness of the characters themselves, dull, old, dead. . . . I don't care so much about what [a] woman *feels*—in the ordinary usage of the word. That *presumes* an *ego* to feel with. I only care about what the woman *is*—what she *is*—inhumanly, physiologically, materially—according to the use of the word: but for me, what she *is* as a phenomenon (or as representing some greater, inhuman will), instead of what she feels according to the human conception. That is where the futurists are stupid. Instead of looking for the new human phenomenon, they will only look for the phenomena of the science of physics to be found in human being. . . . You mustn't look in my novel for the old stable ego of the character. There is another ego, according to whose action the individual is unrecognisable, and passes through, as it were, allotropic states which it needs a deeper sense than any we've been used to exercise, to discover are states of the same single radically-unchanged element. (Like as diamond and coal are the same pure element of carbon. The ordinary novel would trace the history of the diamond—but I say "diamond, what! This is carbon." And my diamond might be coal or soot, and my theme is carbon.)[37]

The point of the letter—which Lawrence does not put as clearly as he might, struggling as he was with a new conception and against the advice of a respected critic and friend—is that the personality, the self, consists of far more than the ego's conception of the self, but that literature has not done justice to those nebulous aspects of personality. Lawrence's objection to the practice of the Russians would be clearer if he had left out the word "moral"—a red flag to most present-day critics. What Lawrence objects to in these writers is their narrow conception of their characters—for the author's conception functions in fiction much as the ego functions in ordinary psychology, as a conceptual constraint upon the fullness of self. In fiction, especially nineteenth-century fiction, such a conception inevitably has a "moral" aspect, since the character is acting ("rightly" or "wrongly") in a world of other characters. But Lawrence's objection is not to the *morals* of these writers or their characters, but to the narrowness of their psychological conception.

Confusing, too, is Lawrence's use of "nonhuman" and "inhuman" when he means "precognitive" or "pre-individual." However "generic" Lawrence's conception of his characters is, they are still recognizably human. Lawrence, however, minimizes the individual aspects of character he believes to be often overemphasized at the expense of deeper elements. His professed indifference to what the woman *feels* exemplifies this: he does not wish to confine his presentation to feelings that are sufficiently clear and coherent to be given sanction by the mind. Rather, he strives also to depict "states of being" that are almost physiological rather than mental—for example, Isabel's sense that Bertie is indispensable to her living—but are nevertheless distinctively human. Lawrence is, then, dissatisfied with the individualism at the heart of modern literature. He objects to identifying the self with the mind's conception of the self—a tendency fostered by stream-of-consciousness technique, purporting as it does to present the flow of thought in the mind—and he strives to forge techniques to evoke the self more fully, such as his use of third-person indirect presentation.

One feature of Lawrence's presentation commented on by several critics (and by Lawrence himself in the foreword to *Women in Love*) is the evocation of a rhythm, a pulsating quality, that works through the character's psyche. On the page such rhythms are suggested mainly by the repetition of words or images or situations—a technique that some critics have found objectionable. But since he wishes more fully to present the psyche, Lawrence must somehow suggest those rhythms, for, as he has said, "every natural crisis in emotion or passion or understanding comes from this pulsing, frictional to-and-fro which works up to culmination" (foreword to *Women in Love*).[38]

Lawrence's multileveled presentation of character is complemented and supported by something in the works that might be called "psychic texture." This texture arises out of a more general psychic milieu in the works, not generated simply by particular characters and not identifiable with individual states of mind; it is conveyed through the authorial voice that "contains" the characters, uniting them in a pervasive medium that grows out of setting and event and is more palpably psychological (or "psychic," in Jung's generic sense of that term), than mood or atmosphere. The modern worldview militates against the conception of any psychic element not directly associated with some individual mind; there is in Lawrence's works, however, a quality that is "psychic" and yet cannot be equated with the attitude of any character or of the narrator. This dimension may be suggested by the term "spirit of place," for it owes a great deal to description of setting, but it draws upon the psychological states of individual characters, and it is manifested in the authorial voice even when that voice does not directly reflect the personality of any individual character. Psychic texture, then, both grows out of and is the necessary medium for Lawrence's sense of personality as continuous with environment.[39]

This quality is to be found in the opening paragraph of "The Prussian Officer":

They had marched more than thirty kilometres since dawn, along the white, hot road where occasional thickets of trees threw a moment of shade, then out into the glare again. On either hand, the valley wide and shallow, glittered with heat; dark-green patches of rye, pale young corn, fallow and meadow and black pine woods spread in a dull, hot diagram under a glistening sky. But right in front the mountains ranged across, pale blue and very still, snow gleaming gently out of the deep atmosphere. And towards the mountains, on and on, the regiment marched between the rye-fields and the meadows, between the scraggy fruit trees set regularly on either side of the high road. The burnished, dark-green rye threw off a suffocating heat, the mountains drew gradually nearer and more distinct. While the feet of the soldiers grew hotter, sweat ran through their hair under their helmets, and their knapsacks could burn no more in contact with their shoulders, but seemed instead to give off a cold, prickly sensation.

This largely descriptive passage is presented authorially; it speaks for no identifiable character. Yet the first word, "They," involves a human perspective basic to the tenor of the passage. The heat and glare of the road, the shade of the thickets of trees have meaning only as experienced by someone, as do the contrasts suggested by the fecund crops in the valley and the snow-touched mountains. And this *experienced* dimension of the passage becomes more tangible in the reference to the "suffocating" heat, and in the explici̇̃ (but still generic) references to the sensations of "the soldiers" in the last sentence. The description generates an energy, an intensity, a tension (somehow accentuated by the distant but unavailable mountains) that is the appropriate psychic backdrop for the story. The brief second paragraph, beginning "He" rather than "They," is so continuous with the first that the individual referred to is easily absorbed into the milieu, almost as if the first paragraph had expressed his sense of things: "He walked on and on in silence, staring at the mountains ahead, that rose sheer out of the land, and stood fold behind fold, half earth, half heaven, the heaven, the barrier with slits of snow, in the pale, bluish peaks." The milieu thus established acts as a kind of psychic equivalent of the electromagnetic field and contributes a great deal to the distinctive energy of Lawrence's works.

Another insufficiently recognized and understood attribute of Lawrence's work is its "contextuality"—a scrupulous fidelity to the full psychological context of the characters depicted. It is, for instance, only in the light of the full context of "England, My England," that the Egbert of the pleated brow and the disillusioned heart can be seen to have moved so long a way down the road of self-disavowal. And it is only in the whole context that there can be found some explanation as to why Egbert responds so irresponsibly to Joyce's accident. By the time the accident occurs, Egbert has come to take an irrevocable stand against not only authority but also responsibility, so that no matter how much his heart may be anxious about Joyce's knee (*CSS*, 2: 320), he will not act; action, authority, and responsibility have been relegated to the Marshalls. Then as Winifred becon :s more purely the Mater Dolorata, suffering the seven swords in her breast (*CSS*, 2: 322), Egbert becomes more fully the alien, evasive serpent turning away now even from sympathy (*CSS*, 2: 324).

Lawrence's contextual integrity, his development of a full, detailed psychological context, involves him in a fidelity to reality that many readers are not prepared to credit, largely because of assumptions that Lawrence manipulates characters in order to illustrate some aspect of his "doctrine." Actually, Lawrence is trying to do justice to the complexity of the living situation he is depicting, and he often succeeds so well as to all but obscure any thematic "point." Contextuality is integral to the exploratory aim of Lawrence's art, in that a true and subtle exploration can occur only if a character's situation is rendered with attention to all the strains, uncertainties, and ambiguities involved.

To understand why one of Lawrence's characters thinks or acts as he does, the reader should refer not to the social class the character "represents," nor to the traits of his biographical "original," nor to the Lawrentian doctrine he presumably embodies. He should refer first to the character's psychological *context*, with all its stresses, fears, enticements to role-playing or to evasion, etc. Only if the reader has sufficient faith in the subtlety of Lawrence's art that he is willing to re-create in his own mind the situation of the character will he grasp the forces working upon that character and see why he reacts as he does. Further, because of this precisely adjusted contextuality, each character's situation is different, and his proclivities in that situation should not be generalized into a Lawrentian rule of conduct. Many of Lawrence's stories depict a crisis that a character must respond to either through self-assertion or self-effacement. But simply because self-assertion is the appropriate response in one situation, we should not infer that Lawrence advocates self-assertion, or even that this character should always act assertively.[40]

The ending of "Odour of Chrysanthemums" shows Lawrence's contextuality at work, and at the same time illustrates the divergence of his psychological modes from the "epiphanic" revelation that many modern stories turn upon. Critics of "Odour of Chrysanthemums" tend to focus on Elizabeth's realization dramatized in the story's closing pages. But the aim of the story is not so simply cognitive, and Lawrence's true interest lies in exploring and faithfully representing a fuller range of Elizabeth's reactions to this trauma. Among the most interesting of her reactions is self-castigation for having denied Walter, and a consequent exaggeration of how cruelly she had injured this man and how clearly she now sees her fault. But she can afford so categorical a view only because Walter is dead. It is much easier for her to tell herself that "She denied him what he was—she saw it now. She had refused him as himself," than it would have been to come to terms with the living, willful, and inscrutable man. And so it is too neat to say that death has "restored the truth"—quite the contrary, death has allowed Elizabeth a simplification that life would never have permitted. But Elizabeth should not be judged harshly, for this simplification of her relation with Walter is precisely what is needed by someone in her situation.

Does the story's ending convey some valid "life-realization" that Elizabeth has come to, or does it rather, with great fidelity, explore the psychology of such a loss? Is the first reaction after bereavement likely to be the "true" one? Is it not more likely to be colored by fear, by guilt, by the need to find some simple conception of things to hold onto?

The complexity of Lawrence's characterization is further compounded by the kinds of judgments he does and does not make about his characters. Presuming that Lawrence's stories intend to inculcate some doctrine or to redress some personal vendetta, many critics seek to distinguish heroes from villains according to how characters "represent" Lawrence or his ideas. In practice, Lawrence's characters are judged primarily on whether they are life-affirmers or life-deniers. The most important question is to be asked about a character in Lawrence's works is whether he is trying, however imperfectly, to open himself to life, to run the risk of engaging the new, to have faith that the present life-crisis can be broken through into some new direction; or whether he is trying to protect or insulate himself against life, trying defensively to maintain some status quo that he fears represents the best, or the safest, he can ever achieve. As straightforward as this criterion may seem, in application it becomes quite complex. The life-affirmer must on occasion break off a relationship or go through a phase of retrogression or withdrawal; the life-denier, on the other hand, may be subtle in his evasions—so subtle as to turn to sexual passion or to the clichés of Christian charity as a means of escape from what he lacks the courage to face. Nor is any one act likely to reveal the character's true orientation; for that, the larger context of the story is required.

Furthermore, judging a character in these terms must be distinguished from the attitude we are asked to take toward him: having judged a character to be making a wrong decision about his life, the reader may yet sympathize with him in his failure. For example, the more we come to understand Egbert in "England, My England," the more clearly wrong appear some of his acts, but the more too we come to sympathize with him, to wish we could help him set right what is clearly seen as a wrong life-course. After the accident to Joyce, he sells out entirely his earlier best qualities; "when the war broke out his whole instinct was against it: against war" (*CSS*, 2: 326), and yet he seizes upon the opportunity war provided to bring his negation to a culmination. The progressive development of Egbert's fatalism and despair, so terribly reflected in the details of his death, prompts the reader's sympathy, and yet Egbert must also be judged as one who has surrendered to a dissolution that seems to him far more real than the abandoned struggle for synthesis and for life.

Finally, none of these adjurations denies that Lawrence's works can and should be read in conjunction with the ideas he proposes more directly in his essays, reviews, and letters. But two points must be emphasized: first, such ideas should be turned to only after some basic sense of the story as story has been arrived at; second, the story will always involve some "special case," some exception to the general principle. For example, having come to an understanding of the human relationships between the Officer and the Orderly in "The Prussian Officer," the reader may then approach these characters in terms of the categories of mental consciousness and blood consciousness. But insofar as the Orderly "represents" the blood consciousness, his mechanical, reflexive response to the life-challenge presented by the Officer, and his subsequent collapse and death, hint strongly of limitations in that mode of consciousness. Surely the young Orderly had a great deal to live for, and surely it would have been better had he been able to summon up the cunning or the understanding to elude the Officer's challenge before it reached life-destroying proportions. But, limited creature that he is, the Orderly cannot do this, and so he dies almost as an animal would in response to an attack—not a very good illustration of Lawrence's presumed belief in the superiority of the blood consciousness.

To sum up, then, attention to the categories of point of view, contextuality, and evaluative judgment is necessary in order to appreciate Lawrence's subtle, distinctive modes of presentation. Too schematic an approach to Lawrence's works inevitably fails to do them justice, especially if the point of view of the presentation embodies the character's own confusions and evasions. So subtle can this contextuality become that Lawrence may depict a character who is basically a life-affirmer but who is so confused by the life-crisis he is facing (as one is always confused in a true crisis), that he makes a wrong move, but the reader is supposed to be sufficiently attuned to the larger context of the story to understand and sympathize with what is happening. Whatever peril such subtle contextuality may involve for the reader, whatever opportunity for misreading, it is nonetheless necessary to Lawrence's deepest artistic purposes that he depict his characters' situations in their fullest complexity. How realistic, and how worthwhile, would it be to purport to depict a crisis and yet to show the characters who are caught up in it acting lucidly? It is precisely this audacious subtlety, this fidelity to experience, that is so valuable in Lawrence's art and makes his short stories so different from those of his contemporaries. To abort these qualities by forcing preconceptions upon the stories is to destroy what is finest in them and to deprive us of both pleasure and insight.

Weldon Thornton

University of North Carolina
at Chapel Hill

VIRGINIA WOOLF AND
KATHERINE MANSFIELD

Virginia Woolf wrote novels, essays, biography, diaries, and letters. She also wrote twenty-four short stories.[1] Amid the brilliant richness of the other work, however, the stories lie neglected. They are said, even by Woolf herself, to hint at the accomplishments of the novels.

Yet the short story form is superbly suited to her famous vision. The title of one story, "Moments of Being," can serve as a metaphor for her particular knack of seeing into the center of those specks of time and space where reality becomes transparent. Reality is perceptible only in "orts, scraps, and fragments," says the scriptwriter, speaking for Woolf in her last novel, *Between the Acts*. She knows how to expand as well as condense time in order to uncover those suspended fragments. Moreover, she has a lyrical gift that fits the outburst of the short form. In fact, a typical story by Virginia Woolf could be an ideal model of Frank O'Connor's definition of the genre as a "significant moment" from which past, present, and future may be viewed simultaneously.[2]

The moment is her subject; the moment is her method. Perhaps there never was another short-story writer for whom form and content were thus merged. An excellent example is "The Searchlight." Its opening captures a party of sophisticated people paused on a London balcony between dinner and theater. Casually drinking coffee, smoking, and chatting, they watch an air force searchlight probing the night skies. In one burst of light, Mrs. Ivimey "sees" something. She sees the setting and action of a story told her by her great-grandfather about his youth. It seems that he lived in a lonely tower on the Yorkshire moors. One day, using his telescope, he saw a kiss between a man and a girl. He saw love, and, leaving his tower, he ran miles across the moors to find that girl, whom he would later marry. That's all: "The light . . . only falls here and there." Present time restrictions intervene: "Right you are. Friday." But with her story, Mrs. Ivimey has swept away one hundred years. She has had a glimpse of love observed, as with books and telescopes, as opposed to love embraced. Once again life has happened between the acts, between, in this case, dinner and the theater.

Like "The Searchlight," almost all the other Woolf stories have at their center a philosophical theme expressed in tones reserved by many writers for sensual experience. She cares passionately about the precise nature of reality and the values of existence. She worries about philosophical dichotomies; the "knowing" versus "being" dilemma, for instance, is central to "The Searchlight." Woolf is likewise intrigued by the opposition of art and life, appearance and reality, subjectivity and objectivity, the self and the not-self, vision and fact. Even when she writes about social class division or, as she so often does, the man-woman confrontation, her concerns are as much philosophical as political or psychological.

Above all, Woolf investigates the Imagination as a tool for knowing, unifying, and finally transcending its environment through love. For her, short stories are also "religious." They constitute a search for lasting significance in natural and human phenomena. The sea, the landscape, animals, and above all the mysterious human figures themselves, beckon to her, then depart through mists: "If I fall on my knees, if I go through the ritual, the ancient antics, it's you, unknown figures, you I adore; if I open my arms, it's you I embrace, you I draw to me—adorable world!" ("An Unwritten Novel").

Her work had this philosophical and religious emphasis from the beginning. One of her first short stories, "Monday or Tuesday," manages in just three hundred words to present both details and panoramas of reality while simultaneously questioning its essential qualities. The story opens far from the human activity that is always for Woolf only one component of an overlapping universe. A heron, who can afford to be "lazy and indifferent" because he knows his way instinctively, passes over the human sphere and under the sky. The sky is even more self-absorbed. Indifferent to lakes, mountains, and stars, the sky—though she "moves"—"remains." Heron and sky, male and female, are contrasted with the active world of men, women, and children, of jarring omnibuses, reflections in London shop windows, and Miss Thingummy, who sits in her office drinking her tea. Could anything be more real than Miss Thingummy?

"And is truth then a list of observable details?" the narrative consciousness seems to be asking. So many details are simply reflections of something else. So many are transient and incomparable—"squandered in separate scales." So much happens parenthetically. Though the questions are difficult, the searching long and laborious, still the mind behind this story is "for ever desiring truth." Above it all, not needing to desire but simply to be, are the heron and the sky. The gap between the two worlds is traveled—"voyaging," Woolf says, using her favored water metaphor—via the imagination. In the penultimate paragraph someone very like a conventional narrator takes shape, home from all that activity, sitting by the fire, reading her way into the reality behind the flames, smoke, and sparks—Platonic imagery for this Platonic search. The view in the last lines drifts upward from the dross of everyday activity. Visions of mosques enter the consciousness, followed—higher up—by the Indian seas, then by blue space and the stars themselves. Is this perhaps truth at last? Or is it only psychic "closeness" with the vast elements, which is all we have and all we need to have? As if in answer, the sky first covers the stars, those bright specks of near certainty, then uncovers them to our hungering gaze.

This human miracle of connectedness has happened amid the most ordinary facts of life. Realizations about the mind, the way it knows, and its involvement with the world outside itself, await us any Monday or Tuesday.

The abundance of her speculations sometimes threatens to dilute Woolf's considerable energies. A period of abstract questioning can drive her back to facts, to "Solid Objects" (to mention another story title), to the Miss Thingummys. There she roots happily among direct experiences. But as soon as she describes the solid objects, she brings them sensuously to life. And once she has done that, she cannot help herself—she must daydream. So, like all of us, Woolf oscillates between experience and interpretation.

She speaks of these matters directly in "The Mark on the Wall," as charming a piece of philosophy as has ever been written. Glancing up from her daily concerns one day, Woolf—for it is surely proper to identify the voice here as hers—notices a small black mark against a white wall. Is it a large nail mark? Thus begins a series of meanderings through, among other topics, the nature of fantasizing, selfhood as an infinite series of reflected phantom images, the male-induced fraudulence of social convention, and the vast ignorance behind what learned professors call factual knowledge. Life, she decides, is an accidental matter in spite of all our civilized attempts to control it. Very little sticks to us: "Why, if one wants to compare life to anything, one must liken it to being blown through the Tube at fifty miles an hour—landing at the other end without a single hairpin in one's hair! Shot out at the feet of God entirely naked!" Therefore, it is useless to get up to see just what the mark on the wall really is. What it "really" is, is just another particle of so-called solid reality, which will not connect. Staying where she sits, this pensive Woolf wants "to sink deeper and deeper, away from the surface, with its hard separate facts."

Just here she gets caught. To be sure, she opens up the world of speculation. But she does so by daring to deny the importance of long-established convention, such as which Anglican archbishop precedes which Anglican archbishop, thereby forcing Nature to protect herself. No one's thoughts must collide with

Nature's reality. People must not be left dangerously adrift in solipsism. So in spite of her love of the daydream, Woolf finds she must learn what the mark on the wall is, and thereby hang onto something as definite and real as "a plank in the sea." She seeks salvation by "worshipping solidity, worshipping reality, worshipping the impersonal world which is a proof of some existence other than ours."[3]

When Woolf turns from the speculative story to a more recognizable version of the genre, she is nonetheless often working through the same issues. "The Introduction," for instance, dramatizes one of Woolf's lasting concerns, the endangered self. The theme is embodied in a shy, intellectually ambitious young woman who is introduced to an arrogant young man and learns that her role in civilization is merely to adorn him. One of several stories about people meeting and parting without significantly altering their isolation, "The Introduction" builds its feminist theme on the question of what is real. As Lily Everit drives to the party in a cab, she looks through the glass between her and the driver to see "her own white phantom reflected in his dark coat." Her personality, as in "The Mark on the Wall," is an infinitely possible rather than definitely knowable thing. She responds to this situation, as other Woolf characters do, by calling life a series of dualisms between which one must steer the craft of one's self. "One divided life . . . into fact and into fiction, into rock and into wave." At the beginning of the story, Lily's rock is her essay on Swift, for which she has just that morning received high praise from her professor. But in the hands of the unwittingly brutal Bob Brinsley, a gem of conventional English manhood and harder, more assertively real, than her essay, she feels her own sense of reality melting away. Everything turns to water, "leaving her only the power to stand at bay." Mrs. Dalloway, a "steamer" of a woman, flings her "into a whirlpool where either she would perish or be saved." But in this whirlpool of the man-woman involvement, though there is "a kind of passion," there is no salvation. Lily has entered naked and vulnerable—like Eve, Woolf's language would urge us to remember—"in some shady garden" from which she is evicted, "a naked wretch," knowing at that moment of vision that "there are no sanctuaries."

Even in the relatively plotted stories (which Woolf wrote for money, thinking plot was what people wanted), she cannot turn her mind completely from metaphorical thinking. In "Lappin and Lapinova" she creates a plot that is saved from being cloying by the universality of its conceptual underpinnings. That the story is in addition romantic, sad, and filled with longing makes it among the most appealing of her short works of fiction. Rosalind and Ernest, a newly wedded young couple, are tucked into their own private, enchanting world. There she calls him King of the Rabbits, and she is his Queen Lapinova. With this construct, the honeymooning couple for some time control their outer worlds, for they can turn any disagreeable aspect of it into fictional shapes. An unpleasant sister-in-law is thought of as an ugly ferret in their woodsy kingdom. A bullying mother-in-law becomes the Squire. Rosalind and Ernest are very much in love. Their created world sustains them both, but especially Rosalind. Without the collusion of her husband in the play, she is threatened with "being melted; dispersed; dissolved into nothingness." At the end, that is just what happens. Rosalind is almost literally disenchanted by the now prosaic Ernest, who has given up the game and forfeited her spirit to death. The author's terse conclusion is: "So that was the end of that marriage." The statement is a variant of the Gogol phrase quoted by Frank O'Connor as a description of what any successful short story "means": "and from that day forth everything was as it were changed and appeared in a different light to him."[4] Everything appears in a different light to Rosalind because she can no longer use her imagination to achieve the delicate balance of art in life.

To the service of her themes, Woolf brought an astonishing array of technical skills. Some of the stories are, in the first place, so unusual as to merit, sixty years after they were written, the label "experimental." Stories like "Monday or Tuesday" and "Kew Gardens" have not so much a concealed narrator or shifting points of view as what has been called, with respect to the New Novel in France, "the experiencing mind."[5] Frequently that mind makes the distance between observer and observed seem to disappear. Then there is the magic of what Woolf does with time. In the time it takes Fanny Wilmot in "Moments of Being" to search for a pin, she re-creates Julia Craye's lifetime and pinpoints her essence. Woolf also performs magic with space: in "The String Quartet" a piece by Mozart sends Woolf's readers racing around the sensual universe—to a pear tree on top of a mountain, to the silver fishes in the Rhone. Perhaps only with Proust is language equal to these same tasks. A further very contemporary touch in "The String Quartet" is the telescoped dialogue, which is like Harold Pinter's but without his overtones of absurdity, fear, and cruelty. Yet there are rich and ancient iambic rhythms to Woolf's language as well: "How lovely goodness is in those who, stepping lightly, go smiling through the world." In fact, what marks Woolf's techniques throughout her fiction is this combination of the experimental and the traditional. In a story like "Monday or Tuesday," for instance, there are not true characters and only the haziest of actions. The setting floats; the conflict is intellectual. The piece is too philosophical to qualify as a traditional story, too personal and sensual to be called a traditional essay. And yet we can find our way back to Addison as one of its progenitors.

Much has been made of the visual elements in Woolf's style. She lived among painters and knew well the technique of impressionistic pointillism. She adapted it perfectly to her philosophy that reality appears to us in light-illuminated moments rather than in big slabs of uninterrupted truth. Woolf is the prose painter in such pieces as "Blue and Green" (published in *Monday or Tuesday*, 1921, and never reprinted), where she demonstrates that color is not static; and the beautiful "Kew Gardens," the first paragraph of which is a profuse palette of primary colors and light.

In other stories Woolf is more photographer than painter, very much the great-niece of the famous Victorian photographer Julia Margaret Cameron. Brilliantly, in "The Lady in the Looking-Glass," she contrasts immutable mirror images with the daily world, where change is constant. How can she fit a portrait of the unknowable Isabella, now moving about in the garden, into the fixed truth the mirror seems to offer? A Platonic exercise again. If the mirror seems at first dependent upon older photographic techniques, it becomes startlingly contemporary once Isabella moves into the reflection. At this point, the scene is reminiscent of the relatively static parts of Robert Altman's film *Images*, which uses mirrors to depict the multiple phantasmagoria of personality, and of Bergman's *Persona*. In "Kew Gardens" the point of view is as flexible as that of a film camera whose lens is resting in a flower bed. Sometimes it rises just above the bed to watch people as they pass, the audio turned up for a time, then turned down as in another Altman film, *McCabe and Mrs. Miller*. Sometimes it zooms in for a close-up. A snail fills the frame. The way heat and color move through the air is as much like time-lapse photography as like cinema. Then the camera pulls back to reveal the larger design: couples are promenading along the grass paths, the glinting glass of the palm house is seen in the distance, an airplane is heard in the summer sky. (Woolf is very fond, too, of using the camera perspective for sweeping panoramas, as in the opening of "Monday or Tuesday.") A little like Alain Renais's *Last Year at Marienbad*, and yet mysteriously beautiful in its own way, "Kew Gardens" remains an avant-garde piece.

When we have spoken of the rhythms of her language and the bond between her outer and inner eyes, we have not yet explained the beauty of Woolf's style. We must underscore the fact that her prose moves as often through sensuous images, one leading directly to another, as it does through the linear method dictated by discursive reasoning and normal chronology. She writes a lyrical short story, not a mimetic one. She needs the freedom of prose to explore the corners of her mind, but the resources of poetry to record her discoveries. She writes telescopically. She condenses and intensifies. So elliptical are some of her stories that one must explicate them as one would a poem by her friend T. S. Eliot. Her sentences, her paragraphs, are long and elegant, yet not "feminine" as she feared, but sinewy, with anatomical strength achieved through the exercise of rewriting.

Behind all Woolf's short fiction is a complex motivation. To speak of it is to add to our understanding of the genre. It can be argued that Virginia Woolf was haunted by impacted grief and ambivalence toward death; between the ages of thirteen and twenty-five, she lost first her mother and father, and then their substitutes, her half-sister and beloved brother. Art, and its handmaiden the imagination, worked wonders with her pain, but just at the point of its greatest beauty, art also "unseals . . . sorrow" (as she expresses it in "The String Quartet"). It may be that the short story is particularly dissatisfying in this regard. In Woolf's hands it creates an illusion of perpetual being, something of an antidote to grief. Then the moment ceases, leaving, as a residue, joy but also yearning. Along the continuum between time and eternity, the novel can mark more moments; so it was as a novelist that Woolf found her deepest pleasure.

Eventually, of course, all fictions failed to sustain her. She committed suicide by walking into a river. It was an interesting choice in that water always has dichotomous potentials in Woolf's stories. Water either unifies conflicting elements or it dissolves the self utterly (see, for instance, the discussion of "The Introduction," above). Unification and dissolution: these, it seems, are the two aspects of death for Woolf.

They are invoked again in "The Haunted House," and shown to be not two aspects, but one. Mysterious, elliptical, and bursting the confines of time, the story names the ultimate separation: "So fine, so rare, coolly sunk beneath the surface the beam I sought always burnt behind the glass. Death was the glass; death was between us." Death comes between the narrator and the couple who died in her house hundreds of years before. Death—the fact and the fear of it—comes between any potential "us." It is the frightening reflection in the glass. Of the ghostly couple who haunt the house, the wife died first, we learn. The bereaved husband first went north, east, and south—his wife, in the language of folklore, having gone west. But finally he returned to their house, where the narrator encounters them, joyfully reunited in each other. The reunion occurs in a structure that seems to be both a house and a body. For the most part, the "pulse of the house" beats regularly. It says, "Safe, safe, safe . . . the treasure buried." In this state the house merges with human factors, both dead and alive. It dissolves too into natural factors—the woodthrush and the rose, the wind and the trees. Death is thereby overcome. In the midst of all the activity, however, the narrator hears the pulse stop short. Until she can find the buried treasure, she is at the mercy of death. Happily, the ghostly couple, gazing down at the sleeping narrator and her husband, see that they have fallen asleep with "love upon their lips." The pulse of the house now beats strongly its message of perpetual security. The beam, in a sense, breaks through the glass. Waking, the narrator knows that the hidden treasure is "the light in the heart." The treasure is love. The story's title is ironic, for in this story all sorts of ghosts are laid to rest for the moment.

• • •

Katherine Mansfield lived precociously. In 1908, at twenty, the young New Zealander had already committed herself to freedom in London, daily writing, and serious publishing—which is just as well, for Mansfield was destined to live only half a lifetime.

When she died at thirty-four of tuberculosis, she left a substantial body of writing. Poems, diaries, and letters there were, but chiefly short stories, of which she is arguably her generation's best practitioner in English. A definitive collection of her work has not yet been made, but John Middleton Murry, who was both her husband and her editor, published a posthumous volume of eighty-eight stories.[6]

The urge to make sense of her truncated life must not lead us to impose a sentimental pattern on those stories. Nevertheless, Murry's chronological arrangement of them, as well as the biographical accounts we have of their author, makes it clear that within her short lifetime Mansfield grew markedly in intellectual discernment, aesthetic accomplishment, and emotional maturity. Ultimately, she became a creator of worlds that are, at their best, as honest, compassionate, and formally exquisite as those of her spiritual mentor, Anton Chekhov. To be sure, at the end of her life, she was still occasionally turning out a merely clever story, polished and not thoroughly felt. But on the whole, the previous judgment stands. It is helpful, therefore, to an overall understanding of Mansfield to follow the phases of her development.

One of the earliest of these seems to have grown out of her ability to amuse her family and friends with impersonations—quick, vivid, enacted presences. That skill, added to a relatively contrived turn of plot or control by the author, is the basis for several of the so-called "German stories" collected as *In a German Pension* (1911). The hilarious "Germans at Meat" is representative. Just a few gestures vividly capture the characters around the table at a health spa. The Widow plucks a hairpin from her head and, before returning it, casually uses it to pick her teeth, all the while intoning axioms on the relation of vegetarianism, the English suffragettes, and fecundity. Herr Rat, blowing on his soup, alludes just as casually to his sexual experience, en masse, as it were. The Germans' enormous appetites are matched by rotund self-satisfaction. The mood darkens when the Germans suggest to the narrator, a young Englishwoman of refinement, that England ought to fear an invasion, but her stance of mild sarcasm and complete self-possession keeps the gluttons merely funny and in their place.

There are deliciously wicked delights here and there in the German stories. The opening of "A Modern Soul," for instance, has some of the qualities of Restoration comedy. But on the whole, "Germans at Meat" is probably the best of an unsatisfactory lot. They are the work of a bright, young writer with a strictly limited vision. Mansfield's Germans are indeed arrogantly vulgar, but they are set up too easily as targets. Moreover, the uneasiness that some readers are certain to feel in the presence of ethnic humor is reinforced in these stories, particularly in "Germans at Meat," where the title and the reference to potential political hostilities oil the way to inflexible conclusions. Amusing stereotyping— a constant danger for comic short fiction—is what is really going on. More important, in terms of what Mansfield will do with her narrative voice later, the narrator of these German stories manipulates her fellow boarders in order to bring out the worst in them for us to laugh at. Responding to Herr Rat, for instance, she reports to her reading conspirators: " 'How interesting,' I said, attempting to infuse just the right amount of enthusiasm into my voice." This narrator is smug. She is telling us about herself rather than dramatizing herself so that we can thoroughly believe in her. She is also protecting herself, of course. No one can deny that this young woman is the most superior person in the group, however difficult she may be to know well, or perhaps because of that difficulty. There is a certain cruelty and cynicism here that will not be purged for several years.

In addition to the rigidly satiric voice in these early stories, there is one other striking tone. The young Mansfield is angry about woman's lot. She has a self-devouring anger that runs to bitterness, a quality that makes stories such as "Frau Brechenmacher Attends a Wedding," "A Birthday," and "At Lehmann's" less artistically appealing than some of her later treatments of women's roles, such as "Mr. Reginald Peacock's Day" and the masterful "Prelude" and "At the Bay."

"Frau Brechenmacher" and "A Birthday" are essentially the same story narrated from the points of view first of the wife, then of the husband. The village wedding in the first story is the occasion for the men to humiliate the bride, who has borne an illegitimate child (a daughter and no happier than her mother). The groom, it is said, literally stinks, but, as the village women put it, "Every woman has a cross to bear." The story's sexual innuendos become blatant after Frau Brechenmacher, the overworked mother of five young children, the eldest another burdened female, goes home to remember her wedding night, for which she had been completely unprepared. Not that she is much better prepared now for sexual abuse: "She lay down on the bed and put her arm across her face like a child who expected to be hurt as Herr Brechenmacher lurched in."

Mansfield carries the universal condemnation perceived by the Frau—"all over the world the same . . . how *stupid*"—into the middle-class household of "A Birthday," where the abuse is more subtle, but equally violent. Andreas Binzer condemns himself: "I'm too sensitive for a man," he wails, but everywhere is evidence of his insensitivity to his wife's situation. She is in painful labor with her third child in four years, but she worries about her husband. He pities himself because he does not have more support. It is surely disloyal of him to find his wife's photograph unattractive and to imagine her as dead as he awaits the results of her confinement. The servant girl, here and elsewhere in Mansfield a choric commentator on the main action, returns to her kitchen, loathing men and vowing sterility. Her real problem—hers, Frau Binzer's, Frau Brechenmacher's—is that she is "bursting for want of sympathy."

Mansfield came to dislike her German stories. They represented in her mind clever but trivial juvenilia. As for the themes in her stories—particularly the relationship between men and women and the isolation of the young woman— these she would continue to write about, refining them as her sensibility matured. But first she would write another sort of story altogether. In turning toward her homeland, she treated ethnicity with a completely different emphasis from that of her early stories. Her stories set in New Zealand were comparable, in fact, to some of the first of the American local-color stories, with the addition of a certain amount of psychological subtlety.

The change of locale and tone is remarkable. "The Woman at the Store" (1911) opens with a description of the New Zealand wilderness that would have struck English readers as exotic: "there was nothing to be seen but wave after wave of tussock grass, patched with purple orchids and manuka bushes covered with thick spider webs." Then, equally surprising from an author who had been presenting herself as a sophisticate, comes her attempt at rough dialect: "It's six years since I was married, and four miscarriages. I says to 'im, I says, what do you think I'm doin' up 'here? If you was back at the coast, I'd 'have you lynched for child murder. Over and over I tells 'im—you've broken my spirit and spoiled my looks, and wot for—that's wot I'm driving at." The plot is also startling. Two men and a woman, who is the narrator and may be the men's sister, have been riding in the wilderness for a month. They come upon an isolated store, where a woman is alone with her nasty, pathetic six-year-old daughter. Claiming that her husband has been gone as usual for weeks, she welcomes the trio to the extent of sleeping with one of the men. During the night the child, to spite her mother, draws a picture for the visitors. It shows her mother shooting her father and burying him.

Upon reflection, this and the other New Zealand stories of this phase do not seem so far removed from Mansfield's early artistic choices. The first-person narrator, for instance, while socially and psychologically more attuned to the main participants in these stories, is still superior to the action in the old way. From the German stories, Mansfield likewise carries over her skill in accurately hearing the voices of her characters. And her adeptness at portraying social classes other than her own had been demonstrated not only in the German stories such as "Frau Brechenmacher Attends a Wedding" and "The Child-Who-Was-Tired," but as early as her first story published in England, "The Tiredness of Rosabel." As in these stories and others, in "The Woman at the Store" we have an exhausted female at the mercy of a brutal man and childbearing. "Wot for?" is the question Mansfield has been asking from the beginning.

Now the violence in the male-female relationship explodes outward. Somewhat controlled in the European settings, it becomes murder in New Zealand. The woman in the store kills the husband who has all but destroyed her. She is half-mad as a result of her psychological and physical isolation. "Ole Underwood" presents another "cracked" New Zealander; he has murdered his wife. In "Millie" we see a third isolated person, torn between what Mansfield regards as feminine aspects of character—chiefly maternal feelings—and masculine—the primitive, eye-for-an-eye justice of the men, who are out to punish a murderer. Millie is so far from civilization, as represented rather mawkishly by the print of a garden party at Windsor Castle, that she easily gives in to the hot, mad joy of killing.

As dramatic as these New Zealand stories are, the plotting is not so very different from, say, "The Sister of the Baroness," which turns on contrivances only slightly less subtle. Furthermore, Mansfield is still resorting to clever versions of the nineteenth-century surprise ending. Linked to the emphasis on action is the de-emphasis on character. In all these New Zealand stories, Mansfield puts a wide distance between herself and the characters, comparable to the distance achieved by the satire in some of the German stories. The distance is as much moral as aesthetic. Simple explanations for the murders are made, but no interpretations are drawn. Finally, we do not care very much about any of these people. A coldness thus is cast over the exciting plots, whose action is, in any case, off-stage. At this point in her work, Mansfield is far more interested in art than in humanity.

She was not yet ready to return, heart and soul, to her homeland. She had first to prepare the way by mining her childhood. Suddenly, in the middle of the wilderness New Zealand stories, she writes "The Little Girl," a story so fine as to set her on the way to becoming—with, say, Isaac Babel and Frank O'Connor—one of our greatest portrayers of children in short fiction.

Mansfield depicts children sympathetically; at the same time, in her best stories she achieves the right distance on childish emotions. In "The Little Girl" the sensations of little Kezia, who is perhaps five years old, are always expressed in terms of her size: her father is huge, his voice loud, the far jollier father next door perceived through a hole in the fence. Father beats her unjustly. He intimidates her and is a hard giant compared to her soft, comforting grandmother. Then, one night when mother and grandmother are out of the house, the little girl awakens from a nightmare to find her father by the bedside. He scoops her up and takes her to his bedroom, an eminently masculine place, with newspaper and half-smoked cigar, which he now casts out to make room to warm his little daughter in his bed. Then tired out from working so hard, he falls asleep. Kezia reflects: "He was harder than the grandmother, but it was a nice hardness. . . . 'Oh,' said the little girl, 'my head's on your heart; I can hear it going. What a big heart you've got, father dear' ". an insight which, if she can retain it, may one day allow Kezia to trust men and to marry satisfactorily.

There were five years between these early New Zealand stories and the magnificent "Prelude" (1917). During that time Mansfield wrote, apparently, very few stories, and only one completely good one, the famous "The Little Governess." But clearly she was changing enormously in those years. So, of course, was the European world. The war was as stimulating and devastating an event for Mansfield as it was for every other young person with a mind open to experience. For Mansfield there was, in addition, the personal grief over the loss of her younger brother, Leslie, with whom she had grown increasingly intimate before his death. The English writer Vita Sackville-West, who was also one of her country's finest gardeners, used to say that her garden at Sissinghurst—its beauty, she supposedly meant, its wild suggestiveness within a strictly controlled form—was an answer to war. Mansfield could have meant "Prelude" to counter the international and personal horror in something of the same manner. She is never directly political in her stories, rarely even makes reference to matters in the so-called larger world, but the domestic "Prelude" is such a complete, beautiful, and fully human a world as to make international battle seem a very passing phenomenon indeed.

The method of "Prelude" is in many ways its content. Its title the name of a musical form, the story reflects Mansfield's early training—she played the cello, sang, and for a time thought of a career in music. The prelude as developed by Bach is a very free form, and with Chopin becomes highly suggestive and imaginative, almost appearing improvised. In Mansfield's hands, the form is plotless. People move; there are clearly identified "scenes," each with completed action; but there is no strictly linear cause and effect. (What a distance she has come from "The Woman at the Store.") Connecting the scenes is a larger movement consisting of exactly pointed rhythms and balances. For instance, the story moves gracefully toward the mother, Linda Burnell, giving detailed attention to the other characters, but preparing us subtly for the penultimate scene, section 11, with its pivotal weight on Linda and her vision. The final section settles into a more objective tone through the device of a letter from Beryl to someone in the outside world. Thus are some details firmly rooted, and yet the story ends airily. The whole is much like the aloe plant, which provides the central symbol for the story: "High above them, as though becalmed in the air, and yet holding so fast to the earth it grew from, it might have had claws instead of roots." The lyrical composition is attached to a mimetic base and never allowed to become wispy impressionism.

And where is the narrator in this composition? Far from the self-conscious teller of the German satires and the reporter of action in the early New Zealand adventures, Mansfield's narrator has here magically hidden herself. She conceals herself first in one character, then another—a child, a woman, a servant, a man . . . a duck. She switches so fast from perspective to perspective that we do not see any movement at all. Nor have we the usual sense of the omniscient narrator, a voice distinct from all the others and somehow above the action, even when she describes a phenomenon like the dawn in section 5. The narrator conceals herself in the rising day as skillfully as in the other characters, though without in any way personifying the natural experience. So completely in control is this author that she can afford to give up more obvious methods of control. It is as if Mansfield were not the composer of this prelude so much as its performer.

Yet the method never overpowers the people. Each is vividly drawn. None is judged. The flirtatious, yearning, self-loathing Beryl is accepted just as she is. Mrs. Fairfield is the ideal comforter, but she is no more important a thread of this richly human tapestry than are any of the children—themselves affectingly distinct from one another—or the compelling, mysterious Linda Burnell herself. "Prelude" is the story of a family understood so compassionately that what might otherwise be seen as faults are simply taken as aspects of living. We are as inclined as Mrs. Fairfield is, for instance, to accept Linda's inability to mother her children intimately. Partly that is owing to our sympathy for her lot—the old one, too many children too fast—but it is due even more to the sharply delineated tenderness of her characterization.

The husband, Stanley, also profits from the method. To be sure, the household is overwhelmingly female. So is the element that holds it together: "she spoke to her mother with the special voice that women use at night to each other as though they spoke in their sleep or from some hollow cave." In addition, Stanley Burnell comes in for his share of criticism, here and in the sequel story, "At the Bay." Here, for instance, Linda knows him to be a big, loyal dog of a man, but too dominating, too easily hurt. She loves him, she says, and admires him, but simultaneously she hates the hooks by which he anchors her. On attaining her Lawrencian vision, she is freed to laugh. Lest the reader come to feel condescending toward Stanley, we also see him in the light of devoted husband. We see the joy with which, when his wife asks him at night to light a candle, "he leapt out of bed as though he were going to leap at the moon for her."

The portraits of husband, wife, and the child Kezia firmly mark Mansfield's new maturity. The Burnells' is a satisfactory marriage in spite of woman's lot. All the ingredients of the relationships—the sweet dailyness, on the one hand, and the painful loss of independence, on the other—are suspended in a gel of family strength. The husband is no longer an ogre. More admirable still, Linda Burnell, based on Mansfield's mother, whom she felt had not loved her enough, is here given the right to her own values. Through the charming Kezia and her entirely realistic adventure, Mansfield recaptures the little girl she was, the one she was chasing in the story called "The Little Girl." In "Prelude," Mansfield demonstrates her newly honed ability to use her art to focus life both within, and above, the fray.[7]

In the same year, 1917, Mansfield's experimental stories began to appear with greater frequency. Technically, these stories are of two distinct types. One is dialogue, an example of which she apparently wrote as early as 1911. Of course, the ancients used this "experimental" form; and her stories were based, we are told, on Theocritus.[8] "Late at Night," "Two Tuppenny Ones, Please," "The Lady's Maid," and "The Black Cap" belong to this type. The first three are actually monologues and startlingly like the "dialogues for one voice" by Colette, a writer whose life-style Mansfield admired, and whose work was currently being published in Le Matin. The second type is a more truly experimental form—a very short tone poem doubtless intended to be as colorful and luminous as a post-impressionist painting. Examples are "See-Saw," "Spring Pictures," and "Bank Holiday." None of these short experimental stories is of the least moral or aesthetic interest to the general reader. But they provide important sources for speculation about Mansfield's continued development as an artist.

Both types of experiments are attempts at objectivity. In the visual ones Mansfield describes something that exists out there, as it were, and that can be simply taken down as data. And the dialogues are bits of drama, commonly understood to be the most objective of literary genres. They are all in some way related to the freedom she was achieving in 1917 as she created and revised the grand experimental design of "Prelude." The earlier New Zealand stories—"The Woman at the Store" and the others—are falsely, coldly, objective by comparison. She may have been trying to refine her self and her narrative voice out of existence, as Joyce's Stephen Dedalus advised the artist. There would then be psychological payoffs too. Her self, frequently elusive, unlovable, and now subclinically tubercular, might thus be avoided. The experimental stories disappointed Mansfield, and the public gave them scant attention. Even "Prelude" was received in silence; so she had no encouragement to continue in this vein. She may also have learned that objectivity of the sort she sought was a temporary illusion on both the aesthetic and psychological levels. Whatever the case, after the experimental stories of 1917, various strong narrative voices reenter her fiction. Subtle stances are taken that nonetheless leave characters and ideas their freedom. Still, Mansfield did learn something positive from the experiments. Just as scientists often labor long with negative or little results and suddenly come via that very route to meaningful discoveries, so did Mansfield create her best work after the experimental stories. In other words, the experimental stories were in some way like artist's sketches for the larger works. This is very clear in the case of "The Lady's Maid," which directly precedes "The Daughters of the Late Colonel" in Murry's chronology, and which we know from biographical sources is to a degree based on Mansfield's intimate woman friend, "Leslie Moore" (Ida Constance Baker), just as is Constantia in "The Daughters." It is likewise clear in the case of another more-or-less experimental story, the exciting "The Wind Blows," which in method and content helps to set up "Prelude." In some mysterious way, when good writers are writing badly, they are often on the eve of writing better. (Curiously, in her last story, "The Canary," she returns to an experimental form.)

A cluster of justly admired stories followed the experimental work: "Bliss" (1918), "Je ne parle pas français" (1918), "The Man Without a Temperament" (1920), "The Stranger" (1920). Mansfield's creative power had been released. Beginning with "The Daughters of the Late Colonel" (also 1920), she completed nineteen successful stories in as many months. That a few of these are trivial does not matter in the midst of the almost unbroken string of gems: "Life of Ma Parker," "The Voyage," "Miss Brill," "Marriage à la Mode," "The Doll's House," "The Fly." Her second long masterpiece, "At the Bay," also belongs to this period. Its recapturing of the thematic and technical perfection of four years before demonstrates Mansfield's agility. She had hit her stride: she had slipped her methods on like a dress and with them focused her themes.

In maturity, Mansfield learned to write sotto voce, as the narrator in "A Married Man's Story" puts it. He continues: "No fine effects—no bravura. But just the plain truth, as only a liar can tell it." The narrative voice became a quiet undertone—its function to reveal simple, preferably concrete, reality, not in some slice-of-life mode, but polished by the tricks of the crafty fictionalist in order to focus upon the kernel of meaning. It delicately furthered broadly moral ends.

This means that the narrator takes extremely subtle stands, intimately close to the action. For instance, even in her comedy the mature Mansfield never mocks as she did in her German stories. Her naive girls and women ("The Daughters of the Late Colonel," "The Singing Lesson," "Her First Ball," "Taking the Veil," and the superbly Austenian "The Doves' Nest") are protected from their own silliness by the author's intimacy with them. Even when Mansfield chooses some ironic distance, as in the unusually skillful handling of the corrupt but naive narrator in "Je ne parle pas français," she hovers nearby, never too superior. But she gently directs the reader's reactions, making the stories of this period different from "Prelude" and "At the Bay," where she successfully attempts to withhold almost all judgment. Comparatively, the last stories show a return to plot—nothing like the adventurous New Zealand stories, but a line that moves softly to an end. Sometimes those endings are neat, entirely too clever no doubt, and even "thematic," but normally they underline the ambiguity and tolerate it: "Rot!" whispers the Man Without a Temperament; "*Isn't* it, darling?" concludes Laurie in "The Garden-Party" about life itself.

In these last stories, Mansfield further refined her special skill for narrative description. For instance, in "The Voyage" the descriptions monitor the little girl's mood, and underscore in a lovely, indirect manner, the theme of the story: "It was dark on the Old Wharf, very dark. . . . Here and there on a rounded woodpile, that was like the stalk of a huge black mushroom, there hung a lantern, but it seemed afraid to unfurl its timid, quivering light in all that blackness; it burned softly, as if for itself." The method here consciously comes from music. It is rhythm and timbre as much as content. Occasionally Mansfield will modulate the description into something that carries the heavier weight of symbolism: the pear tree in "Bliss," the fur neckpiece in "Miss Brill." She plays no games about this sort of thing. Either the symbols are a natural part of the setting, or she makes the point straightforwardly. Tidily married couples are doves ("Mr. and Mrs. Dove"). Our lives may be snuffed out like flies' ("The Fly"). A canary's lyrical sweetness and sad fragility is as close to an analogue of life as we shall get ("The Canary").

In the best Mansfield stories both description and dialogue brilliantly bring the characters to life. Although they do not evoke the reader's deepest affections, there is a certain very moving quality about her people. William in "Marriage à la Mode" is a good example. So, of course, are all the children—those in "The Doll's House" and "The Voyage"—and the childlike adults like Miss Brill and the speaker in "The Canary."

The range of characters and social settings is broad. Mansfield can convincingly create women, men, children, and, sometimes, animals. In addition to the very young—even an infant in "At the Bay"—she depicts older people like Mr.

Neave in "An Ideal Family" and Miss Brill. She presents people in isolation, in romantic or marital couples (not necessarily the same thing for her), and in families. If there are rarely large groups, that is due to the nature of the short story genre as much as to Mansfield's abilities. In terms of social class, she is most thorough about the middle class, but from the beginning she was able to portray working-class girls, particularly servants. Because she was one of life's alert wanderers, Mansfield observed enough cultural and natural detail to be able to set her stories in several countries: Germany, France, New Zealand, and England.

Her themes, however, are not as varied, but that fact scarcely distinguishes her from many other first-rate writers. She wrote most often about innocence challenged. She brilliantly portrayed characters looking back on that innocence like the remains of a dream, as in "Sun and Moon." Often her girls and women suffer unfairly; they have too many children; they have too little money ("The Child-Who-Was-Tired," "The Doll's House," "Pictures," and "Miss Brill"); men are insensitive to them ("The Little Governess" and "This Flower"). She wrote about narcissism in both women and men, and how it causes people, particularly couples, to drift apart ("Prelude," "Marriage à la Mode," "The Man Without a Temperament," "Bliss," "Mr. Reginald Peacock's Day," "Revelations," "The Stranger," "Honeymoon," and "A Cup of Tea"). Innocence lost, unfairness to women and children, the penalties of isolation and narcissism: these few themes, with one important exception to be discussed later, are the bases for most of Mansfield's work.

If there is a quintessential Mansfield story, it is "The Garden-Party." When a man says to the heroine in Jean Stafford's "The Interior Castle," "My dear, you look like something out of Katherine Mansfield," it is this story that he has equated with its author's sensibility. Its typical elements and treatments include: a New Zealand domestic setting; a family consisting of a down-to-earth father, a frivolous mother, three daughters, and one son; pretty feminine clothes and gestures; a fashionable party; flowers (lilies) described as to seem gently symbolic of both the gaiety of the party and the approaching death; empathy with a working-class widow, who has five little children; offstage violence; self-involvement leading unwittingly to cruelty; and an innocent young heroine, who walks the line between sentimentality and real experience.

The story opens onto a setting reminiscent of the romantic comedy of an Austen or a James. The mood is upbeat: "ideal," "perfect," "delicious." Even the rose bushes have been blessed. The comic figure of the mother is introduced, saying something superbly egotistical: "Treat me as a honoured guest." Laura has a charm as lacey as a garden-party dress. She flies, she skims, over the lawn. Childlike, she adores her bread-and-butter, her cream puff. She blushes. She and her brother Laurie are as close as Shakespeare's Violet and Sebastian. In addition, the leader of the party of workers has the deepest blue eyes and a nose for lavender. Life is sweet and amusing. It moves gaily, full of potential.

Without spoiling that scene in the least, Mansfield begins to present the oppositions to the "ideal" that will create story. One of the workmen is pale and haggard. The splendid yellow-fruited Karaka-trees must be hidden by the marquee. The canna lilies are "wide open, radiant, almost frighteningly alive on bright crimson stems." Jose begins singing a lyric about the death of hope, the waking from a dream—while wearing a smile that undercuts the song's warning. Still, the mother keeps the laughter fueled. Her handwriting as reckless as she is, she thinks she has ordered "egg and mice" sandwiches for the party.

In the exact middle, the story turns. "Something had happened," writes Mansfield bluntly. A young workman from one of the cottages at the foot of the hill has been killed, leaving a wife and five children.

As we have been slyly led to expect, Jose has not the imagination to empathize. She substitutes prejudice for understanding, assuming that the man must have been drunk. Laura, who has already been identified as "the artistic one," has the beginnings, at least, of true imagination. Realizing that the sounds of the forthcoming party will be offensive to the widow, she insists upon canceling it. But soon the picture in her mind's eye becomes "blurred, unreal," and she can no longer sustain the reality of other people's pain (especially since at the moment she looks absolutely smashing in a new hat). The story is once more at a romantic pitch, and the reader is almost as willing to postpone confrontation with the incident as Laura is. The stream of life overwhelms us: "The band struck up; the hired waiters ran from the house to the marquee. Wherever you looked there were couples strolling, bending to the flowers, greeting, moving on over the lawn. They were like bright birds that had alighted in the Sheridans' garden for this one afternoon, on their way to—where?"

That is the question, of course, and its answer has already been implied. They are on their way to the universal stopping place. After the party when the father is "tactless" enough to reintroduce the subject of the "horrible affair," it is inevitable that Laura, who has a "different" view of matters, should be the one to call on the widow. Her bright frock and her pretty hat are grotesquely out of place as she enters the world of poverty and death, now far more real than garden parties. For one awful moment she looks into the face of grief—the young widow's "face, puffed up, red, with swollen eyes"—and then upon the face of death itself.

What can Mansfield say about a young person's first look at death? How can she honestly render this nearly indescribable event? Wisely, she forgoes her own insights to let Laura's nature shape the experience. The denouement may be taken as superficial if this division of author from subject is not kept constantly in mind.

We know Laura to be artistic, a little sentimental (Jose is correct on that point), and, with the possible exception of her brother and father, with whom she shares certain family characteristics, more imaginative than the rest of the Sheridans. She bears the marks of youthful narcissism, but she has flashes of real empathy for people around her. In fact, for her there is something mildly erotic about working men, so unlike the "silly boys" who come to supper on Sundays. Delicately rebellious, she flaunts social conventions by eating bread in public. Most important, she has refused to shut her eyes to anything. When she thinks of the poverty-stricken scene at the bottom of the hill, it is "disgusting and sordid" to her. "But still one must go everywhere; one must see everything." In short, at this stage of her life, Laura is in search of undifferentiated experience.

When this charming child-woman looks at the dead man, she sees, therefore, what her nature dictates. The young man is dreaming. "He was wonderful, beautiful. . . . All is well, said that sleeping face." "This marvel," Laura thinks: "While they were laughing, and while the band was playing, this marvel had come to the lane." Death has come in the back door to the garden party as the most important guest. Laura knows that something ritualistic is required by way of acknowledging that the dead young man has reached a place beyond frivolous arrangements. Sobbing childishly, she offers the nervous, poignant, "Forgive my hat"—which, as a response to death, may be as useful as anything else.

Waking then from the dream, running from everything, from the beautiful face of death as well as the swollen face of grief, from party frocks and those poor dark people with their oily voices, she experiences an emotional high. Like many such feelings, its component parts are fused so tightly that it cannot be analyzed. "What life was she couldn't explain." But that does not matter. She is in the loving arms of her brother, who understands that Laura has been reborn into her own world.

So to the short list of Mansfield's major themes, we must add a final one. In "The Garden-Party," "At the Bay" (section 7), "The Daughters of the Late Colonel," "Life of Ma Parker," "Six Years After," and in her last two stories, "The Fly" and "The Canary," she looks at death in its living aspect, grief. Wedged between her brother's death and her own, these stories represent an interesting compromise between being awash with grief in life and coming to terms with it, however briefly, in art. Only the unfinished "Six Years After" fails to provide a satisfactory artistic stasis. Written with some of the finest insights of her career, this shipboard story of a mother's grief for her adored young son remained unfinished because the grief as expressed was unendurable and the story drifts off threateningly: "And the little steamer, growing determined, throbbed on, pressed on, as if at the end of the journey there waited . . ."

The grief in the completed stories is usually handled by being forgotten, or, as in the pathetic case of Ma Parker, being unutterable because there is no one to hear. In other words, grief is not really *handled* at all.

Life is so full that grief gets displaced. Grandmother and Kezia, thinking of two deaths in "At the Bay"—one past, one (the Grandmother's) to come—are diverted back into life by tickling each other. Soon both have "forgotten" what they were talking about. Similarly, the colonel's daughters are caught up in the conventions of postfuneral courtesy. In any case, grief is not the operant emotion in response to the death of their comically brutal father. That event simply resurrects the old grief for their mother, thirty-five years dead—not that the sisters realize this fact. Looking at a photograph of their mother, the middle-aged, unmarried Josephine wonders how their lives would have been different had their mother lived. Then, hearing some sparrows peeping on the window-ledge, she feels their "crying, so weak and forlorn" inside her. By the end of the story, both sisters have "forgotten" what it was they needed to say to each other.

In Mansfield's sharpest depiction of grief, "The Fly," the main character, called "the boss," finds that after six years of mourning for his son, he can no longer "arrange to weep." Instead, he experiments sadistically with a fly—as do the gods with us mortals. When the poor creature finally dies, the boss is seized with "a grinding feeling of wretchedness," but he too has forgotten the grief he had been trying to experience: "For the life of him he could not remember."

In Mansfield's last story, "The Canary," someone is finally able to express grief in the customary manner. Speaking directly, through a monologue, the narrator recalls the small details of the dead bird's life and acknowledges what he meant to hers. She also attempts to interpret the bird's life and death in larger terms: "I must confess that there does seem to me something sad in life. It is hard to say what it is. I don't mean the sorrow that we all know, like illness and poverty and death. . . . But isn't it extraordinary that under his sweet, joyful little singing it was just this sadness—ah, what is it?—that I heard?" Transmuted into a floating feeling of diffuse sadness, wretchedness, or simply unreality, grief in the Mansfield stories falls residually like ash.

• • •

What, besides editorial convenience, can be meant by the *and* in the title of this essay? The most dangerous of words, it encourages an exaggeration of similarities and a simplification of differences. True, Virginia Woolf and Katherine Mansfield were born about the same time; they were women, they wrote fiction, they even met. But around them and between them flowed a culture so complex as to make the link logically tenuous.

That is the purist position. The link remains—fascinating, and in some respects natural. To begin with, Woolf and Mansfield were friends. In spite of the seriousness of Mansfield's illness (Woolf was comparatively healthy during the period), they saw each other several times between 1917 and 1920 and exchanged about thirty letters.[9] Inevitably they had mutual friends—Clive Bell; Lytton Strachey; Lady Ottoline Morrell, at whose house, Garsington, both the Woolfs and the Murrys stayed; S. S. Koteliansky, whom both women helped with translations from the Russian. Mansfield was the intermediary when, during one strange interlude in modern literary history, Woolf took temporary possession of the Cornish cottages that had been occupied by D. H. Lawrence. There were publishing connections as well, by far the most important of which was that Leonard and Virginia Woolf printed, as the second offering of their home-based Hogarth Press in 1917–18, Mansfield's masterpiece, "Prelude."

The friendship was not, however, one of those intimacies for which the term "Bloomsbury" has become synonymous. Indeed, a certain sadness hovers over their relationship because they missed the best in one another. If Mansfield was openly eager, privately she was intimidated and angry about what she saw as Woolf's aloofness. For her part, Woolf was ambivalent. She longed for closeness to just such a woman as Mansfield, but prejudice intervened. There was something about Mansfield's racy life-style and her colonial background that made it impossible for the two women to "coalesce," as Woolf would later put it (*LVW*, 4:366). Mansfield, she thought, was hard, cheap, and superficial. She smelled obviously of perfume. Too late, Woolf would recognize that she had simultaneously been attracted to Mansfield's worldly experience, saying—and the remark probably had aesthetic overtones as well—that the younger woman brought to the association a "sharpness and reality" that Woolf needed then.

But parallel sympathies repeatedly drew the two women together. At the time of their meeting, for instance, neither knew well another serious woman writer. Now here was a female friend who also made art a religion. Unfortunately, the great comfort they found in their long talks about art was a little soiled by their feeling that in the future they would be the top contenders for that backhanded prize, "the best woman writer of our time." They were equally ambitious, but Woolf felt the competition more keenly: "Katherine is the very best of women writers—always of course passing over one fine but very modest example" (*LVW*, 2:241). The jealousy behind that half-comic statement, made explicit elsewhere, was matched by Mansfield's envy of Woolf's situation as a woman: "No wonder she can write," the ill, poverty-stricken, and wandering Mansfield wrote to her absent husband; "her roof over her, her possessions around her, and her man somewhere within call" (*LJM*, 419–20).

Other, more secret, reverberations existed but were not fully explored. Both Mansfield and Woolf suffered from a serious recurrent illness, the omnipresence of which was met with courage; each had the capacity to look upon other women sexually; each had her grief—a beloved brother dead, children unborn: deep rhythms that were turned successfully into art. Each must have sensed in the other someone who was driven to write, or perhaps called to it—depending on whether one believes in the psychic push or the cosmic pull.

Artistically, they met as equals. Respect for each other's intelligence and commitment was the basis for the friendship. As critics of each other's work, however, they were less than generous. Mansfield disliked Woolf's second novel, *Night and Day*, for its concern with art as against life. There was not enough punch for Mansfield in Woolf's stories either, though she greatly admired "Kew Gardens" and found in its daily discovery of the transcendent moment something to which she too was alert. As for Woolf, that brilliant critic—often of dead, minor writers—she was notoriously handicapped by her own insecurities about major contemporaries. Of Mansfield, her opinion shortly after the younger woman's death, was this: "My theory is that while she possessed the most amazing *senses* of her generation . . . she was weak as water, as insipid, and a great deal more commonplace, when she had to use her mind. That is, she can't put thoughts, or feelings, or subtleties of any kind into her characters, without at once becoming, where she's serious, hard, and where she's sympathetic, sentimental." "Prelude," conceived as a work entirely of the senses, Woolf found "exquisite" (*LVW*, 3:59).

Of course, "Prelude" and its sequel, "At the Bay," are remarkably close to Woolf's own achievements in content as well as method. Simultaneously storehouses of static beauty and conveyors of active worlds, the two stories might have been written by Virginia Woolf—a statement meant as a compliment to both writers. Furthermore, if one places "Prelude" and, for example, "The Searchlight" alongside anything by W. Somerset Maugham—to take an extreme instance of a writer of the conventionally-plotted story—or even some things by D. H. Lawrence—a writer who condenses, intensifies, and symbolizes, but whose sense of what is real compels his pen—then Woolf and Mansfield appear as allies. They seemed so to many of their contemporaries, we must remember. In 1921, the year of Woolf's *Monday or Tuesday* collection, following close on Mansfield's *Bliss and Other Stories* (1920), readers found them alike in their creation of dreamy states of being through the methods of suggestive language and psychological sophistication. They were discussed together as those highbrow lady writers of postimpressionist fiction. Mansfield recognized the similarities herself. After one of their talks, doubtless about the sublime possibilities for form in fiction, she wrote to Woolf: "We have got the same job, Virginia, and it is really very curious and thrilling that we should both, quite apart from each other, be after *so very nearly the same thing*" (*LKM*, 71; my italics).

She could have made the same remark about certain of their subjects. They both wrote, when young, satirical stories that they abjured on later reflection. Mansfield refused to have *In a German Pension* reprinted, though after her death Murry made the stories available. In contrast, Leonard Woolf respected his late wife's wishes about "A Society," a feminist satire loosely based on the all-male "Apostles" society at Cambridge. The story is frequently hilarious, but must have seemed to an older Woolf topical, rambling, and defensive. Her later treatment of strongly feminist themes (as "feminist" is understood today) is echoed in Mansfield. Putting their politics where their art was, they gave voice to certain voiceless members of society: to shopgirls, actresses, cleaning women, and fecund wives, in Mansfield; to quiet, "ordinary" women, easily crushed by a male-built civilization, in Woolf. They found their women characters in domestic situations rather than in the world of politics and business. They depicted them in love and on honeymoons. If their characters ventured out, it was often to give or attend parties, of which both women have written famously.

At this point comes controversy. For the answer to the next question—did Woolf and Mansfield write what they did, and the way they did because they were women?—lies not in criticism or psychology but in politics. Is the *and* in "Woolf and Mansfield" a noxious form of segregation by gender? Or is it symbolic of aesthetic sisterhood based on shared traditions?

Whatever the changes in intellectual fashion about this intriguing matter, the fact remains that both wrote frequently about "women's subjects"—marriages, parties, endangered female psyches, and so on. In addition, their work seems to bear out one of the oldest observations about women writers, that they are unusually attuned to the delicate details of daily life—a statement which, if it were not so often tangled up with prejudiced assumptions about there being more important subjects and more solid techniques, would be worth further investigation. Readers who complain that their characters are cold, hard, or nonexistent—indeed Mansfield and Woolf make versions of this charge against each other—sometimes appear to expect more warmth because the authors are women. Woolf feared having her work called "feminine" (meaning "pretty" or, worse, "precious") more than any other criticism. She knew the term was usually a condemnation to minor status. And Mansfield, it would appear, deliberately practiced writing from a male's point of view in order to achieve a liberated vision.

Perhaps the similarities between Woolf and Mansfield can be explained in a more specific way. If it is true that "Prelude" (1917) is to *To the Lighthouse* (1927) what "At the Bay" (1921) is to *The Waves* (1931), is it appropriate to speak of Mansfield's "influence" on Woolf? When Woolf was setting the type for "Prelude," did something of its substance imprint itself on her mind? Woolf says nothing of the sort in her letters or diaries, just as she is reluctant to acknowledge the obvious parallels between Joyce's work and her own. She probably did not, in any case, know the truth. But it was at the height of Woolf's conversations with Mansfield that the former wrote the famous essay in which she calls for the abolition of conventional plot, comedy, tragedy, love interest, and catastrophe because "Life is not a series of gig lamps symmetrically arranged; but a luminous halo, a semi-transparent envelope surrounding us from the beginning of consciousness to the end."[10] She might as well have been praising "Prelude" by Mansfield, whom she does not name, as Joyce and Chekhov, whom she does.

A more particular, if ultimately more mysterious, instance of possible influence is presented by Mansfield's most careful biographer, who argues that Woolf's "Kew Gardens" was written to Mansfield's prescription.[11] Apparently Mansfield wanted to write "a kind of, musically speaking, conversation *set* to flowers," and almost immediately afterwards was shown "Kew Gardens," which is just that plus a good deal more. This astonishing argument is more persuasive when it is known that Woolf had published no short stories at all before meeting Mansfield, and, aside from essays, had written only fantasy sketches and relatively traditional fiction, in form if not content. Mansfield's "Spring Pictures" (1915) was written long before Woolf wrote anything similar.

One of the problems with positing the connection is that Mansfield herself did not seem to think her friend was influenced by her. She may have been too polite, or too awed, to say so, and in fact says something to the contrary. Praising "Kew Gardens" in a letter to Woolf, she also writes—in the statement quoted earlier with a different emphasis—"it is really quite curious and thrilling that we should both, *quite apart from each other*, be after so very nearly the same thing" (my italics). There may be no precise facts about the direct influence of Mansfield on Woolf, but it is undoubtedly true that Mansfield, who talked so intelligently about form in fiction over tea, instructed as well as entertained her visitor.

Today we can make finer distinctions than Mansfield could. "Prelude" and "At the Bay" apart, no experienced reader of short fiction is going to mistake a typical Mansfield story for one by Woolf. Mansfield's depend more on plot and probability; Woolf's on self-determined tone. Comparatively, Mansfield takes broader sweeps at establishing the truth; Woolf, more delicate, beautiful ones. Mansfield has dozens of sharply outlined characters, clearly separated from their creator—in fiction, if not in fact. Woolf produces emanations from the self or figures sketched at their centers. She writes more directly about feelings and ideas. Given the long-established and still useful definition of the lyric short story as a counterpart to the conventional, realistic mode, Woolf is the more lyrical because her subjects tend to be thoughts expressed in imaged sensations rather than characters depicted in chronological events. Her symbols are more organically connected to the rest of the narrative. (Think of the searchlight in the story of that title as compared to the lilies in "The Garden-Party.") In fact, only by enlarging the definition of the genre to the borders of poetry on the one hand and essays on the other can we include Woolf as a short-story writer at all.

These distinctions confirm the foolishness of speaking too quickly about a shared fictional tradition. With Woolf especially it is hard to trace a straight line back to her models. She had read far more widely than Mansfield. Also, whereas Mansfield knew from a very young age that her talents could best be expressed in the short story, Woolf never made firm divisions into genres either in her reading or her writing, so she drew freely on novelists, essayists, dramatists, and even poets. Then there is that element in Woolf that it is perfectly safe to call genius. Though she read with superb analytic skill, there was yet an idiosyncratic aspect in her piecing together of information. Following her own path through the Western tradition, she probably learned to write her short fiction from the Greek and Elizabethan dramatists, Joseph Addison, Walter Pater, George Meredith, Henry James, James Joyce, Dorothy Richardson, Katherine Mansfield herself, and Anton Chekhov—among others.

But what of Chekhov, that seemingly omniscient presence for later story writers: was he not teacher to both Woolf and Mansfield? Certainly Woolf saw in his work an affinity with her own *Monday or Tuesday*. As we have seen, she discusses him, together with Joyce, as one of those moderns who take a slight situation and reveal in it the profundities of life. Chekhov's "Gusev" is, she says, so marvelously "vague and inconclusive" that she wonders whether it can be called a short story at all in the conventional sense.[12]

If Woolf admired Chekhov, Mansfield adored him. She read all the Russians fervently, but one does not speak loosely or merely repeat platitudes in saying that Mansfield was Chekhov's disciple. She modeled certain of her stories—most clearly "The Child-Who-Was-Tired" and "Life of Ma Parker"— after certain of his: "Sleepyhead" and "Misery." After her satirical vein was mined out, her youthful decadence lived out, and her lessons from Theocritus practiced, she sought like a pilgrim her master's technical perfections, depth of sympathy, tolerance for human limitations, range of portraiture, and, more practically, his facility for seeing in a situation the kernel of truth. She valued his life too, especially near the end of hers. He was an artist and tubercular, like herself. In addition, he was a doctor, and through reading him she devoutly wished to be healed of what she imagined was a spiritual lesion symptomatic of profound disunity of being.

One conclusion is certain. They sustained their life's work in different fashions, but after that work was done, Woolf and Mansfield passed into the tradition of the English short story at neighboring points. One might validly speak of them as having together exercised a certain power over later writers. Mansfield, a prolific writer of stories, has been the more direct influence. Woolf's effect has come chiefly through her great experimental novels, forms in which for eighteen years after Mansfield's death she continued many of the same methods and themes as in her shorter pieces. In 1920, as she was about to begin those novels, she envisioned them as growing out of the short stories: "conceive mark on the wall, K[ew]. G[ardens]. and unwritten novel taking hands and dancing in unity."[13] To the names of Woolf and Mansfield, one must add that of James Joyce in order to see the tradition clearly. His famous concept of the epiphany, after all, is nearly synonymous with Woolf's moments of being theory, which both women practiced. Following Joyce, following Virginia Woolf and Katherine Mansfield, the most important element in our short stories has not been external action, or even change, but that precious though daily miracle, human awareness.

Joanne Trautmann Banks

Pennsylvania State University
Milton S. Hershey Medical Center

SAKI AND WODEHOUSE

"Saki" (Hector Hugh Munro, 1870–1916) and Pelham Grenville Wodehouse (1881–1975) were practitioners of the well-made short story, roughly analogous to the late nineteenth-century well-made play.[1] Their worlds were essentially Edwardian, the society they portray is relatively fixed and hierarchical, with aristocratic assumptions. Most critics agree that they will survive as high stylists primarily, despite their debt to theater; Munro is traceable to Oscar Wilde, Wodehouse perhaps most of all to W. S. Gilbert. In their fashion they are dandiacal, in which they resemble Sir Max Beerbohm. Their stories are humorous and deliberately limited; Saki's most memorable tales are grimly ironic, but the comic dominate in number. Wodehouse is out for fun completely. Their short works are "self-destructing artifacts," though not in the sense that Stanley Fish has made familiar to literary scholars; they are made to be read quickly, to be devoured as delectable tid-bits, concocted with an art that conceals art. Munro's original audience was English, upper-class, sophisticated, and homogeneous: in brief, London society, more specifically Mayfair. Wodehouse, in some respects more idiosyncratic, commanded a wider public, first in English, later in American magazines. More commercial in intention than Munro, he was no less an artist.

The patterns of their lives were similar in youth, and peculiar to the English nineteenth century. They came of empire-builders stationed in the Far East, who sent their children home to be brought up by English relatives. The Wodehouses, a milder lot, were civil servants; the Munros had been military for generations. It is frequently pointed out that Munro and Wodehouse were raised by aunts in early childhood, and that little good is credited to aunts in their fiction: most biographers feel that both writers were wounded in childhood. Saki was emotionally arrested; perhaps nothing was capable of materially harming Wodehouse, but his remoteness is a bit unnatural. Thus both men came of an oft-described and documented society and class, and to some extent were typical. The psychic stresses of their slightly unusual childhoods may have made them humorists who saw life from a special angle.

Their fictional "worlds" had the presuppositions of their upbringings; in neither is the prospect of social change important or seriously envisioned. Wodehouse conceived a kindly Paradise of Fools, which he viewed with benevolent and boundless mockery. Sean O'Casey described him in a famous phrase as literature's performing flea, which Wodehouse characteristically accepted and utilized: it would be more accurate to say, however, that his characters were the fleas and Wodehouse the flea master who trained them in symmetrical and comic gyrations. His tolerance was almost boundless, as was his mockery. Saki's world, though strange, is more recognizable, and far more competitive; in it the foolish and incompetent receive no mercy. They are not comic, but contemptible. Munro himself was an effective man of action in a position and a world where physical action was governed by rules and physical labor was performed by inferiors; his combats were largely artificial, his comic heroes elegant epicenes who believed only in the unimportance of being earnest. But these are fighters too, although the chosen field may be the restaurant of a fashionable hotel. In "Reginald at the Carlton" the hero lunches with the Duchess (presumably she is paying), and the story consists wholly of dialogue, a merciless and unequal battle of wits: the Duchess has pretensions, and is therefore hopelessly handicapped. At the end she is let down softly: "And now, if you can tear yourself away from the salted almonds, we'll go and have coffee under the palms that are so necessary for our discomfort." Reginald has taken over.

· · ·

Wodehouse is in a sense timeless; Munro had temporal opinions, from which Saki's fiction is not free, despite the mask of humor. He was fascinated by the contemporary political scene, and his convictions were instinctively Tory, as became his background. The results were complicated and self-contradictory, as was of course the era he portrayed. His first successful humorous writing, *The Westminster Alice*, is political and topical satire, concerned with current events and figures in a parody of Lewis Carroll. It is inspired nonsense, borne on the wings of its progenitor, but it deals with such realities as the Boer War and its message is imperialist. When he turns to the short story itself, his opinions are not invisible: suffragettes are harpooned, for instance, along with reformers of every kind, and most especially pacifists, specifically George Bernard Shaw; in the world of high society social climbers are relentlessly savaged. And, while he admires men of action, he detests tycoons; in fact, the entire bourgeoisie—the high, the middle, and the low.

This would seem to leave little that is positive, and one might well point out that Munro's successful work is satiric humor and leave it "at that." Yet unlike Wodehouse he is a romantic—in a simple version of romanticism, an escapist, a lover of the elemental, the strange, the exotic. He evidently doted on J. E. Flecker's *The Golden Journey to Samarkand* (see his story "A Defensive Diamond"): I do myself, but Flecker has undoubtedly been long overpassed. Saki's romanticism is a form of romantic irony: he craves the heart's desire, the lost Paradise. His intellect tells him that the Romantic Quest seeks impossibility, but he persists; World War I was his final quest, which he found, incredibly, romantic. His last word on reality is brief, too brief perhaps to bear great weight; it resembles the more persistent word of A. E. Housman in its unalterable rejection of all that is. The cat is Saki's favorite beast, and its glory is defiance: "it dies fighting to the last, quivering with the choking rage of mastered resistance, and voicing in its death-yell that agony of bitter remonstrance which human animals, too, have flung at the powers that may be; the last protest against a destiny that might have made them happy—and has not" ("The Achievement of the Cat").

Saki's published short stories number about 150. Most of them appeared originally in the *Westminster Gazette*, a few in the *Morning Post* and the *Bystander*. They were collected in *Reginald* (1904), *Reginald in Russia* (1910), *The Chronicles of Clovis* (1911), and *Beasts and Super-Beasts* (1914) in his lifetime, with posthumous additions in *The Toys of Peace* (1919) and *The Square Egg and Other Sketches* (1924). They are widely available in well-known reprints except for six published but uncollected tales which A. J. Langguth has printed for the first time in book form in his recent *Saki: A Life of Hector Hugh Munro* (1981). Munro's career in fiction substantially commenced with "Reginald" in 1901 in the *Westminster Gazette*, though one story in *The Toys of Peace* is dated 1891, and two others also preceded it. The canon includes compositions that are stories by courtesy only: monologues, essays, sketches, and topical apologues or allegories.

It commences with the witty commentaries of "Reginald" on the London social scene, with an occasional look-in at country-house parties. He is Wildean, agreeably epicene, a dandy like the persona of Beerbohm's early prose, though a little more strident. Reginald is youth incarnate, and a comic figure; in Saki's pages he will not age. " 'To have reached thirty,' said Reginald, 'is to have failed in life,' " and he doesn't. He is wholly flippant, a characteristic brought out by interlocutors who are less so; he is, of course, the vehicle of Saki's wit, which develops into story through his interaction with them. He is charming, disarmingly selfish, and a rebel against the society to which he nevertheless firmly belongs; he knows the ropes too well to get in serious trouble. Some of his escapades, always intentional and self-assertive, are outrageous, but he does not expose himself to real ostracism, only temporary coldness ("There was *rather* a breath of winter in the air when I left those Dorsetshire people.")

In this instance ("Reginald on House-Parties") he has been invited for the shooting, at which he is inexpert: "And they tried to rag me in the smoking-room about not being able to hit a bird at five yards, a sort of bovine ragging that suggested cows buzzing around a gadfly and thinking they were teasing it." So he rises at dawn the next morning ("I know it was dawn, because there were lark-noises in the sky, and the grass looked as if it had been left out all night"), and blazes away at the most conspicuous bird in sight, a peacock. "They said afterwards that it was a tame bird; that's simply *silly*, because it was awfully wild at the first few shots." He then has it dragged into the hall, where everybody must see it on the way to the breakfast room. "I breakfasted upstairs myself. I gathered afterwards that the meal was tinged with a very unchristian spirit. I suppose it's unlucky to bring peacock's feathers into a house; anyway, there was a blue-pencilly look in my hostess's eye when I took my departure."

The deed is horrific; it is clear that Reginald is guilty of deliberate "pavonicide," though he says not; and there is an added touch of demure perverseness in a particular touch. Reginald has remembered the jibe about hitting a bird at five yards, and has "measured the distance as nearly as it would let me." The *telling* of the deed is exquisite in its quiet precision, its undeviating pretense of innocence and gentleness. "What else," he seems to ask, "could I have done?"

Saki's "cruelty" is often mentioned; it is certainly responsible for some of his most striking effects. Reginald is his first comic protagonist, and most dominant in that the *Reginald* collection is wholly devoted to him. He is a shadowy figure compared to the later Clovis Sangrail, and the Reginald stories are slighter than those that came after, in which the "cruelty" theme is more noticeable. Yet we think first of Reginald when we think of Saki; he has a pristine freshness, a purer comic strain, self-delighting. One might find a parallel in another practitioner of cruelty, Evelyn Waugh, whose early *Decline and Fall* has a humor that exists for itself, unburdened by later responsibilities. To put the case differently, Saki had one hero, the brilliant and insouciant youth. Reginald is the prototype, and he is ever-young. Nothing can really touch him, he is as close to Paradise as a position in London society will permit. He is theoretically aware of the state of thirtyishness, but he will never reach it. His selfishness and insensitivity are attributes of youth, untouched by trouble, and his creator has endowed him with intelligence, taste, and enormous *savoir vivre*. This hero has no future; the later Clovis has some intimations of mortality. To see what Reginald would have become we go beyond the limits of the stories to a novel, *The Unbearable Bassington* (1912); Comus Bassington ends in dishonor, exile, and miserable death. He is not really Reginald, though; Reginald has never fallen.

The tales that celebrate him usually employ interlocutors. There are exceptions: the general theme is Reginald upon his world, and he sometimes monologizes on such topics as the Royal Academy, worries, house parties, besetting sins, and tariffs. Invariably, however, the presence of a listener is understood, even when silent, and there is always narrative, since he illustrates his mock-opinions with copious examples and anecdotes. At their simplest the Reginald stories are still tightly organized: apparent digressions are actually a device to display his inventiveness, and there are no loose ends. As structures they move from "turn" to "turn" without (since they are brief) relief or lapse, and conclude climactically with an O. Henry–like "snapper," a final twist at once relevant and surprising.

Thus in "Reginald on Besetting Sins" we have the sad example of "The Woman Who Told The Truth." "Not all at once, of course, but the habit grew upon her gradually, like lichen on an apparently healthy tree." Reginald kindly finds excuses: "her life was a rather empty one, and it is so easy to slip into the habit of telling the truth in little matters." The situation deteriorates, however, "until at last she took to telling the truth about her age; she said she was forty-two and five months—by that time, you see, she was veracious even to months. It may have been pleasing to the angels, but her elder sister was not gratified," and as a result gives her for her birthday a view of Jerusalem from the Mount of Olives, instead of the opera tickets she has hoped for. "The revenge of an elder sister may be long in coming, but, like a South-Eastern express, it arrives in its own good time."

Things go on worsening. "And after a while her friends began to thin out in patches. Her passion for the truth was not compatible with a large visiting list. For instance, she told Miriam Klopstock *exactly* how she looked at the Ilexes' ball. Certainly Miriam had asked for her candid opinion, but the Woman prayed in church every Sunday for peace in our time, and it was not consistent." She tries "to recall the artless mendacity of past days" with her prestigious and imperious dressmaker, but "habit had become too strong." As always, the result is disastrous. "Madame was not best pleased at being contradicted . . . , and when Madame lost her temper you usually found it afterwards in the bill."

The end arrives, capped by perhaps the most famous sentence in the Saki canon. "At last the dreadful thing came, as the Woman had foreseen all along that it must. . . . On a raw Wednesday morning, in a few ill-chosen words, she told the cook that she drank. . . . The cook was a good cook, as cooks go; and as cooks go she went." This would seem to be enough: turn after flashing, unexpected turn; but there is still the snapper, an added twist that tidies up one tiny piece of unfinished business. "Miriam Klopstock came to lunch the next day. Women and elephants never forget an injury."

The avenging Miriam appears in several stories, as a standard though presumably oversized member of Reginald's set. She "takes nines in voices," and "They had to stop her playing in the 'Macaw's' Hockey Club because you could hear what she thought when her shins got mixed up in a scrimmage for half a mile on a still day." As an interlocutor she is perhaps less significant than the also-recurrent Duchess because she calls forth fewer of Reginald's powers than that pretentious *grande dame* and is engaged chiefly in farce situations; in which, however, she is vigorous and entertaining. She is mentioned here at more than appropriate length because she may have been remembered notably by Wodehouse later on: one story pursues her, "poor Miriam Klopstock, who *would* take her Chow with her to the bathroom, and while she was bathing it was playing at she-bears with her garments. Miriam is always late for breakfast, and she wasn't really missed till the middle of lunch" ("Reginald on Tariffs"). This has its sequel: later on, Reginald plans a book of personal reminiscences, to the terror of most of his acquaintances, especially Miriam, who "began at once about the incident of the Chow dog in the bathroom, which she insisted must be struck out." He pretends to demur, at which she "snorted, 'You're not the boy I took you for,' as though she were an eagle arriving at Olympus with the wrong Ganymede" ("The Innocence of Reginald").

Now, long after in his Blandings Castle series, Wodehouse adverts repeatedly to the story of Sir Gregory Parsloe-Parsloe and the prawns, which is never told because people are too overcome with laughter to recite it; and in the same series the Honourable Galahad Threepwood frightens his entire society with his book of reminiscences—which he *has* written, but is accidentally destroyed. There is a good chance that Wodehouse is remembering Miriam Klopstock. For the matter of that, his Bertie Wooster is a *genuinely* innocent (and half-witted) Reginald.

After *Reginald* the Munro collections vary in point of view. There is no strict progression, but in general the dominant figure is diffused into various storytellers in particular social situations, often glamorous. *Reginald in Russia* is appropriate only to the title story, since neither Reginald nor Russia appears again. Some others he could have told; some, such as "The Blood-Feud of Toad-Water," do not fit him; a few are straight third person; and one, "The Baker's Dozen," is arranged as a playlet. Taking the canon as a whole, there is *typically* a perceptible narrator, evident in confidential asides or engaged by an interlocutor. Saki does not use the framework of a general audience, as do Lord Dunsany in his Jorkins stories or Wodehouse at the Angler's Rest with Mr. Mulliner holding forth in the bar parlor. One might speculate that this device was so familiar that the fastidious Saki disdained it; and one cannot imagine a Saki audience that would sit still for a story; his atmosphere is too competitive. There would be Reginalds and Duchesses, or more exotically Baronesses and Gräfins, engrossed in outdoing each other. To return to *Reginald in Russia*, for various reasons it is the least homogeneous of the story collections of his lifetime; Munro's career as a political foreign correspondent distracted him, while at the same time he was developing as a writer. His increasing prestige made more space available to him in the journals and his stories grew longer, while his sense of the unifying narrator temporarily diminished.

To categorize Saki's tales is not particularly profitable. It might be possible to distinguish degrees of narrative development. Those who are interested in establishing his convictions could proceed by degrees of "seriousness," but very few of his stories are completely "straight," and these are least attractive. He was fond of allegorical sketches, usually political and topical; these appear occasionally from *Reginald in Russia* on. Their topicality dates them, along with their opinions—most of all the ones that derive from the Balkan wars of the early 1900s, of which Munro had firsthand experience as a correspondent on assignment. Concerning these he was most earnestly warlike, and his reminiscent "The Cupboards of the Yesterdays" (in *The Toys of Peace*) is one of his dullest productions.

To do them justice, these sketches are often witty and dramatic; they tend to be chiefly monologues, but with interlocutors who offer enough opposition to strike out sparks. It may be said, too, that as satirist it is Saki's function to attack the absurdities and illogicalities of all social and political life. He is not fond of activists of any kind, especially suffragettes, but their opposers do not escape unscathed either. His wit plays upon all society, even upon all civilization. In full narratives he is weakest when snobbish, as in "The Wolves of Cernogratz" (in *The Toys of Peace*), where it is evident that he has loved the *Almanach de Gotha* not wisely but too well, or in "The Easter Egg" (in *The Chronicles of Clovis*) too melodramatic, in which he commits the tactical error of being too respectful to a character both wise and courageous, Lady Barbara, whom he overexposes. The tale is perhaps prophetic as a serious treatment of propagandist terrorism, but it is well-known that people were planting bombs before World War I.

To venture a sweeping generalization, Saki's best and most characteristic short stories are founded on practical jokes. His youth had been full of them; in their embattled early years the Munro children had been severely repressed, and vented their explosiveness in their more privileged teens in elaborate and sometimes horrendous pranks, in which young Hector was an inventive leader. No doubt there are many psychological explanations, both simple and complex. The practical joke is an assertion; it may be revengeful and retributive, rebellious; an expression of superiority; a means of preserving threatened individuality; an act of aesthetic creation, pure and self-delighting; an embodiment of elemental and eternal disorder, like the medieval vice.

In the Saki tales there are many literal practical jokes: their general function is the preservation of flippancy against the threats of all conventional assumptions. They are particularly evident in the Reginald and Clovis collections: these young men are determined to take nothing seriously, to preserve their independence, and to master all conventional thinkers, whether sincere or, more frequently, hypocritical. (It is not always easy to distinguish.) On one memorable occasion ("Reginald's Choir Treat"), "the vicar's daughter undertook the reformation of Reginald" with considerable temporary success. At first repulsed by his pyrotechnical dialectics,

Anabel began to realize that the battle is not always to the strong-minded. With the immemorial resource of her sex, she abandoned the frontal attack and laid stress on her unassisted labours in parish work, her mental loneliness, her discouragements—and at the right moment she produced strawberries and cream. Reginald was obviously affected by the latter, and when his preceptors suggested that he might begin the strenuous life by helping her to supervise the annual outing of the bucolic infants who composed the local choir, his eyes shone with the dangerous enthusiasm of a convert.

Unfortunately he is left to his own subversive devices: "The most virtuous women are not proof against damp grass, and Annabel kept her bed with a cold." After tricking them out of their clothes, he organizes the choristers into a Bacchanalian procession through the village, with the happy addition of "a he-goat from a neighbouring orchard. . . ." Properly, Reginald explained, "there should have been an outfit of panther skins; as it was, those who had spotted handkerchiefs were allowed to wear them, which they did with thankfulness." Of the tout ensemble he remarks mildly that "he had seen something like it in pictures; the villagers had seen nothing like it in their lives, and remarked as much freely." The effect on the unfortunate Annabel is left to the imagination, but "Reginald's family never forgave him. They had no sense of humour." (It is to be noted that he *has* a family, which is mentioned in several stories, but it seems to exist only to be helplessly scandalized by him.) Mythically Reginald is Bacchus, or Pan with his flair for Panics, or a Lord of Misrule; and his effect is enhanced by his imperturbable affectations of innocence, as in his account of his "pavonicide" in the similar tale of "Reginald on Houseparties." As a mortal he inflicts poetic justice on those who try to change his nature; in his defense it may be said that he protects his identity by leaving his attackers in confusion. To change would be to die—and from the point of view of his creator there would be an end to Reginald stories.

Saki's most famous practical joke is "The Schartz-Metterklume Method" (in *Beasts and Super-Beasts*), in which one Lady Carlotta is mistaken by an overbearing Mrs. Quabarl for the new governess she has come to meet at the railroad station.

"You must be Miss Hope, the governess I've come to meet," said the apparition [Mrs. Quabarl], in a tone that admitted of very little argument.

"Very well, if I must I must," said Lady Carlotta to herself with dangerous meekness.

The Quabarls are affluent social climbers with ill-based pretensions to position and culture; they are prepared to run roughshod over an expected docile and powerless governess for their young children. Lady Carlotta falls upon them like an avenging fury; she is the genuine social article, intrepid, intelligent, and endowed with a merciless sense of humor. In her brief stay with her employers she puts them utterly to rout. In her crowning exploit she resembles Reginald, a veritable deity of discord, or in Saki's words "a Goddess of Battles." She teaches history "on the Schartz-Metterklume method" of putting her charges to act out great events dramatically, and she chooses to start with the Rape of the Sabine Women, with explosive results. Interrupted ("Miss Hope, what on earth is the meaning of this scene?"), she explains: "Early Roman history; the Sabine women, don't you know? It's the Schartz-Metterklume method to make children understand history by acting it themselves; fixes it in their memory, you know. Of course, if, thanks to your interference, your boys go through life thinking that the Sabine women ultimately escaped, I really cannot be held responsible."

Dismissed, Lady Carlotta leaves further problems with the unhappy Quabarls: her (imaginary) luggage will need to be forwarded. "There are only a couple of trunks and some golf-clubs and a leopard cub," which is, according to her, actually "more than half-grown, you know. A fowl every day and a rabbit on Sundays is what it usually gets. Raw beef makes it too excitable." The arrival of the real governess causes "a turmoil which that good lady was quite unused to inspiring. Obviously the Quabarl family had been woefully befooled, but a certain amount of relief came with the knowledge."

As was earlier said, "The Schartz-Metterklume Method" is Saki's most famous jape, and there is a good deal more to say about the practical joke motif in his work—but first, a word about the story's special quality. Lady Carlotta herself is notable among Saki's women, more fully drawn than is usual in the tales; she is eccentric, powerful, and firmly moral, while she is also supremely witty, more so than a summary can reveal. She has more reverberations than most Saki characters; one is tempted to look for literary parallels, which he does not ordinarily evoke. In her case one might range from Dickens to Wilde, though as a *combination* she is unique. While relentless, she has no stain of cruelty; she does the Quabarls no actual harm, while she metes out comic retribution.

The Quabarls are of course fakes, and it is delightful to see them exposed. Yet the very completeness of their rout makes them objects of sympathy. One shares in their relief, participating with them in a kind of comic catharsis, when their nightmare ends. After all, they play their game like others in Saki's world of one-upmanship, and their failure endows them momentarily with innocence (we do not see how they treat the *genuine* governess). The tale reflects Munro's convictions and prejudices, no doubt. The aristocrat is not to be challenged; she knows the rules, her *savoir vivre* is absolute, and the justice of her world is not in question. The "Schartz-Metterklume Method" is a double-stab itself, at German pedantry, under the general assumption that Teutonism is comprehensively ridiculous, and at the sentimental fripperies of "progressive education," perhaps too democratic in its implications, and not the traditional and real thing. But in this story the wit carries all, and the cruel claws are sheathed.

The literal practical joke is very frequent in Saki, and more figuratively it could be magnified into a general principle; the tales are jokes upon the reader himself; the constant turns, the "snapper" conclusions, his startling metaphors, perpetually surprising, which jest even with language in their exploitation of clichés, the common, easy, thoughtless phrases we use to counterfeit meaning—all these are literally subversive of our expectations. If we seek for Munro's opinions behind them, we may come upon the cat's death yell, "that agony of bitter remonstrance which human animals, too, have flung at the powers that may be; the last protest against a destiny that might have made them happy—and has not." But this would be getting beyond a joke, and his own death was presumably not unhappy, though warlike.

Saki's practical jokes are undoubtedly sometimes cruel. Commentators have generally attributed them to a state of arrested development that made him an unsentimental Peter Pan. His recent biographer A. S. Langguth suggests that his writing has ceased to shock, and is prophetic of the absurdism and black humor of the later twentieth century. These are deep waters, as Sherlock Holmes was wont to remark; too deep for dogmatism. Saki achieves effects that are striking and unique; their source may be, as has been frequently suggested, in some inner lack, but his effects are calculated. Their context cannot be replaced; he wrote with a classical elegance that heightened their shock with its contrasting imperturbability, and his world itself is inimitable.

His style could be reproduced now only as parodic tour de force, though we can find similarities, British and Anglo-Irish. There were, of course, Wilde and Shaw, Beerbohm, Chesterton, Dunsany; later on Evelyn Waugh, who rivaled him in cruelty jokes. John Collier was more like him than any other twentieth-century writer, and a natural parallel because he specialized in short stories and had a similar audience to Saki's. Wodehouse himself is similar in elegance and in wildly inventive figures, but he was pervasively a parodist, unlike Saki, and never by intent cruel, though his unvarying mockery and farcical plots can bring him to the verge. Lawrence Durrell belongs to the Saki tradition; in his case, however, there *is* absurdism, a wild humor beyond Saki's wit. The similarity is in elegance and virtuosity.

The practical joke, literal or figurative, is almost omnipresent in Saki, some degree of cruelty very frequent, and imperturbability invariable. "Esmé" (in *The Chronicles of Clovis*) is his most outrageous achievement in comic cruelty: a hapless gypsy child is devoured by a fortuitous hyena in the presence of the narrator and a companion, who represents the normal reaction.

"How can you let that ravening beast trot by your side?" asked Constance.

"In the first place, I can't prevent it," I said; "and in the second place, whatever else he may be, I doubt if he's ravening at the present moment."

Constance shuddered. "Do you think the poor little thing suffered much?" came another of her futile questions.

"The indications were all that way," I said; "on the other hand, of course, it may have been crying from sheer temper. Children sometimes do."

At the end of the story, after the hyena has been accidentally killed by a passing motorist, there are no repercussions. The hyena has strayed from a private menagerie, and for excellent reasons the owner never advertises his loss. The narrator (a Baroness), an imperturbable opportunist, herself poses as the owner of the dead beast, which she passes off as a valuable thoroughbred dog to the disturbed driver, disposing of the evidence by requiring him to bury it. "The gypsies were equally unobtrusive over their missing offspring; I don't suppose in large encampments they really know to a child or two how many they've got." In the sequel she profits to the extent of "a charming little diamond brooch" from the motorist, who is grateful for her forbearance. She does lose the friendship of her companion Constance, a setback she accepts with equanimity. "You see, when I sold the brooch I quite properly refused to give her any share of the proceeds."

The story is successful because, unlike its casualties, it is thoroughly alive. It moves lightly, and it has its decorum. It is drily told: the Baroness understates. To summarize where argument could be endless, "Esmé" holds comedy and horror in fruitful tension, each element supporting the other: it has many implications that are rigidly restrained, but linger in the mind. The Baroness herself, the narrator, has enough potentiality to furnish a Henry James novel—though perhaps it is the art of this highly compressed tale that it seems so, since Saki could not have written a Henry James novel, as he demonstrated in *The Unbearable Bassington*.

"Esmé" is at the outset a battle for dominance; the Baroness is evidently matching wits with the arrogant and formidable Clovis, who challenges her to interest him. She seems to have announced a "hunting story," which he immediately discourages: "All hunting stories are the same." "My hunting story isn't a bit like any you have ever heard," she replies, and proceeds to prove it: for some moments he tries to intervene, but is quickly forced into silence. She commences with a throw-away that is also a self-characterization. The Baroness dominates both Clovis and the story; she herself is horrifying and imperturbable. Yet she *might* be unhappy, and fascinating, if the reins were loosed.

It happened quite a while ago, when I was about twenty-three. I wasn't living apart from my husband then; you see, neither of us could afford to make the other a separate allowance. In spite of everything that proverbs may say, poverty keeps together more homes than it breaks up. But we always hunted with different packs. All this has nothing to do with the story.

"The Story" is so compact that we do not learn her nationality, but it impels us to wonder. She may be foreign. She may be English but married to a foreign nobleman, probably French, at which she is proficient: "I stormed and scolded and coaxed in English and French and gamekeeper language" (she is certainly a huntress). The title "Esmé" is itself a French joke: not knowing the hyena's sex she gives it a name that may be either male or female. Her levity has the effect of cruelty, in contrast with the brainless normality of her English companion Constance Braddle. Whatever she is, she has a cosmopolitan flavor; it may be that Saki, writing for an English audience, plays for safety—the tale has its decorums, as has been suggested above. More deeply, it may be that she represents Munro's own ethos: this is a world of cruel accidents, which the wise accept undismayed; she is not unfeeling, but unshaken. Less favorably, it might be averred that she has the feelings of a huntress. Perhaps her sympathies are with the hyena. After the killing of the child, "When the beast joined us again, after an absence of a few minutes, there was an air of patient understanding about him, as though he knew that he had done something of which we disapproved, but which he felt to be thoroughly justifiable." Beasts will be beasts. In any event, "Esmé" is a most suggestive story.

As elsewhere, the joke motif is present in Saki's serious stories of cruelty and violence, but in these the joker is usually Nemesis, and the author's sympathies easier to discern than in his comedies. *Easier* rather than *easy*, perhaps; the distinction is relative between serious and comic, and the better "serious" tales are the more complex. The simpler verge on melodrama, although not devoid of wit and irony. As in the Reginald tales, violence and disorder intervene to save

the protagonist from insensitive authority and tyrannical custom. In the celebrated "Sredni Vashtar" (in *The Chronicles of Clovis*) the struggle is mortal. Conradin, a ten year old, is being slowly stifled by his cousin and guardian, Mrs. De
Ropp. "One of these days Conradin supposed he would succumb to the master-
ing pressure of wearisome necessary things—such as illnesses and coddling restrictions and drawn-out dulness. Without his imagination, which was rampant
under the spur of loneliness, he would have succumbed long ago."

His only refuge from his guardian is a disused tool shed, which is peopled by
phantoms of his imagination and two living creatures: a hen, "on which the boy
lavished an affection that had scarcely another outlet," and, secreted away, "a
large polecat-ferret," whom he makes his god under the name of Sredni Vashtar,
and worships with strange ceremonies. Mrs. De Ropp, visited by hubris, uncovers his refuge, disposes of the hen, and finally and fatally discovers the ferret,
which tears out her throat and escapes. The shock of the story lies in Conradin's
unbounded exultation in this result. At the end, in the midst of the clamorous
dismay of the household, he has leisurely toasted and buttered and eaten a piece
of bread, which he had always been forbidden to do because Mrs. De Ropp had
decided that toast was bad for him and troublesome to prepare. " 'Whoever will
break it to the poor child? I couldn't for the life of me!' exclaimed a shrill voice.
And while they debated the matter among themselves, Conradin made himself
another piece of toast."

Like "Esmé," "Sredni Vashtar" reverberates beyond its limits. Saki is never
diffuse, but his account of the creation of the ferret-god in the boy's mind is
sympathetic, acute, and objective. He originates in a dreadful necessity; we are
convinced that without him Conradin cannot survive, and this strengthens the
story, though hard on Mrs. De Ropp. The probability of a different conclusion
is glanced at, with a blasphemous echoing of "Lord, I believe; help Thou my
unbelief." "He knew as he prayed that he did not believe. He knew that the
Woman would come out presently with that pursed smile he loathed so well on
her face, and that in an hour or two the gardener would carry away his wonderful god, a god no longer, but a simple brown ferret in a hutch." Instead, his
prayers are rewarded, his god confirmed. It is likely enough that "Sredni Vashtar" is a fantasy of the sickly boy Hector Munro, pursued by the worse of his
two dreadful aunts; if so, Saki is able to find a context for it

The other serious "cruelty" stories are slighter, though all of them are striking. Like "Sredni Vashtar" they are grim jokes played by Nemesis upon the
insensitive and presumptuous, and like "Sredni" they are pagan, but they spring
from a shallower fount; relatively, they are arbitrary and modish. We cannot
accept the Wood Gods who wreak vengeance in "The Music on the Hill" (in
The Chronicles of Clovis) as we accept Conradin, nor the good-looking werewolf in

"Gabriel-Ernest" (in *Reginald in Russia*), the savage surrogate of Reginald and Clovis. Broadly, these tales can be accounted for by alluding to Saki's simple and pervasive romanticism. He hated commonplace, he was primitivist; more profoundly, he was a depth-psychologist who found more in human nature than civilized creeds explain, though he did not *analyze*. This would describe his seriousness; what it leaves out is the all-important fact that his stories fundamentally are jokes.

• • •

P. G. Wodehouse is "Edwardian" partly in the elegance of style he inherited from writers like Wilde and Saki, and partly because much reality as he dealt in originated in a special world of Edwardian younger sons of the British aristocracy, for which he claimed historical and sociological authenticity. The claim is not wholly serious; Wodehouse was consistently self-deprecatory, and he advanced it facetiously as his *only* link with reality. Reviewing his career in *Author! Author!* (1962), he tells of finding himself with great ambitions but no material, no knowledge of the world, till it occurred to him that he had been brought up among pleasant, idle young men with tastes beyond their means, and prospects at once assured and precarious, floating on the surface of a society still firm enough to bear them up, but only by temporary favor. Looking backward, their world has the glamour of distance, which he utilizes in fiction; historically, this state of things may come again, and the fiction be justified as reality, his vision vindicated.

At seventy-nine years of age, Wodehouse reviewed the charge that his world "has gone with the wind and is one with Nineveh and Tyre."

This is pointed out to me every time a new book of mine dealing with the members of the Drones is published. "Edwardian!" the critics hiss at me. (It is not easy to hiss the word Edwardian, containing as it does no sibilant, but they manage it.) And I shuffle my feet and blush a good deal and say, "Yes, I suppose you're right, dash it." After all, I tell myself, there has been no generic name for the type of young man who figures in my stories since he used to be called a knut (or Gilbert the Filbert) in the pre-first-war days, which certainly seems to suggest that the species has died out like the macaronis of the Regency and the whiskered mashers of the Victoran [*sic*] era.

Of course the actual situation is vastly more complicated than this suggests. In the vast canon of Wodehouse's fiction his archetypal Edwardianness does not emerge until the 1920s, when he finally settled into the pattern that distinguished him; and the tales of the Drones Club represent a single grouping, though the "knut" is proteanly pervasive.

In 1961 Wodehouse calculated that he had written (and presumably saw published) 315 short stories, scrupulously recording that two of them had plots supplied by his friend William Townend. The end was not yet, but by his account the market had slackened by World War II, and his heyday was the 1920s and 1930s. He had reached his peak in the short story, from which he never fell, by the 1920s, and never quite gave over; Richard Usborne speaks in 1976 (in *Wodehouse at Work*) of "the hundred and fifty or so short stories that he has published since 1920."

Few critics have focused strongly on the short stories as a separate genre, since Wodehouse was also writing novelettes and novels throughout his enormously long and productive career, and does little separating of his own: what he says of fiction is easily applicable to both the long and the short form, and his literary development is likewise generally parallel. He commenced with "school stories," based on his experience as a public school boy at Dulwich College, which he loved faithfully. The school story was recognized as a genre, and a number of English magazines devoted themselves to it. It had a ready-made audience of "old boys" and doubtless those who wished they had been or aspired to be. The first published story was "The Prize Poem" (in the *Public School Magazine*, July 1901), which incidentally was a remarkably expert beginning. Trying his luck in the United States, Wodehouse moved on to the humorous-romantic story, influenced by the preferences of such journals as *Collier's* and especially the *Saturday Evening Post*. The third stage is succinctly described by David A. Jasen: "then he created specific characters and placed them in comedy situations. He evolved eight different series characters, with separate and distinct casts, who occasionally met in other series." Bertie Wooster developed from an Edwardian "knut" named Reggie Pepper; Jeeves, who had been faintly adumbrated in earlier butlers and valets, emerged full-blown from a particular necessity.

In Wodehouse's account of it in *Author! Author!*, "At this point—early 1916—Bertie Wooster hogged the entire show and I never looked on Jeeves as anything but just one of the extras, a nonentity who might consider himself lucky if he got even two lines. It was only when I was writing a thing called *The Artistic Career of Corky*—late 1916—that he respectfully elbowed Bertie to one side and took charge." The author goes on to explain that Jeeves was advanced to solve a particular problem, which neither Bertie nor the Corky of the title was equipped to handle. " 'Jeeves,' " says Bertie on page four of *The Artistic Career of Corky*, 'we want your advice. And from now on,' he might have added, 'you get equal billing.' "

As these comments imply, Wodehouse thought of his fiction in theatrical terms. His first requisite was tight dramatic structure; he worked out his plots in scenarios, then cast his characters. Sometimes he was uncertain at the outset who they were, or even whether he was writing a short story or a novel; he was a writing-machine, self-adjusting. Things almost always worked out; a few short stories betray uncertainty in bursting seams, but very few.

He was not a great critic, or perhaps his critical abilities are subsumed in the consummate art of his finest fiction. He has no theories of absolute value; he is inveterately unpretentious and self-effacing, and his criteria are wholly empirical. By long experience, especially theatrical experience, he knows what will work, but not the why of it. One may venture to say that he was wiser than most of his fellow technicians in the commercial theater with their insistence on "points" and dependence on audiences, since he had a better sense of wholeness, but as a good team man he suppressed his capabilities.

Aiming at pure entertainment, he sought rigorous structure, as his comments in *Author! Author!* indicate. Plot comes first: coming late in life upon Trollope, he is fascinated by his realistic characterizations but bemused by what seem to be his methods. For himself, he says, he never permits his characters free play or development. There are to be no dead spots; his characters exist to be used, each in his proper place, and they are to be engaged with each other from first to last. They divide naturally into major and minor, and major figures are never to be wasted on minor situations. True to his "dramatic" analogy, he is greatly preoccupied with exposition, and justly prides himself in his increasing skill in dealing with his difficulties. Dialogue is to be introduced as soon as possible, and his is highly studied.

In general, he seeks *liveness*. After the "school stories," he begins to make use, as does Saki, of the surprise or "snapper" ending, with its witty reversal, under the influence of O. Henry (its final haven would seem to be our contemporary sports pages). Likewise, having conceived the character of Psmith in his school stories, he diffuses Psmith's functions as "buzzer," the enlivener, among the heroes of his humorous-romantic tales; the hero's outrageous volubility and wit keep things stirring while the romantic plot develops. Later on, when his tales have evolved into sagas with established central characters, Wodehouse employed the framework device of a central storyteller with a set audience to deal with the problem of introductory exposition; this was far from original, and at one point he apologized for it, but he could use it with consummate skill, especially in the Mulliner tales of the 1920s and 1930s.

The first phase, the "school" stories of the early 1900s, is respectable. Wodehouse was quite happy with the public school conventions of the magazines he wrote for, and frequently expert. Within the limits of the form he is realistic and genial. His first published tale, "The Prize Poem," is finished, and it genuinely portrays a school situation. Competition for the prize is compulsory. Through a series of accidents involving wind-blown copies of an *editio princeps*, three reluctant contestants submit the same set of verses. The headmaster, scandalized, forgives the culprits after an inquiry: all the characters are essentially decent, the headmaster is understanding, and the point is the inadvertent foolishness of the assignment itself, which is canceled *sine die*. Wodehouse works very close to school routine, it may be noted; quite a number of tales concern examinations and assignments. There are sports stories, mainly involving cricket, on which Wodehouse is said to be authoritative and conscientious. (They sound authentic to an American, and are supported by Britons.) The tales avoid melodrama and sentimentality: the main interest is the conflict between schoolboy and schoolmaster, a game with rules, and fundamentally moral. Within certain limits the boys evade their school work, and violate the regulations on boundaries, constantly testing the tight system; there is a steady balancing of stresses between the realities of human nature and the school's ideal presuppositions about industry and good conduct.

The tales accept the ethos of the public school and the class system (of the 1890s). Outsiders are likely to be ridiculed, and all lesser breeds without the law. But Wodehouse's pervasive humor and geniality prevent offense: there are few of the stock confrontations between gentleman and cad, though the assumption of the schoolboy's superior wit and physical prowess is not entirely avoided. (The characteristic humor is already present in these early stories, though tied to reality, and it can convey contempt for the underdog in its objectivity. The problem, however, is not at this stage urgent.)

Wodehouse wrote from a broad background of school fiction, but a few high points of reference will suffice to place him. Like many others he admired Thomas Hughes's *Tom Brown's School Days*, but exposed what he regarded as the inane and unrealistic sentimentality of its latter half in an extravaganza called "The Tom Brown Question," in which he alleges that Hughes's later chapters were written under extreme pressure from the Secret Society for Putting Wholesome Literature Within the Reach of Every Boy, And Seeing That He Gets It. ("The second part of your book must be written to suit the rules of our society. Do you agree, or shall we throw you over that precipice?") The second exhibit or rather exhibits are Dean Farrar's notorious *Eric or Little by Little* and *St. Winifred's or the World of School*, famed for their unbridled moralizing, and mercilessly mocked by Kipling in *Stalky and Company* (1899). Hughes is chided for lapses, Farrar dismissed out of hand for didacticism and lack of verisimilitude. Kipling's *Stalky* stories are quite another matter, and a most positive influence, since Wodehouse admired them.

Briefly, Kipling seems to have encouraged Wodehouse to try for verisimilitude, and he surpasses his master on the level of commonsense reality. With enormous skill the older writer managed to impose upon his reader the illusion

that here at last was the Real Thing, boys as they are; actually, his schoolboy
heroes were impossibly intelligent and invariably successful; conversely, his
schoolmasters were gullible, petty, and in general easy marks. The boys always
won, and always justly. Stalky, the title character, is a youthful deux ex machina,
though Kipling manages to make him seem possible and human. There is nothing entirely like him in Wodehouse, who was struck by Stalky and essayed to
emulate him in "The Manoeuvres of Charteris," but stayed his hand by common
sense. Charteris embarks on his exploits out of pique and bravado; he is only
partly successful, and is finally rescued after a series of embarrassing and farcical
mishaps by accident and his headmaster's magnanimity. The meaning of the tale
is his reconciliation with his world of school; unlike Stalky, he has never been in
control of it himself.

The school stories of Wodehouse, though slight, are neatly plotted, balanced,
even in tone. There are many literary allusions and quotations in them, pointing
ahead to a future when these become indispensable hallmarks of Wodehousian
art. It may be paradoxical to emphasize their modest good sense and realism,
since their author was to move steadily away from all ordinary reality, but the
contradiction is only an appearance; he understood the ground that was his
takeoff point. In accepting the conventions of a preestablished genre the stories
also foreshadow his later oeuvre, which accepts and utilizes—and parodies—
the conventions of popular fiction. These early tales are still readable, though
perhaps they stand rather on the feet of the later P. G. W. than their own.

Richard Usborne, the chief critical authority on early Wodehouse, remarks
that he "gave up writing short stories about English public schools as soon as he
started to sell to America. His first two subsequent collections, *The Man Upstairs*
[1914] and *The Man with Two Left Feet* [1917], are of interest now only to remind
us that young Wodehouse, though possibly a born writer, had a long period of
hack apprenticeship before he found his form and, jettisoning sentimentality and
seriousness, came into his birthright." These two volumes represent the humorous-romantic stage that precedes the long period of full achievement beginning
about 1920, and first evident in book form in *The Clicking of Cuthbert* (1922).
Wodehouse himself speaks of them as belonging to "what, if I were important
enough to have such things, would be called my middle period." Significantly,
he was at least mildly offended that Usborne, his first serious student, spent a
disproportionate amount of effort on the early work, especially the school
stories, and contented himself with general approval of the later and finished
product. (This is Usborne's own report, which I cite because it is characteristic
of Wodehouse criticism to content itself with praise. The author himself encouraged this by his flippancy and self-depreciation, but he wished to be appreciated for taking care, and wanted to be taken at his best.)

Wodehouse, looking backward from the 1970s, regards his humorous-romantic tales with nostalgic affection as apprentice work. In his preface to a reprint of *The Man with Two Left Feet* he charges himself with "slanting." "A slanter," he reflects, "is a writer who studies what editors want. He reads the magazines carefully and turns out stories as like the ones they are publishing as he can manage without actual plagiarism. It is a deadly practice." Despite advice, he had persisted: "At that time every magazine was clamouring for O. Henry, so I gave them O. Henry and sat back. . . ." As a result, ironically "every one of these stories had to find a home in the pulps." Besides O. Henry, as R. B. D. French has acutely suggested, their sentimental whimsy may owe something to English practitioners like W. J. Locke and Leonard Merrick, with a more valuable and enduring influence from the "well-made" stories of W. W. Jacobs.

These stories are literate and ingenious, with something of the geniality of the later P. G. W. Some of them come close to self-parody, which also points toward the future. Most are happy-ending love-tales, as is often true later; the difference is that these are "serious" without conviction, perfunctory counterfeits of real life and emotion. They leave their author wallowing in pits of his own digging, rather than standing above them. Their basic materials are similar to later work, but Wodehouse has not established his attitude, has not imagined his characters.

The mature stories are wholly humorous, and they are stylized, with symmetrical farce-plots. They are incredibly accomplished; Sean O'Casey's notorious phrase, "performing flea," is partly accurate, for Wodehouse does indeed perform, and far beyond the requirements of mere duty or necessity. Despite his enormous popular and financial success, he achieved a self-delighting art. Usborne states the commercial situation from which the stories came—perhaps too succinctly: "In the 1920's and 30's there were many illustrated magazines on both sides of the Atlantic paying high for good humorous short stories, five-to-eight-thousand-word episodes, complete with sunny plot, a beginning, middle and end, and the young happily paired off in the fade-out. Wodehouse wrote for this profitable market. He became one of the golden boys of the magazines and, not necessarily the same thing, a master of his craft."

Wodehouse himself addressed the problem of commerce and art directly (it is his unique wedding of art-and-mart that is in question). It is true that prices enter frequently into his literary discussion. In *Author! Author!* he remarks, "It occurs to me, reading over these letters, that there is a great deal about money in them. . . ." Conceding that "We pen-pushers, as a class, are business-men," he concludes at last that "What urges a writer to write is that he likes writing. Naturally, when he has written something, he wants to get as much for it as he can, but that is a very different thing from writing for money." In his case, that is, he wrote "self-destructing artifacts" to a formula of proven popularity, but with pains that went far beyond the requirements of success, in a unique style of incredible virtuosity for his own delight.

In his mature stories he turned wholly to humor, but he theorizes little, though he frequently meditated the humorist's plight. Humor, he says, is "a disorder of something. To be a humorist, one must see the world out of focus. You must, in other words, be slightly cockeyed." As to the plight involved, "This leads you to ridicule established institutions, and as most people want to keep their faith in established institutions intact, the next thing that happens is that you get looked askance at." Like Saki and most professional humorists he deliberately resists analysis, since analyzing humor notoriously analyzes it away. "Oddly, considering that humor is so despised, people are always writing articles or delivering lectures about it, generally starting off with the words 'Why do we laugh?' " Deriding psychological explanations, he conceives of humor as deliberate distortion effecting incongruity, without distinguishing it from wit or intentional nonsense, in which he sometimes indulges.

To Evelyn Waugh the secret of Wodehouse was escapism. "For Mr. Wodehouse there has been no fall of Man; no aboriginal calamity. His characters have never tasted the forbidden fruit. They are still in Eden. . . . Mr. Wodehouse's idyllic world can never stale." This is to say that the humor of Wodehouse exists purely for itself, quite free from reality. (Rather ironically, Waugh's own closest approach to the type is in a novel entitled *Decline and Fall*.) Malcolm Muggeridge, who was officially concerned in the greatest disaster of Wodehouse's life, the World War II debacle that brought him close to formal charges of treason, explains the author's strange indifference to what was going on as comic fatalism: all human affairs are entertaining insanity, which must simply be accepted. Muggeridge, however, has attributed social significance to Wodehouse's humor as an accurate picture of a declining society, and narrowed it to "a certain brand of English humour, doggedly held onto by the natives. . . . In essence, it is a sort of mystique of failure." He concludes that "The whole edifice of Wodehouse's humour is founded on this glorification of failure and inadequacy." To accept this generalization provisionally, in this respect Wodehouse is the exact opposite of Saki.

To him, at any rate, all pretensions are comic, all idols false, all humans limited, though usually amiable. (*All* generalizations are subject to exception, it should be added.) Max Beerbohm in an essay on "Laughter" suggested that humor derives from the breach of solemnity of situation or character, a release of tension; an accident in church, for example, with its contrast between public ritual and private reaction. Humor in Beerbohm is a release from embarrassment; and this is even more evident in Wodehouse, who seems to have shrunk from all public occasions and formal demonstrations. Dismayingly, he is on record as disliking Beerbohm, who resembled him significantly. Probably he felt that Beerbohm was affected and "put on side," but his own situations were Beerbohm-like; a bored choirboy surreptitiously making faces at the congregation, or Bertie Wooster's dread of presiding over a children's Christmas party in Santa Claus costume. Unlike Beerbohm he was fond of broad horseplay, but they were akin as elegant stylists and consummate parodists.

To Wodehouse all human activities are absurd, and consequently all men of action, though he is good-humored about them. As to the military, they are "heroes all, and it gets them greatly disliked," while adventurous explorers and great hunters are uproarious shams, who boast magnificently and exist to be shown up in crises. More conventional occupations are also comic: the financiers, the professions, authors, clerics, aristocrats, especially at the opposite extremes of baronet and duke; confidence-men, and thieves, are subject to boundless mockery. Even blackmailers have their funny side, although these, with Roderick Spode the Fascist, are borderline cases. Failures and underdogs get the best treatment, as the most humble of beings.

The "mature" short stories of full achievement can be categorized in various ways. They come chiefly, as has been remarked, in the 1920s and 1930s, though Wodehouse never wholly abandoned the genre. Several groups of them have been collected and recollected in omnibus form. The most substantial are the Mulliner tales (*The World of Mr. Mulliner* [1974] and *The World of Jeeves* [1971], first collected as a whole in omnibus volumes quite early). Six stories deal with Lord Emsworth and Blandings Castle; there are distinctive tales of the Edwardian Drones Club, and nineteen that chronicle the picaresque Ukridge and have been separately collected. There is one story, "Uncle Fred Flits By," about the fabulous Earl of Ickenham, who has Drones Club connections; it is a Wodehouse masterpiece, though he owed the plot to his friend William Townend. Some groups intermingle, and are further intertwined with the novel-canon, particularly the Jeeves-Wooster and Drones Club tales. The Golf and the Mulliner stories are most easily separable from entangling alliances; the Golf saga is perhaps most homogeneous, the Mulliner tales most numerous, brilliant, and varied. Faced with the Wodehouse cornucopia, I shall focus on them, though Jeeves-Wooster are oftener discussed.

The Mulliner tales are very tall. Wodehouse describes their origin in a retrospective preface. He had been using Jeeves and the Drones Club as main story-bases, and wanted a change. Meanwhile, "I had been getting ideas for stories and shoving them down in the old notebook, but it seemed to me that they were all too bizarre for editorial consumption." He found a way of introducing them in a familiar device "I particularly dislike," the club yarn. "You know the sort of thing I mean; you must have read them by the dozens. We were sitting round the fire at the club that winter night. . . ." Then comes the tall tale. It occurred to him, "Why not have those stories of mine told by a fisherman, whose veracity would be automatically suspect? And at the same moment the name Mr. Mulliner occurred to me." His publisher liked the first sample and suggested a series, "I took Jeeves off, transfer[r]ing him to novels, and put Mr. Mulliner on at the pavilion end, where he has remained ever since."

Richard Usborne remarks that Mulliner "was Wodehouse's favorite mouthpiece for the really tall story. He tells his 'stretchers' with determination, grace, ease and solemnity," adding that "He has a vocabulary of phrase and situation dredged almost wholesale from popular bilge literature." As to this, it has been said more than once that Wodehouse was the world's most omnivorous reader of trash, which he ingested genially, with profit and delight. It would be impossible to distinguish his sources accurately, but the lady-novelists deriving from *Jane Eyre* were favorite targets. To speculate, Ethel M. Dell would be the best of them, and Ouida, Marie Corelli, the Baroness Orczy, Ethel Hull, and Elinor Glyn would be probabilities.

Wodehouse used his framework with enormous skill. Mr. Mulliner is perhaps a type: he exists only to tell stories. We know he is a fisherman and are not further curious, but his involvement with his audience is elaborate and delightful; the introductory byplay is itself dramatic.

We have noticed that Saki's storytellers struggle for mastery and usually win, though sometimes vigorously opposed. Lord Dunsany's *Travel Tales of Mr. Jorkens*, club yarns of a master-liar, depend strongly on Jorkens's assertions of verity. The situation is very similar to the situation of Mr. Mulliner in the bar parlor of the Anglers' Rest, and the comparison emphasizes Wodehouse's technical skill; perhaps it is not quite fair, since Jorkens tells genuine tall tales, excellent in themselves, while the Mulliner stories, also excellent, are parodies. Jorkens is serious, and a real person with emotions; Mr. Mulliner also insists upon his truthfulness, but he is a magician and superhuman. The opposition to him is weak and comic. Amid roughly contemporary storytellers perhaps Kai Lung, the Chinese professional of Ernest Bramah [Smith], might represent the fullest competition and parallel to the Mulliner relationship of teller-audience-tale, in complexity of relationship and exquisite, stylized artificiality.

Mr. Mulliner speaks always of Mulliners, and (at least generically) with unqualified approval. "My nephew George (said Mr. Mulliner) was as nice a young fellow as you would ever wish to meet." "There is probably no family on earth more nicely scrupulous as regards keeping its promises than the Mulliners." "George had the dogged, honest Mulliner streak in him." "All we Mulliners have been athletes; and George, when at the University, had been noted for his speed of foot." It is at one point favorably noted that "No Mulliner has ever taken a prize at a cat show. No Mulliner, indeed, to the best of my knowledge, has ever been entered for such a competition." "All the Mulliners have been able speakers." "As a family the Mulliners have always been noted for their reckless courage." They have, perhaps, one shortcoming: "It is a curious fact that, gifted though the Mulliners have been in virtually every branch of life and sport, few of us have ever taken kindly to golf." Needless to say, Mulliners are noted for physical beauty.

Most of Mr. Mulliner's inexhaustible supply of relatives are nephews, with an infrequent niece or so. As it happens, his brother Wilfred is the most distinguished, "the clever one of the family," and there are occasional uncles and cousins. As individuals they do have their limitations, like all Wodehouse characters, but most of them are amiable, especially the younger ones. Usually unworldly, they yet have enormous powers of survival and amazing resourcefulness when they are (as they are invariably) thrust into difficult situations. In the main the love-plot is standard: Mulliner boy woos girl; he is opposed by formidable rivals, hostile families, misunderstandings with the loved one, his own inadequacies. In a variant ("Honeysuckle Cottage") "My distant cousin James Rodman" is rescued from an inappropriate match with a sentimental heroine by an outrageous mongrel who is eventually revealed as the faithful dog who saves his master. All the characters are stock-figures of sentimental romance, including the cottage with its evil spell, but everything is turned upside down. "James turned. Through the trees to the east he could see the red roof of Honeysuckle Cottage, lurking like some evil dragon in ambush. Then, together, man and dog passed silently into the sunset."

Being parodies of popular love-stories and thrillers, the Mulliner stories depend heavily upon false motivation, which Wodehouse developed into high art. The tightness of his plots prohibits genuine motivation and character development, as with O. Henry; he seeks perpetual motion and "liveness," and the incessant turns, twists, and reversals of a typical story, with a "snapper" at the end, make for outrageous transformations of mouse into lion, fumbler into supreme performer. Wodehouse, in short, thrives on the limitation of his formula. Closest to real motivation are the occasions when his protagonist throws his weight around too much and has to be sharply corrected, as when like Bertie Wooster he mistakes himself for a true hero, or otherwise misconceives reality.

Archibald Mulliner, for example, is an outstanding pinhead. He falls in love with the beautiful and majestic Aurelia Cammarleigh, and assumes that to win her he "would have to be a man who Did Things." What he *can* do is an imitation of a hen laying an egg, at which "he was admittedly a master." In pursuit of the queenly Aurelia he denies this one great gift, masquerades as a deep thinker, a nonsmoker, and a total abstainer, and in consequence almost ruins his prospects. He has greatly misunderstood Aurelia, who likes him for what he really is, and only recovers himself at the last moment by "giving the performance of a lifetime" in imitation of a hen laying an egg. The performance, which is fully described, does the trick ("The Reverent Wooing of Archibald"). The heroines are likely to be more down-to-earth than their Mulliner adorers, as a matter of fact. Archibald tries to be a romantic hero and has to be put straight.

The many Mulliners have various occupations. Aside from hen-imitating, Archibald is quite simply a Drone. Wilfred, the clever one of the family, is "the inventor of what are known to the trade as Mulliner's Magic Marvels—a general term embracing the Raven Gipsy Face-Cream, the Snow of the Mountains Lotion, and many other preparations," especially Mulliner's Buck-U-Uppo, which has important repercussions in several stories. Augustine Mulliner, one of its recipients, is a curate, as is "my cousin Rupert's younger son, Anselm." Lancelot Mulliner is a free-verse poet until he reforms: another Lancelot (a lapse of memory, presumably) is a Bohemian artist. James Rodney of "Honeysuckle Cottage" is a writer of sensational mystery stories. Fussy Cousin Cedric is a mystery: "Some said he was writing a monumental history of Spats, others that he was engaged upon his Memoirs. My private belief is that he was not working at anything." Clarence Mulliner ("The Romance of a Bulb-Squeezer") is a fashionable photographer of great repute; his eventual happy wedding "was attended by almost everybody of any note in Society or on the Stage; and was the first occasion on which a bride and bridegroom had ever walked out of church beneath an arch of crossed tripods." Perhaps the lowliest is Wilmot, a Nodder in Hollywood, "a position which you might say, roughly, lies socially somewhere in between that of the man who works the wind-machine and that of a writer of additional dialogue. There is also a class of Untouchables who are known as Nodders' assistants, but this is a technicality with which I need not trouble you." It is cheering to learn that Wilmot becomes an executive "With brevet rank as a brother-in-law" ("The Nodder"), and escapes his superiors completely in "The Juice of an Orange" as business manager of a movie star at $3,000 a week.

To Wodehouse all callings, including his own, were absurd. There are few doctors and I think no lawyers in the Mulliner tales, presumably because they are traditionally too busy for glorious adventure, but here and elsewhere he takes note of their well-known fondness for their fees. In the earliest story, "The Truth About George," the hero is seriously discommoded by his stammer, which prevents him from proposing to Susan Blake, with whom he is associated through a common devotion to crossword puzzles. He consults a specialist, "a kindly man with moth-eaten whiskers and an eye like a meditative cod-fish," who proceeds to give him advice so ridiculous that it furnishes the rest of the plot. "And having requested the young man—in a voice of the clearest timbre, free from all trace of impediment—to hand over a fee of five guineas, the specialist sent George out into the world."

George follows the doctor's advice, with such shattering results that he is shocked into one of Wodehouse's greatest displays of rhetorical virtuosity, a fantastic flood of alliterative mixed-metaphors. I quote his eventual proposal at length:

His voice rang out clear and unimpeded. It seemed to him incredible that he had ever yammered at this girl like an overheated steam-radiator. "It cannot have escaped your notice that I have long entertained towards you sentiments warmer and deeper than those of ordinary friendship. It is love, Susan, that has been animating my bosom. Love, first a tiny seed, has burgeoned in my heart till blazing into flame, it has swept away on the crest of its wave my diffidence, my doubt, my fears, and my foreboding, and now, like the topmost topaz of some ancient tower, it cries to all the world in a voice of thunder: 'You are mine! My mate! Predestined to me since Time first began!' As the star guides the mariner when, battered by boiling billows, he hies him home to the haven of hope and happiness, so do you gleam upon me along life's rough road and seem to say, 'Have courage, George! I am here!' Susan, I am not an eloquent man—I cannot speak fluently as I could wish—but these simple words which you have just heard come from the heart, the unspotted heart of an English gentleman. Susan, I love you."

Naturally, he is accepted. Susan, like George a crossword-puzzle expert with a knowledge of the dictionary of synonyms, yields completely and exhaustively. " 'Yes, yea, ay, aye! Decidedly, unquestionably, indubitably, incontrovertibly, and past all dispute.' "

Wodehouse was an incredibly accomplished performer, who succeeded so often that we lose sight of his achievement from its sheer magnitude, and he was at the top of his form in most of the Mulliner tales. As Keats advised Shelley to do, he loads every rift with golden ore. His own terse advice to his friend William Townend (in *Author! Author!*) concerns preparatory exposition, and getting to dialogue as soon as possible. He emphasizes condensation, citing his own mistakes with superfluous characters and incidents. He is great on symmetry of proportion and proper subordination: major characters are not to be wasted on minor situations; neutral figures should have neutral names, while names themselves should be characteristic (he did not descend to crude allegorical labels, in the Victorian fashion). In "Came the Dawn," for example, Lancelot Mulliner is thrown out physically by three consecutive butlers, whose names are impressive as befits the awe that surrounds Wodehousian butlers, but shaded to fit their several employers. Bewstridge, the first, serves Lancelot's uncle Jeremiah Briggs, a wealthy pickle manufacturer; the second, Fotheringay, is the chief minion of Lord Biddlecombe; while the third, Margerison, is the hall-porter of the Junior Lipstick club for debutantes. (A hall-porter is the best the club can offer in an emergency.)

Wodehouse shuns the episodic, but he is a master of significant repetition, whose sense of rhythm is unerring. His use of *threes*, as in the example just cited, may come from stage experience, perhaps the blackout sketch of musical comedy; indeed, his structural principles come mainly from the theater. Life and motion are primary, rounded off in final surprise. His tenets aim toward unity of impression, but his practice provides much more than is required for smooth functioning: continuous wit in word and situation. Mr. Mulliner in particular combines the imperturbable understatement of Oscar Wilde with unbridled mock-heroic hyperbole; Wilde and his follower Saki are terser than Wodehouse and less homely, but these three most aptly represent "the world out of focus," the "slightly cockeyed" vision that distinguishes Wodehouse's humor.

The Golf Stories (*The Clicking of Cuthbert* [1922] and *The Heart of a Goof* [1926]) have the same framework as the Mulliner tales, with the Oldest Member their narrator. The introductory by-play is usually furnished by the unsuccessful efforts of his fellow club members to avoid hearing them. Usborne remarks that "Wodehouse established The Oldest Member, himself full of reverence for the sacred game, to tell some of the most irreverent stories about it in all its literature," but the fun is affectionate. The Golf Saga is naturally more homogeneous than the Mulliner, since it is mainly confined to the club and the golf course, while the Mulliners wander freely in time and space: "The Story of William," for instance, springs from the great San Francisco Earthquake of 1906, "The Nodder" from Hollywood in the 1930s. The Golf Stories have the same love-story formula, occasionally varied by the escape-motif of the fearsome Agnes Flack, where the happy ending consists of the getaway of her involuntary suitors. The central assumption that Life is Golf renders them mock-heroic, and as in the Mulliner stories Wodehouse supplies prodigious ornament far beyond plot-necessity, with fantastic detail.

Mr. Mulliner's clergy, for instance, quote chapter-and-verse with wonderful comic effects, as in " 'Oh, that I had wings like a dove. Psalm XIV. 6,' muttered the bishop" ("The Bishop's Move"). The golfing equivalent would be Wodehouse's loving descriptions of matches, hole-by-hole, the course itself magnified into epic proportions, or the enormous respect for golfing authority: " 'Those rules were drawn up by—' I bared my head reverently 'by the Committee of the Royal and Ancient at St. Andrews'" ("The Long Hole," in *The Clicking of Cuthbert*).

Stanley Featherstonehaugh Ukridge is unique in Wodehouse, his only rogue-hero. After figuring in one early novel he is starred in a collection of ten stories (*Ukridge* [1924]), and appears scatteringly over the years as late as 1966. His status is high, almost on a level with Jeeves and Bertie Wooster. Unlike them, he is not to be found in the later novels. Perhaps there was no room for him; utterly flamboyant, he would be wasted as a minor character, and it may be too that Wodehouse recognized that he is best in short hauls. Ukridge lives in an amoral, entertaining world of his own imagination; he is a confidence-man in search of the perfect caper. He manages prize-fighters, with side-bets at long odds; he combats dishonest bookies dishonestly. He wages constant warfare with his formidable aunt, who represents conventional propriety, and plagues her with knavish and outlandish tricks. (As a successful female novelist, in the Wodehouse world she deserves him doubly, as aunt and by occupation.)

Ukridge's schemes are always comic, and he is never in serious trouble with the law, especially as he is irrefragably an upper-class Briton. He is a vast inconvenience to his reputable friends. His technical function is to stir up the maximum of disorder, productive of farce-plots. Continually on the brink of disaster, he is (like most of the Mulliners) remarkably resourceful in emergencies, and usually aided by happy accidents. Unlike Mulliner heroes, in the later stories he is himself the narrator, but he has an interlocutor, Corky, to act as foil. Corky, who like the young Wodehouse himself is a struggling, frugal, industrious writer, is a neutral figure, respectable, and constantly victimized by his brigand friend. The device is skillful: Ukridge can only be adequately represented from his own point of view, and the unobtrusive Corky, who is intelligent and humorous but never gets into Ukridge's act, is his ideal introducer.

Drones Club members are especially to be found in *Young Men in Spats* (1936) and *Eggs, Beans and Crumpets* (1940), though they often appear in Jeeves-Wooster tales and novels, and Archibald Mulliner "was having a thoughtful cocktail in the window of the Drones Club, looking out on Dover Street," when he first glimpsed Aurelia Cammarleigh. They mainly tell their stories in the Drones bar, and these always concern fellow members. They are all in some degrees pinheads like Bertie Wooster, who is one of them, and they belong to his Edwardian world. They are generally well-born younger sons existing on allowances from older relatives, though there is a club millionaire, Oofie Prosser, and Bertie himself is wealthy and employs a "gentleman's personal gentleman"—Jeeves. They have duties only when their relatives, usually aunts or uncles, can get hold of them: sometimes these duties furnish story-plots, but more often they find their problems by themselves.

In particular, they are given to falling in and out of love with great speed, usually with estimable but inappropriate girls; though expert courtiers they have little staying-power. They dish themselves, and have formidable rivals. Freddie Widgeon has his (characteristic) problems:

I suppose, all in all, Freddie Widgeon has been in love at first sight with possibly twenty-seven girls in the course of his career: but hitherto everything had been what you might call plain sailing. I mean, he would flutter round for a few days and then the girl, incensed by some floater on his part or possibly merely unable to stand the sight of him any longer, would throw him out on his left ear, and that would be that. Everything pleasant and agreeable and orderly, as you might say. But this was different. Here he had come up against a new element, the jealous rival, and it was beginning to look not so good. ("Trouble Down at Tudleigh")

Drones are eternally young in the short stories. They have standards of loyalty, generosity, and propriety; their love-affairs, for example, are remarkably innocent. Their chief lack is caution. Around the club bar are hangovers at noon, but these are humorous inconveniences: alcohol is always comic in Wodehouse, and important to him as an action-starter, or merely an atmospheric token of conviviality. Edwardianly, the Drones do not drink with women beyond a polite bottle of wine at a picnic. There is one exception, their least amiable member, Oofy Prosser, the Club Millionaire, who is addicted to night clubs and cuties, and even he is comic, and supplies one of the greatest moments in perhaps the funniest of all Drones stories, "Sonny Boy," ushered in by this pronouncement: "On his return home this morning, Mr. Prosser appears to have decided not to go to bed. You will find him in the fireplace."

Bertie Wooster is not the greatest pinhead of the brotherhood of Drones: Barmy Fotheringay-Phipps and one or two others are said to surpass him. He is more complex, and of course receives far more attention, along with "the inimitable Jeeves." Both go back to the beginnings of Wodehouse's maturity, antedating the Mulliners. In supplanting Bertie with Mr. Mulliner for short stories, Wodehouse is correct; the Mulliner tales have more glitter and variety. Bertie goes on, but is most fully developed in the novels. It has been claimed that Jeeves adds a further dimension to the Wodehouse short story, and thus achieves preeminence for Wooster-Jeeves in the short-story canon: the comic twists always turn out to be designed by *him*, with superhuman foresight, and go beyond the convenient coincidences of the farce-plot. Jeeves is the mysterious and omnipotent Sherlock Holmes, and Bertie the struggling Watson, who misunderstands the action until Holmes explains it at the end.

Like Holmes, Jeeves has his methods; it might be objected that they are too rough, since he lands Bertie with a (false) reputation for insanity on two continents, and otherwise victimizes him. Sometimes the only recourse is a speedy exit down a water pipe or fire escape, en route to the closest railway station. As to extra dimensions, Mr. Mulliner almost always has his own final twist, engaging his audience before, during, and after the happenings he narrates. Perhaps it should be conceded that in some respects the Wooster-Jeeves combination elicits more of the quintessential Wodehouse in their wealth of literary allusions, Bertie's complicated mock-heroic narrative voice, and the general interplay; we suspect that Bertie's fatuity is feigned, as when he forgets himself and bursts into idiomatic and perfectly correct French. Finally, the central device of these stories, like the Mulliner cycle, is the utterly false motivation of the sentimental trash they spring from, interwoven with Bertie's amiability. He is the "parfit gentil" knight (White Knight); he follows the code of the Woosters, who did their bit on the field of Crécy. The code demands absolute loyalty to a pal, particularly an old school pal. Confronted with the outrageous demands of his unscrupulous friend Bingo Little, he protests weakly, then instantaneously yields—and this always happens:

"You don't mean to say you think you're going to lug *me* into it?"
He looked at me like Greta Garbo coming out of a swoon. "Is this Bertie Wooster talking?" he said, pained.
"Yes, it jolly well is."
"Bertie, old man," said Bingo, patting me gently here and there, "reflect! We were at sch—"
"Oh, all right!"

And thus begins the ridiculous action.

Richard Harter Fogle

*University of North Carolina
at Chapel Hill*

A.E. COPPARD AND
H.E. BATES

In 1971 Granada Television produced a series of dramatic adaptations entitled "Country Matters" from some of the stories of A. E. Coppard and H. E. Bates. Critically successful and highly popular in England, "Country Matters" was later exported to the United States and shown on the Public Broadcasting Service stations. The series both drew on and reinforced a connection between the two writers in the general critical and public consciousness, which thought of them as practitioners of the short-story form dealing unpretentiously with rural English life and representing something both ordinary and quintessentially English. From the perspective of "Country Matters," the two writers were regarded as virtually synonymous despite the fact that Alfred Edgar Coppard (1878–1957) was more than a quarter of a century older than Herbert Ernest Bates (1905–74). The difference in age was somewhat obliterated because Coppard, a self-educated clerk, did not begin to write seriously until toward the end of World War I; and his first volume of short stories was published in 1921. Bates had his first novel, *The Two Sisters*, accepted for publication in December 1925 when he was only twenty years old. Both writers had numerous volumes of short stories published in the late 1920s and 1930s (Bates also saw publication of novels, novellas, essays, a book on the short story, children's books, and a few poems; Coppard four volumes of poetry). For a considerable length of time they shared the same publisher, Jonathan Cape. Both continued writing during and after World War II, still appealing to many readers while seeming to others anachronistic, insulated, or sentimental. Bates himself, in 1971, in the second volume of his autobiography, made the connection between the two writers both evaluative and explicit, contrasting his and Coppard's capacity for rendering English life judiciously and justly with the "lumps of offal" produced by the young writers of the 1950s and 1960s.[1]

More significantly, both Bates and Coppard were articulate defenders of the technique of the short story as distinguished from other forms of fiction. Both recalled Turgenev, a master of the shorter form, as a model, an acknowledgment of influence they shared with writers as diverse as James, Conrad, Ford, and Galsworthy. For Bates and Coppard, Turgenev initiated the focus on unity and compression in the short story, although Bates added the almost equivalent influences of Chekhov, Maupassant, and Crane.[2] In 1948, in a preface for an American collected edition of his tales, Coppard maintained that the short story was not simply a compressed or stripped-down version of the novel but, rather, a form altogether different in nature and origin. The story originated in folk tales and oral transmission, its unity most frequently inhering within the mind or consciousness of a single character. In this, Coppard asserted, he was following the principles of another of his masters, Henry James. Later, in his autobiography, written shortly before his death and published posthumously, Coppard repeated his reverence for James, although he did not always incorporate the master's technical dictates in his stories. For example, James followed the notion, deriving from Turgenev, that a storyteller began with a character and invented episodes to bring out the character's significance. Coppard said that he worked in the opposite direction, beginning with the episode and finding or inventing a character to illustrate it.[3] He added that the episodes derived from his own experience but were not literally true and thus had merely "the sensation of truth" (IM, 216). Coppard applied his interpretation of the short story to his autobiography, which is a series of anecdotes, impressions, and opinions, with no attempt at a coherent version of self; he claimed at the very beginning that autobiography, in its selection, omission, and exaggeration, is a form of fiction like the short story (IM, 9).

Bates considered the short story less as anecdote than Coppard did. Concentrating on the elements of unity and compression, Bates saw the short story as the effectively distilled novel—even praising his own powers of compression by rather grandiosely claiming that he got more "atmosphere" in a sentence than Thomas Hardy characteristically managed in a page (BW, 63). In his later years, Bates acknowledged his debt to Coppard; in the third and final volume of his autobiography he wrote that Coppard had once told him that the story could learn a great deal from cinematic art in the use of quick cuts, close-ups, and other techniques with a sharp pictorial impact, an influence that Bates asserted had appeared more visibly and consciously in his fiction as he had grown older.[4] For both, the effect of the story was primarily visual. Bates, however, dissented from some of Coppard's opinions and preferences. He cited their disagreement over Stephen Crane, whose work Bates had admired since his school days, and he thought that Coppard was a fine writer except when he was "unwise enough to take that most elephantine of bores, Henry James, as the chief of his models" (VW, 146). In 1940, in a short critical book on the short story, Bates stressed compression and unity as the salient features of the form and described Coppard's work as uneven, claiming that some of his stories were among the best, some among the worst, of recent English examples. He praised Coppard for avoiding any suggestion of Kipling's "loud vulgarities" that sounded like Wagner's music (opinions that Coppard shared, although in more explicitly political terms) (*BW*, 160–61). In his critical book, Bates omitted entirely any reference to Henry James, neither discussing him as an influence on Coppard nor as an original practitioner of literary technique.

Although both advocated and illustrated many of the technical elements in fiction—the unity, the compression, the selection, the restriction to a single point of view, that are characteristic of what has come to be defined as "modernism"—neither Bates nor Coppard can accurately be called a "modernist" writer. "Modernism" can cover a range that includes writers as diverse as Joyce, Lawrence, Kafka, Chekhov, Katherine Mansfield, and Virginia Woolf, but generally and accurately excludes both Bates and Coppard. In part, this may be a judgment, a statement that Bates and Coppard are writers of the second rank. More appropriately, however, it is a descriptive statement about the kind of fiction they wrote and the ways in which they regarded their work. Seldom did Bates or Coppard, especially the latter, consciously place exclusive reliance on symbol or metaphor to convey what could otherwise not be conveyed. Rather, they generally wrote anecdotes or described situations, or defined characters or relationships, with directness and understatement, with no explicit sense that these represented or suggested anything further (in fact, both sometimes explicitly blocked off such suggestion, although neither may have suppressed quite as much as he seemed to think he had). Their fiction radiates the plain man's point of view, the refusal to make more of something than it is. And, in this point of view, they both, explicitly and implicitly, unlike the "modernists," acknowledged no special role or function for the artist, who is as vulnerable or imperfect as anyone else and has nothing of the seer about him, no quality of revelation or representation that is deeper or more significant than that of any other viewer. The disagreement between Coppard's view of Henry James and Bates's is less a disagreement about the nature of fictional art than one about the particular achievement of James. Bates saw in James a high priest of the metaphorical art he rejected; Coppard saw in him only a careful and scrupulous shaper of life whom he endorsed as he would never have venerated a votary of high art. For both Bates and Coppard, the function of the writer, particularly within the short story, was to present life as effectively as he could, not to embroider, but simply to depict the vagaries of the particular. And, in this, both implicitly denied the writer had any special insight; they regarded as pretentious and inflated the making of the particular into the representative—a characteristic that the literary culture has come to associate with "modernism." This is more than a difference in setting, rural as against cosmopolitan, or in voice, the plain man as against the artist. Rather, it is a difference about the way fiction reflects and relates to human experience.

The general critical designation, which has never been developed into thorough critical treatment, of Bates and Coppard as twin examples of rural or home-grown writers expressing tendencies different from the axioms of "modernism" in the midst of the "modern" age, deserves further examination. A. E. Coppard and H. E. Bates, as dedicated writers of a great deal of variously effective short fiction, deserve individual consideration; that individual consideration will follow a discussion of their treatments of "Country Matters" and "Plain Man Speaking." Admittedly, such categories are vaguely wide and far from complete, particularly given the range of each man's work, but the categories can be justified by their popular and critical currency as well as by their function as an introduction to the particular examples of the fiction. To take "Country Matters" first, the designation that deals with subject matter, both Bates and Coppard were very much interested in nature and the rural world, using it frequently as the setting for tales. Yet their approaches to, and uses of, nature are characteristically different.

Coppard's ruralism is often restricted to setting, a thick texture of detail that surrounds a story or an anecdote about people. "The Hurly Burly" begins with a young servant on a farm working and organizing the place efficiently and economically while her young master is in jail. When he is released, he, grateful, marries her but continues to regard her as a servant, placing increasingly large demands on her until she dies from overwork. The emotional force of the story, which Coppard emphasizes, is in her incredibly self-destructive devotion and the injustice of the relationship between owner and servant. The richness of the story, however, is in the detail, the routines of farm life, which Coppard observes carefully but does not seem to integrate into the emotional drama. Sometimes, his stories of rural or natural people do integrate setting and drama more closely and effectively, as in "The Watercress Girl," in which the young girl who cultivates and sells watercress grown in a swamp expresses her feelings and passions directly, apart from any of the conventions of society. Jilted by her lover, she throws acid in her rival's face. Her honest passion, in a story that makes no moral judgment whatever, reunites her with her lover in an example of the stark brutality of rural life. At other times, Coppard's veneration for natural simplicity carries the charm of the deliberately trivial. In one of his best-known and earliest stories, "Arabesque—The Mouse," an indolent, sensitive, and melancholy man sits reading Russian novels and recalling the dead mother he loved and the loved girl who left him. He also feels guilty about the traps he sets to kill the mice who invade his house and ruminates with misery over each mouse corpse. As the story becomes an ingenious and funny debate between the necessity for and the aversion to killing mice, it leaves the heavy and melancholy suggestions of Russian novels and lost loves satirized, undeveloped, and unrelated to experience. In some of his fiction, Coppard uses nature not just to show country character or the hard direct brutality of rural life. Nature also conveys elements of mystery, of living, unknown presences, as in "Ahoy, Sailor Boy!," in which a sailor returning to England senses a frightening and attractive female ghost among the winds, moors, and forests of his native land. Nature is animistic and evocative, in a manner somewhat reminiscent of John Cowper Powys, although in Coppard never philosophically worked out. Nor in "Ahoy, Sailor Boy!" does the use of the ghost invite any of the psychological speculation implicit in James's ghost stories. The animistic Coppard can become trivial, Disneyfied, as in "The Fair Young Willowy Tree," in which the growing female willow tree falls in love with and whispers sweet sentiments to the tall telephone pole placed near her. After several years, the willow's growing branches begin to entangle the telephone wires and the willow is chopped down by insentient man. Coppard as mystic or animist can easily descend into sentimentality; he is generally far more effective in his delineation of country people than he is in describing nature or deriving any meaning from it.

Bates, whose range is considerably wider than Coppard's, is also often effective in depicting the emotions of country people. In "The Daffodil Sky," the title story from one of his volumes, Bates details the emotions of the slow farmer returned after twenty years in jail for killing a man who might or might not have had an affair with his fiancée. Looking for the woman, he finds her daughter (who might or might not be his child) and is attracted to her instinctive sympathy and warmth in the same way he had been attracted to her mother. Nothing happens; the two simply go to the local pub for a drink and her paternity is never revealed. The story exists within the slow, heavy, intense feelings of the farmer and offers a convincing presentation of a man capable of killing for love. Although more lyrical and expansive about such characters in his earliest work, Bates consistently maintained considerable skill and vitality in such description. Bates was also, as Coppard generally was not, sharply observant of all the particulars of nature, superb at describing weather, precise in detailing the configuration of copses and the shapes and colors of anemones. Constance Garnett praised Bates highly as the genuine successor to D. H. Lawrence in his sensitivity to and love for flowers (BW, 32). This may be true, although Bates seldom expands the flower into the metaphor for botanical and organic process in the distinctive way Lawrence does. Indeed, some of Bates's stories seem simply occasions for exercising his skill at precise natural description. In "A Flower Piece," for example, two little girls in a rural house play at being grown-ups, the story concluding that one enjoys acting and one does not. The simple contrast is carried by extensive description of the flowers, trees, and woods surrounding the house, a description unrelated to the contrast between the characters of the girls.

More often, the description functions as a long pause within the action of the story, achieving its significance from placement and from the sense of precise observation rather than from any intrinsic connection with character or event. In "Country Society," for example, an upper-middle-class couple living in the country are giving a cocktail party and are anxious to impress their neighbors by serving white wine and talking of the "distinguished couple" who have accepted their invitation. The "distinguished couple" arrive, bringing with them their attractive young niece, and the host, who had hitherto seemed rather bland and emotionless, finds himself immediately drawn to the niece. At this point, the story breaks off for pages of description of the flowers outside and the deepening shadows of surrounding foliage as evening advances. When the plot resumes, host and niece talk, revealing a sense of mutual attraction, and, then, both party and story end. The natural description is not used to resolve or suggest anything not already suggested by the plot or the conversation in a story that, characteristically for Bates, might be defined as either understated or unresolved, simply a quick reflection of the way life is, just as the description of flowers and trees is simply a precise account of the way they are.

A similar kind of story, with nature interrupting a more eventful and significant plot, is "The Frontier." In this story, an Englishman who owns a tea plantation in northern India meets a young English army nurse while on a short trip to town during World War II. He invites her to spend her few days' leave on his plantation, and, as they travel there, Bates provides extensive particular description of northern Indian flora and fauna (his descriptive powers are far from limited to the ordinary English scene). The exotic description, however, is not connected with what happens in the story, as the nurse, more vital than the planter, is willing to go to bed with him, which he discreetly avoids; the nurse's real aim is to track down a native murderer who has been terrorizing other natives. She finally persuades the planter that they ought to venture into the jungle after the murderer, providing Bates with the opportunity for further description. In the jungle the planter is shot to death, an indication that his time, politically as well as sexually, is over. The description of nature, fascinating in itself, often interrupts but neither advances nor suggests anything further about the story.

Perhaps vaguely in "The Frontier," somewhat more specifically in "The Major of Hussars," the description provides a reflected element of sympathy for the principal character who is sensitive to the landscape around him. In "The Major of Hussars," the description provides a reflected element of sympathy for the principal character, who is sensitive to the landscape around him. In "The Major of Hussars," a retired major, who changes his sets of false teeth for different occasions as he changes his clothes, waits for his wife to join him at a Swiss resort. She delays her arrival several times, while the major takes long walks through the cultivated gardens along the lake, into Alpine meadows, and up mildly mountainous paths. Most of the extensive description of Swiss flowers and scenery is provided by the circumspect and detached narrator, another guest at the hotel. When the major's wife finally arrives, the narrator sees that she is demanding, unappreciative, interested only in herself, and half her husband's age. She destroys the major's holiday, just as she deliberately destroys all his extra false teeth. The narrator only observes, never judges. All the description of nature lingers only as a suggestion of the major's sensitivity and of sympathy for him.

Only very occasionally does Bates endow nature with any of the animistic force visible more frequently in Coppard's work. In "Thelma," the principal character has been a maid at a country inn for many years. She has spent most of her life comforting and serving the commercial travelers who use the inn, although she has always been in love with the first man she took into the beech woods for an afternoon when she was young. He has never returned to the inn. She has often talked with and consoled other men in the same woods. When, thirty-five years after their brief love affair, she learns that her first lover has died, she walks all the way through the woods for the first time, becomes ill, and dies. The extensively described woods seem to represent a strange force, benign or consoling at the edges, malign in the center or when traversed; yet what they represent is far from clear or characteristic of Bates's usual careful and detached control of natural description. Unlike Coppard's, Bates's work contains almost no sentimental personification of nature. Although one of his stories, "Fear," does open with the sentence "On the horizon three thunderstorms talked darkly to each other," Bates shifts quickly to his characters.

In some of Bates's best stories, natural description approaches the metaphorical without being the kind of conscious metaphor that Woolf, Mansfield, or Lawrence would use. Bates's versions of metaphor always emerge through a detached, carefully precise narrator—a seeming surrogate for the author—whose precision becomes itself a form of understatement, submerging the connections it suggests. In "The Flag," the narrator is shown around a country house by its owner, a florid, bombastically patriotic, retired captain. In conversation over the inevitable drinks with the captain and his pale, retiring wife, the narrator picks up hints that the wife may be having an affair with the gardener (never seen). For the narrator, all his extensive observations of the house and its grounds reflect both the vitality of the affair that may or may not be taking place and the decay that is visible in the captain, his house, and his world. Yet such reflections never radiate further than the narrator, are buried by his scrupulous allegiance to verifiable fact—the suggestions about the situation itself subsumed under the emphasis on the narrator's describing simply what he sees. The understatement is terse, effective, authentic; it also seems to limit or devalue something implicit in the situation.

A similar kind of story is "The Evolution of Saxby," in which the narrator meets Saxby numerous times over a period of years, both during and after World War II, on commuter trains to the London suburbs. Saxby invariably talks of the garden he owns or plans, on one site or another, but never fully achieves because he says his wife is ill and her care requires most of his free time. Saxby finally invites the narrator to help plan his newest garden, and the surprised narrator discovers that Saxby's wife is vital and charming, has never been ill, and that she and her husband have, over the past twenty years, made a profitable career out of buying old houses to renovate and sell, moving to a new one as soon as they have finished, and have never taken the time to cultivate a garden. As he leaves, the narrator speculates that Saxby may have wanted his wife recumbent so that he could put down roots and grow his garden—but the speculation, like the garden as possible metaphor, reveals something less of the situation than the situation seemed to promise. Understatement and faithful description, valuable in themselves, seem emphasized at the expense of creative imagination.

The interest in "Country Matters" is, then, different in Coppard and Bates. Coppard's "country" was primarily a veneration for rural and unsophisticated people, material for anecdotes, and a sometimes animistic force. Although Bates shared some of Coppard's interest in subject matter and in rural people, his "country" was far more likely to be precisely rendered detail about the natural world and to suggest as well as to question, perhaps inadvertently, "nature" as a means of conveying human feelings and turmoil in fiction. Coppard was the more earthy of the two, Bates the more sensitive.

The critical designation of Coppard and Bates as exemplifying the perspective of "Plain Man Speaking" is another possible way to connect the two writers. "Plain Man Speaking" suggests an ordinary Englishman's no-nonsense point of view, sharp observations of reality with nothing fabricated, a gesture against high art. This designation, like that of "Country Matters," has a certain superficial accuracy and is a useful introduction, although, finally, examination of it reveals more differences between the two writers than similarities.

Both Coppard and Bates, for example, were always derisive about organized religion and prided themselves on their agnosticism. Bates, although brought up as a Methodist, early denied all faith and later wrote that prelates, politicians, and actors "all come out of the same egg-shell of vanity" (*VW*, 178). Coppard, in his autobiography, used his years as the oldest child in a destitute family on parish relief (when A. E. was only nine, his father died, leaving a wife and three younger daughters) to explain a permanent hatred for all policemen and parsons. Anticlericalism almost never surfaces in Bates's fiction, whereas it is omnipresent in Coppard's.

In some of Coppard's stories, the anticlericalism is the whole point, as in "Abel Staple Disapproves," an anecdote in which a solid, sensible farmer and his conventional brother-in-law are in a pub writing a memorial for the farmer's wife who has just died. The farmer wants no hymn or religious reference included, but his brother-in-law disagrees. They toss a coin to decide; the farmer loses and is resigned to his defeat by cant. Other Coppard stories are reverse mini-allergories, like "Father Raven," in which a pastor, vouching for all, leads his flock to heaven to find himself the only one barred because of his false pledge; or "Clorinda Walks in Heaven," in which a dead spinster on her journey to a rather whimsically conveyed heaven sees a parade of men, all the suitors she denied and thwarted. Sometimes the shaft of the anecdote is aimed particularly at the Protestant clergy. In "Purl and Plain," an amiable and jovial old Catholic father and a stuffy, self-righteous young Protestant curate await the birth of a child of a mixed marriage, the Catholic to baptize the baby if a boy, the Protestant if a girl. The child is a girl, but the parents, having noted the difference between the representatives of the two religions, change their minds and decide to baptize the child as a Catholic. In another slight tale, "Christine's Letter," a rigidly religious young Protestant appeals to his wife, who has run off and become a waitress, to return. Yet, the letter itself makes clear that she has run off because she could no longer stand his arid sanctimony.

Even in some of Coppard's more fully developed and effective stories, religion, particularly Protestantism, is the life-denying villain. Tracing the career of a farm boy who, enchanted with the stage, joins a traveling troop, "Ring the Bells of Heaven" establishes his healthy farm background and even his unrequited love as ultimate aids in his career, having provided him with experience in expressing emotion, but the fundamentalist religion he must abandon is nothing but a barrier. One of Coppard's most moving stories, "Fishmonger's Fiddle," centers on the character of a young woman jilted by her husband and forced by circumstance to live with her puritanically religious aunt and uncle. When she later falls in love with a strange itinerant musician who plays a cello in a fish shop, she realizes that she must suppress her own desire out of gratitude to the aunt and uncle she resents. Her hopes and her failure are conveyed with a searching and convincing complexity. Another story of complex characterization, "The Poor Man," depicts an iconoclastic rustic with a great talent for singing who annoys the puritanical local rector because he is a numbers runner and acknowledges and keeps the illegitimate son he loves. By encouraging the police to arrest the rustic for poaching, the rector helps precipitate the disaster that ruins the rustic's life. Such stories, whether simple or complex, convey Coppard's protest against religion as a force that inhibits or denies humanity.

In his own life, Coppard illustrated the "Plain Man Speaking"—that no-nonsense view of the ordinary Englishman. He entitled his autobiography *It's Me, O Lord!* and provided a subtitle, "An abstract and brief chronicle of some of the life with some of the opinions of A. E. Coppard written by himself." Opinions on issues other than religion, such as quick attacks on capitalism or the pompous follies of government, appear but are never developed or explained. Coppard's fiction always carries the voice of direct and involved statement and has none of Bates's tone of measured detachment. Coppard's autobiography praises or damns directly; it gives lists of those he hated, but almost never provides any justification. He claims to have loved Chaucer, Shakespeare, Milton, Wordsworth, Keats, Browning, early Tennyson, Whitman, Bridges, Masefield, Housman, Yeats, Hardy, Beethoven, and folk music. On the other hand, he had no tolerance at all for Donne, Dryden, Swift, Samuel Johnson, Thackeray, Byron, Shelley, Bach, Mozart, El Greco, or Van Gogh. Coppard always thought of himself as liberal or radical, an unquestioned point of view implicit in the fiction and explicit in the autobiography. He regarded the Boer War as the greatest example of English injustice in his lifetime. In 1950, when he was over seventy, he organized the Authors' World Peace Appeal, which sent a delegation of writers to Russia to try to help ease cold war tensions and alert the public to the dangers of nuclear combat between the United States and the Soviet Union. Coppard organized a steering committee that included Doris Lessing, Alex Comfort, Cecil Day Lewis, Compton Mackenzie, Herbert Read, and Naomi Mitchison. At the peak of the committee's influence, in 1951 and 1952, Dylan Thomas and Christopher Fry were also members. Despite what became, in literary circles at least, the orthodoxy of some of Coppard's opinions, he continued to think of himself as something of an iconoclast, a point of view that often conveyed a quality of quirky charm. For successive issues of *Who's Who*, covering many years, he listed his only recreation as "resting."

Bates is similarly direct and unanalytical about literature, although he makes no such sweeping statements about canonical artists. He does find Lawrence's *Women in Love* "grossly overpraised," although he sees the value of some of Lawrence's other novels and stories (*VW*, 151). Bates usually reserves his acidulous comments about literature for works written after World War II, as in his opinion that Osborne's play should have been called *Look Back in Self-Pity* (*VW*, 157). Bates, however, was far less the iconoclast than Coppard—especially in his later years. The petulance with which he regarded much of the world after World

War II sometimes seems to distort his autobiography, to convert insight into grumbles or social commentary into a generalized litany about decline. He cannot talk about the street games of his youth or the cheap and friendly lunches in pubs without adding that these have all been replaced by "shop-lifting, protest marches, and vandalism" (*VW*, 51). He mentions, at least four times, how anarchic and unpleasant he thinks the universities of the 1960s are. When recalling his own early career as a writer, he could be grandly sweeping: "What chiefly strikes me now about the dawn of the 1930s is the great richness, literary-wise, of the times, not merely on our side of the Atlantic, but on both; we have nothing comparable, on either side, today" (*BW*, 81). But he seems unconscious of some of the infections of the world after World War II, like "literary-wise," within his own prose. A few of his stories, too, carry the same berating tone, such as "Love in a Wych Elm," a slight story in which seven attractive blond sisters in a local family all illustrate the decay and corruption of contemporary affluence.

Nevertheless, it is unfair to overemphasize the cantankerousness of the later Bates or the iconoclasm of Coppard at the expense of a fair appraisal of their work over their lifetimes. Both writers produced a considerable body of work over a long period of time, each writing hundreds of stories—Bates writing dozens of novellas and novels as well—and both dealt with human experience more extensively and centrally than labels like "Country Matters" or "Plain Man Speaking" can indicate. Both merit more penetrating and individual critical treatment than either has received.

• • •

Alfred Edgar Coppard was born in Folkstone on 4 January 1878, the son of George Coppard, a young tailor, and Emily Alma Southwell, a housemaid and the daughter of a hostler. They lived in two rooms in a carpenter's house. Coppard recalled that his mother loved magic and the inexplicable; he described his father as a "free-thinking radical" in an age when tailors and cobblers were "all radical." The elder Coppard objected strongly to the suggestion that his son be sent to a school run by nuns (*IM*, 14). Coppard also recalled his father as fond of flowers, birds, the open air, and reciting long ballads in taverns. In 1883 the family moved to Brighton, then still a cavalry town, where his father had a job with a firm making uniforms. Coppard went to a board school for three years, his only formal schooling, of which he recalled little more than the frequent canings he claimed the headmaster enjoyed giving. In 1887 Coppard's father, only twenty-nine, died of tuberculosis and drink; and his mother, with four young children, found work as an ironer in a laundry, earning twenty-seven pence per twelve-hour day. When he was ten, Coppard was sent to London to live with his father's eldest brother, a more successful tailor, and there became a tailor's errand boy. He later recalled his fear at running through Whitechapel and East End streets at night at the time of the Jack the Ripper murders. He soon found a job as a messenger, running in crises to deliver the latest news to newspaper offices for Reuter's News Agency, which then owned the only world-wide telegraph service in London. He liked the work, but he missed his mother and sisters, and he returned to Brighton in 1891 and found a job as an office boy. While working, he trained as a runner—winning prizes in local races—played cricket and football, and began to write poetry. He thought of himself as a radical, like his father, and a poet by natural inclination, adding in his retrospective account that he knew nothing of history or literature.

Since two of his sisters were established in domestic service and Coppard had a series of increasingly better jobs as office clerk, his mother was able to give up working at the laundry. By 1907, when he decided to leave Brighton, Coppard had married a young girl named Lily Anne, whom he had met when she was working as a stenographer in one of the offices where he was a clerk. Coppard recalled that, when they were engaged, her father once punched him for telling her that she ought not wear stays. The couple moved to Oxford, Coppard finding a job as a clerk. In an Oxford he described as rather like the Victorian slums in Hardy's *Jude the Obscure*, the Coppards moved from one house to another every year or so; he bought a motorcycle, kept and bred dogs, became a vegetarian, and began to write stories as well as poems. Joining first the Liberal party, then the International Labour party, he became more explicitly involved in politics, an interest that led him into contact with university people such as Harold Laski and Aldous Huxley. He attended every poetry reading by W. B. Yeats and was fascinated with the poet's "mystic chant" (*IM*, 196). Toward the end of World War I, Coppard began to see his poems and tales published in magazines. When the war ended, although without savings or other funds, he decided to give up his job as a clerk and spend all his time writing. Proclaiming his need for freedom, he also left his wife and lived alone in a primitive cottage near Headington, eating little more than he could gather in the fields and woods. Reviews and sketches brought him only thirty-one pounds during his first year; he doubled that during the second. Toward the end of 1920, a new publisher (of the Golden Cockerel Press) visited his cottage and asked to publish a volume of short stories, which appeared as *Adam and Eve and Pinch Me* in 1921. At the end of 1922, the farmer-owner reclaimed Coppard's cottage. Coppard returned to Lily Anne for a short time, trying to persuade her to be as unconventional and unfettered as he was. But the marriage soon dissolved. After further years of wandering, in 1931 he married Winifred May De Kok, a young woman from

South Africa. They had two children and, sometime later, settled near Great Dunmow in Essex. Although he was always in a precarious financial position, Coppard's critical reputation grew. Rebecca West called him "the great master of the short story of our time."[5] Over the years, he saw publication of fifteen volumes of his short stories, three volumes of poems, two volumes of sketches, and a volume he edited of selections from Robert Burns's songs. Posthumously, the first volume of his planned autobiography, which ended at his mid-forties, was published as well as additional volumes of collected stories and poems. Coppard died on 13 January 1957.

Since he was often a writer of sketches and anecdotes, a great deal of Coppard's fiction originates in the autobiographical. A number of stories begin with descriptions of lower-class green-grocers' and other shops in a seaside town, seen by a very poor young boy, that directly recall Coppard's experience in Brighton in the mid-1880s. "The Cherry Tree" is a sketch of two young girls who ingeniously pare the housekeeping money to get their poor widowed young mother a bottle of stout and some cherry-tree seeds, an echo of her rural past, for her birthday. "The Presser" uses the character of young Johnny Flynn, often a surrogate for Coppard himself in the early stories, working as a messenger in a tailor's shop in London. In this sketch, Johnny, frightened by the brutality he sees in the East End streets, is also constantly hungry because his puritanical aunt demands all his wages as the price for his room and board yet nearly starves him; but Johnny is fond of the kindly employer and the lively, direct workers in the sweatshop, all of whom reflect the solidarity of the deprived. In this, as in other short sketches, Coppard's description of urban settings achieves a vitality and specificity sometimes missing from his rural scenes.

Other vignettes seem to chronicle Coppard's experience in resigning his clerkship to write. "Luxury" is a rather trivial sketch in which a poor man, having given up everything to write in a country cottage, is enraged by what he sees as his own foolishness. He gives three of his precious bananas to schoolboys who wander by, and, eating the fourth and last banana himself, decides to continue trying to write. "Alas, Poor Bollington," describes a man, living alone in the country, who thinks that he has left his wife, whereas she thinks that she had left him. When they talk this over, four years later, they conclude that he was the one who had really left, and she refuses to see him ever again. Although the conclusion seems simplified and contrived, the early parts of the story, before the confrontation, contain some interesting and complex suggestions about guilt and jealousy.

Some of Coppard's stories and sketches concentrate on the theme of sexual freedom. In "My Hundreth Tale," a long and overwritten story, Johnny Flynn, now a writer living alone in the woods, recalls all his past mistresses. Many were too direct and "vulgar" for his taste; he was too "vulgar" for the last, considerably younger than he. The only conclusion he derives is that no love affair lasts. In another story, "Nixey's Harlequin," the narrator is resentful that another man in the village has the same name he has; he is nonplussed when that name is discovered on the list of twenty-two lovers found recounted in the diary of a married woman who has died. Coppard's point is that the narrator should have been flattered rather than annoyed by the mistake. Here, as often, Coppard venerates promiscuous married women. Less theory ridden and mechanical, and more effective, is "The Field of Mustard," a sharply direct and compressed vignette of hard-working women gathering in the harvest and talking of their past illicit loves.

The theme of sexual freedom is also central to some of Coppard's most thoroughly developed and complex stories, which achieve considerable sympathy for the somewhat unconventional characters they depict. "Olive and Camilla" deals with two middle-aged spinsters who travel together, build adjacent houses in the country, and see each other frequently. Their affection, they come to realize, is based as much on rivalry as on closeness, as much on recalling tales of past and lost heterosexual love as on priding themselves on their capacity to live without men. "The Little Mistress" concentrates on a sensitive, playful, rather fey young woman married to a big, bluff doctor considerably older than she. The wife fires a series of servants, reflecting her own restless and changing affections, even as she corresponds flirtatiously with a young single man off in the colonies. Finally, the wife finds satisfaction by keeping a servant who has had an illegitimate child and allowing the servant to read her correspondence, solely vicarious satisfactions for both of them. The story carries a delicate and convincing sensitivity reminiscent of some of Katherine Mansfield's.

Another effectively sensitive slice of experience is "Doe," in which a middle-aged former bachelor tells his old friend, a vicar with a parish in a rural slum, about his past. As a bachelor, under temporary economic stress and wanting only to write, he had fired the maid who devotedly worked for him. With no other alternatives, she became a prostitute. Discovering this years later, he reclaimed her and married her, but, although both tried, the marriage failed, the habits and perspectives of the prostitute having become too ingrained. After the woman sickens and dies, her widower decides to move in with the vicar, sharing his difficult and impoverished life—the widower using the vicar as the acceptable listener to a guilt he cannot assuage, the vicar using the widower for some sense of experience he himself has never had, the two amiable and dependent on each other in their talk and their constant differences about belief in God and salvation. These stories, so diverse in other ways, all illustrate what Frank O'Connor, in his admiring and discerning criticism of Coppard's work, called both his principal fault and principal virtue, a "pre-occupation with personal freedom."[6]

A number of Coppard's anecdotes or sketches are about ironic reversals of circumstance, characters defeated by what they most desired or defined themselves by. For example, the young runner in "The Third Prize," who needs money and wants to marry, wins the local race and, because of a mistake on the part of officials, collects the prize money twice. Feeling guilty about his greed, he gives one prize to an itinerant blind singer. He then loses the other prize to the charlatan who had arranged the mistake in the first place and threatens the runner with exposure and possible imprisonment if he does not hand over the money. In "Dusky Ruth," a man meets a lovely, mysterious barmaid at a Cotswold inn. Surprised that she is willing to go to bed with him, he is eager until, just as they are about to make love, he suspects that she may be the wife of a murderer, and immediately freezes. The sense of mystery he sought is more than he can handle. Sometimes, in more ambitious and longer stories, like "Silver Circus," the ironic reversal turns into unconvincing melodrama. In this rare fictional excursion outside England, a Viennese porter whose wife has left him is persuaded, for money, to simulate a tiger in a circus reenactment of a fight with a simulated lion. The role of the lion, of course, turns out to be played by the man the porter's wife is now living with. Discovering his identity within the fight, the tiger kills the lion, although it hardly matters to the reader which kills which.

Another story of ironic reversal of circumstance is "A Broadsheet Ballad." It concerns two sisters who have apparently been made pregnant by the same young farmer. He decides to marry the younger sister, although her pregnancy is revealed as a sham designed to win the farmer from her spoiled and demanding older sister. Insofar as the story deals with emotions, jealousies, and sibling rivalries, it is effective, but Coppard devises a melodramatic plot to make the story fit the frame of the "country ballad" and to underline the unexamined theme of primitive country justice. The younger sister is found murdered. The reader knows the older sister did it, but circumstances point toward the young farmer. The girls' father, fonder of his older daughter, suppresses evidence so that the farmer hangs for the crime he did not commit. In the primitive country terms in which Coppard distances himself from his material, presenting it with no indication of an authorial point of view, the crime of murder equals the crime of trifling with a proud girl's affection.

Coppard often uses class issues as a principal theme, sometimes in simple sketches or anecdotes, like "Ninepenny Flute," in which a young working-class man obtains a broken flute, repairs it, and defends it in a pub fight. The sketch goes no further, but the voices and the attitudes in the pub emerge authentically.

Similarly, "The Ballet Girl" is a slight, rather charming tale of a naive young bookmaker's boy in Oxford, sent, as a joke, by his employers to one of the colleges to collect a bill due from an improvident and loutish gentleman. The boy talks his way into and out of situations, is gulled on fools' errands, but, after numerous escapades and parties, emerges from the college with a young girl who dances in the local ballet and "rather" loves him for his freedom from pomp or snobbery.

In a more involved and complicated story, "Judith," the young lady of the local manor house, whose husband is away, as he often is, injures her leg while hunting. The diffident local schoolmaster carries her back to the manor, and the two gradually fall in love. On the night they consummate their love, a local man is murdered. The schoolmaster, having been seen sneaking away from the manor house at dawn, is accused; he lies to protect the lady's reputation and is convicted for a murder he did not commit. The lady, wracked by guilt, writes a long and truthful account of why he lied and then tries to commit suicide. Still in a coma when discovered by her doctor and her returning husband, her letter not believed, she is judged to be sacrificing herself to save the schoolmaster, and he is executed. After her gradual recovery, the lady can no longer recall her letter, which the doctor has burned. The story is a delineation of her vague, class-born guilts and evasions, her buried half-perceptions and her resolves to forget, her dimly seen apprehension about the protections and injustices of class, rather than a story of false accusation and noble sacrifice.

A more consistently successful story is "The Higgler," in which a veteran of World War I, a traveling trader in poultry, eggs, and fruit, manages to survive economically until he stops by a prosperous farm and buys all its eggs and chickens. The farm is run by an intelligent middle-class widow and her educated daughter, and the business connection with the "higgler" continues profitably for both. The woman invites the "higgler" to dinner regularly, and the relationship develops into one of mutual attraction. The woman would marry him, but the "higgler" is fearful about trespassing on class boundaries and feels he can never marry outside his class. He stops visiting the farm entirely and quickly marries his working-class former mistress, but neither the marriage nor the business prospers. Becoming desperate a few years later, he returns to the farm to request a loan. The woman has just died, and the "higgler" discovers that her daughter, whom he had thought would, as a university graduate, particularly abhor the match, had approved all along. The central issue of class guilt and intransigence is conveyed with sensitivity, understatement, and copious detail about both the working farm and the working trade.

Another story, very different in tone although written with equal skill and sharp detail, is "Fine Feathers." In this, young Homer, a clerk in a rural brewery, refuses to follow his father as gardener to the local squire. He criticizes "the three R's of squirearchy—reeving, riding, and rent-collecting." At the same time, Homer is entranced with ideas of gentility, and determines to buy himself an elegant dress suit. Saving money to buy the suit takes fifteen years, his purchase delayed by his father's death and the need to support his mother, as well as by his sister's pregnancy and subsequent marriage. He finally does buy the suit, and is pleased when he thinks the squire's daughter has invited him to a ball at the manor. He arrives, proudly dressed in his finery, to discover that he and the squire's daughter had misunderstood each other and that he had been asked only to help with the serving. It is the only time he wears the suit, for he soon has to sell it to help his sister support her children when her husband's latest store fails. As Homer ages, living out his life as the clerk in the brewery, with almost no social life, the suit remains his obsession, his failed vision of a grander life, a defiance of class. Here, the triviality is Homer's rather than Coppard's. Coppard supplies a perspective of sympathy for the wasted life, the life narrowed by obsession and by class values internalized to a point that subsumes either support or defiance, that sets the terms in which experience itself is apprehended.

The sensitivity, directness, and sympathy of some of Coppard's socially conscious fiction and his concern for personal and sexual freedom explain the considerable popularity of his fiction despite its uneven quality. In addition, his lanaguage and visual description are usually compressed and evocative. Ford Madox Ford may have been exaggerating, as he often was, when he wrote that Coppard was "almost the first English writer to get into English prose the peculiar quality of English lyric verse,"[7] but Ford was underscoring a terse and earthy linguistic power that many others have noted and responded to.

• • •

Although Bates's work has evoked fewer such enthusiastic accolades, it is more even in both tone and quality, and exhibits a careful and prodigious professionalism. Herbert Ernest Bates was born in Rushden, Northamptonshire, on 16 May 1905. Both his grandfathers were cobblers, his mother's father an outspoken Liberal and agnostic who, during a decline in the shoemaking trade about 1910, turned to farming for a living and impressed the young Bates with his encyclopedic knowledge of rural customs. Bates's father, who worked in the office of a small leather-tanning firm, was a religious Methodist primarily interested in music (he led several church choirs) and in learning about nature on long country walks. A long siege of scarlet fever during three months of the hot summer of 1911 permanently accustomed Bates to the solitude necessary for writing. He went to grammar school in nearby Kettering, was influenced by an excellent English master and the prose of Milton's *Areopagitica*, and began to write short stories. After finishing school, he worked for a short time as a local newspaper reporter while writing his first novel. Encouraged by the acceptance of the novel and by Edward Garnett's patronage, he left Northamptonshire and took a job in the children's department of the Bumpus Book Store in Oxford Street. As his books were being published at a rapid rate, he soon left the bookstore, supporting himself entirely by his writing. When he married Marjorie Helen Cox, in 1931, they rebuilt an old farmhouse called the Granary in Little Chart, near Ashford, Kent, and had four children, born between 1932 and 1940. Although Bates claimed that the villagers in Kent were far more insular than those in his native Northamptonshire, he remained there—with the exception of the years during World War II and frequent travel—for the rest of his life. The amount of his published material is truly remarkable: twenty-five novels, eight volumes of novellas, twenty-two volumes of short stories, a number of collected editions, nine volumes of essays, three children's books, a critical book on the short story, a memoir on Edward Garnett, and a three-volume autobiography. Bates also, under the pseudonym of "Flying Officer X," published two volumes of stories about World War II. Having written a one-act play called *The Last Bread* (published by the Labour Publishing Company in 1926), he wrote a full-length play, *The Day of Glory*, published in 1945 and staged in London in 1946. Occasionally, he wrote poetry as well, most of it privately printed. During his later years his work was frequently adapted for radio and television. After Granada's success with "Country Matters," the BBC adapted a number of Bates's novels: *When the Green Woods Laugh, Oh! To Be in England*, and, in a major series of a dozen episodes, one of his most important novels, *Love for Lydia*. *The Triple Echo*, a 1970 novella, was made into a film starring Glenda Jackson and Oliver Reed. In June 1973, at the height of the popularity of the television adaptations, Bates was named Companion of the British Empire. He died on 29 January 1974.

Publication of *Days End and Other Stories* (1928), which was followed quickly by other volumes, established Bates's reputation as a highly skillful practitioner of the short-story form, and has led one recent critic to refer to the period between 1932 and 1938 as that of Bates's "flowering."[8] A number of these stories depend on sexual attraction deriving from chance meetings, an attraction just suggested, as in "The Station," where two truckers pause at a reststop and the wife of the man who runs it invites them to pick plums from the tree in her back garden. Sometimes, the attraction has consequences, as in "The Mill" (like "The Station," published in the 1935 volume called *Cut and Come Again*), in which a seventeen-year-old girl is hired to help a farmer's invalid wife. Insensitive to her own emotions, which are just suggested through superbly precise descriptions of the old mill, the barren junkyard, and the rushing stream, the passive girl is seduced by the farmer. She does not even realize that she is pregnant until the farmer's gentle son returns on leave from the army and talks with her. Finally, she can acknowledge her emotions, a combination of grief and love for her coming baby, and resolves to leave the farm. In some stories, the consequences of sexual attraction are seen as less incipiently positive and less complex, as in "The Kimono," in which an ambitious and conventional young man from Nottingham is in London to take examinations and there meets a sensual woman. The young man never returns to his wife in Nottingham, but remains with the new woman, even after she is unfaithful. He realizes over a period of years that he has wasted his life.

Often, Bates's stories, both early and late, concentrate on the repressed or imperceptive male's denying or not recognizing what the female offers. For example, in "The Lighthouse," a young man, attracted to a married woman who runs a beach café in her husband's absence, is dominated more by his fear of the lighthouse and its height than by his attraction to the woman. Bates's women, almost always portrayed sympathetically, are likely to be left emotionally isolated, like the young jilted waitress whose surroundings so well mirror the life she must accept in "The Flame" or the middle-aged laundress in "The Ox" who stays with her brutal husband and sacrifices all her earnings to send her sons away where they might find jobs and different lives. These stories, as well as many others, show an extraordinary sympathy with human pain, seen as deep and unassuageable. In his preface to the 1963 collection of the "best" of Bates's stories, Henry Miller praised Bates's descriptions of nature, his "fully sexed" women, his bawdy humor, and added that his greatest accomplishment was his "obsession" with human pain, one so intense that "it carries us to another dimension."[9]

Imprisonment and repression are also themes in Bates's finest early stories, particularly in one of his best early volumes, *The Woman Who Had Imagination* (1934). In "The Story Without an End," for example, a fifteen-year-old French boy arrives in London to become a waiter at a relative's grubby restaurant. He fears the brutal owner who orders him to stand against the wall waiting to refill wine glasses or coffee cups. When, one Easter Sunday, the owner leaves for a few hours, the boy is invited for an outing in Hyde Park by the slightly older woman at the cash desk. Sudden rain prevents their going, and they retreat to an upstairs room where they make love. The boy's new confidence is short-lived, for the angry owner returns, sees what has happened, dismisses the woman, and orders the boy to remain "against the wall."

In a story more emotionally complex, "The Waterfall," a forty-year-old spinster and clergyman's daughter walks through the park of the village's manor house, now owned by the parvenu Abrahams, to use his phone, the only one in

the small village, to call the doctor for her ailing father. Although she strongly
wishes to protest Abraham's having locked the gates to some of the park's paths
to prevent their use by the villagers, she represses her feelings and simply uses
the phone. She returns home to find her father dead. Later, Abrahams woos her
with flowers, invitations, kindness; and, passively, after a tearful scene in which
she cries for her father and her own loneliness, she agrees to marry him. Still
prim and withdrawn, she is unable to make suggestions about the house,
grounds, or village, although she knows more about country life than he does.
Finally, she suggests timidly the building of a waterfall to solve a drainage problem in the park. An engineer arrives to supervise the building, and they invite
him to live with them while the work is going on. Always polite and reserved,
the woman cannot tell the engineer that she is sometimes offended by his jokes
or that she disapproves of his fishing in the park lake on Sundays. When the
work is completed, the engineer asks her to pull the switch that will break the
dam and release the waterfall. As she pulls and sees the rushing water, she cries
copiously, a deftly developed metaphor of release that enables her to acknowledge both her respect for Abrahams and her unfulfilled attraction to the
engineer.

Another moving and understated story is "Sally Go Round the Moon," published separately in 1932 and also included in *The Woman Who Had Imagination*
(Bates sometimes published long stories separately, then included them in later
volumes, or published stories in two different volumes, so that his productivity,
although certainly considerable and impressive, is not quite so prodigious as a
quick reading of his bibliography might suggest). "Sally Go Round the Moon"
begins with a fifteen-year-old country girl tending her sister's children in a London slum, while the thin, tense sister and a fat, brutal aunt work at menial jobs
to support the family. Only gradually is the sister's husband introduced as a
remote, delicate man who no longer works mending watches, but spends his
time reading or reviewing books like *The Meaning of God* for obscure publications
that do not pay. Attracted to the girl, the husband trades *The Meaning of God* to
a bookseller (instead of selling it) for an art book with a reproduction of a
picture that reminds him of the girl, and encourages her to return to the country when the aunt strikes her during a trivial domestic squabble. When the
husband takes the girl to the station, she cries and urges him to leave his loveless
marriage and unfaithful wife.

Dramatic conflict in Bates's stories, however, is seldom depicted with much
complexity. More often, the complexity is internalized, and the stories that depend on a dramatic exterior event are likely to be short and relatively simple,
like "Jonah and Bruno," in which a savage schoolmaster brutally beats a slightly
sassy schoolboy. Schoolmasters, in Bates's world, are invariably villains, cold,

demanding, hostile, and sometimes hypocritical, like the schoolmaster father in
"Little Fish," who harrasses his son with petty commands throughout a walk to
town to get the Saturday fish; when they stop at a café for cocoa, he is obse-
quious and deferential as he recognizes the chairman of the local education committee who does not even notice him. Farmworkers, both male and female, in
contrast to schoolmasters, are almost always sensitive, resilient, and kind, treated with considerable respect for their capacity to accommodate themselves to a
hard life. Often, as in "The Gleaner" or "The Plough" or "Breeze Anstay," (the
last in a 1937 collection called *Something Short and Sweet* and reminiscent of
D. H. Lawrence's *The Fox* both in its use of a situation in which an attractive
male intrudes on a lesbian relationship and in its descriptions of farm work), the
respect for the characters is filtered through the mud, thickness, and strain of
rural detail. Many of the rural stories are seen from the point of view of a young
boy, a sensitive, imaginative innocent, interested in the farm, despite its difficulties, or superimposing on it some more imaginative vision, like the young boy in
The Pink Cart who is enchanted by a gypsy couple with an ill daughter who park
their cart for the winter but never return to reclaim it. These stories are simple,
skillfully told, and unequivocal.

Some stories, however, in the volumes published during the 1930s, establish
the point of view of a detached adult narrator. One such is "Beauty's Daughters," in which a narrator on a walking tour rents a room for the night at a deaf
farmer's house. The laconic farmer, who must carry water to the drought-
stricken farm and house in heavy yoked wooden buckets, is disturbed because
his flashy, fleshy wife and two similar daughters spend as much time as they can
at dances and drinking parties and want to turn the farm into a boarding house.
Despite Bates's precise and evocative description of the farm and the fields, the
story seems static because the narrator is totally uninvolved.

A much more ambitious version of a similarly structured story is "The House
with the Apricot," in *Cut and Come Again*. The narrator on his walking tour finds
lodging in a well-preserved and well-furnished old house in a village in which a
semi-senile father and his repressed spinster daughter are elegantly hospitable.
The next morning, the daughter shows the narrator the paths in nearby hills
where he might best find flowers and interesting walks and asks him, if he is
passing a particular farmhouse, to deliver a note. Passing the farmhouse, the
narrator is nearly shot by an irascible, incompetent farmer who accuses him of
trespassing, and who turns out to be the recipient of the note inviting him to
dinner that evening. The farmer asks the narrator in for a drink and regales him
with whiskey and bawdy songs. Later, when the farmer appears at dinner, he
seems entirely different, well dressed, rather prissy, singing hymns all evening
with the daughter. The next morning, the daughter tells the narrator that she

and the farmer have been engaged for years. The narrator wonders, as he leaves, if she realizes what an oaf the farmer is. The narrator's detachment gives the story an estimable clarity and unpretentious authenticity; but that same detachment squelches further possible emotional dimensions of the story.

In his early stories, Bates often returned to his Rushden past, the Evensford of his fiction. Among the stories are quietly moving depictions, such as "A Christmas Song," in which a sensitive and knowledgeable girl who keeps a music shop stays open late on Christmas Eve to find a record of a Schubert song for a shy young man, while friends keep pressing her to join them at a party. She finally goes to the party, an example of the braying joviality of the Midlands middle classes, contrasting it in her mind with her conversation about music with the shy young man. Some of Bates's own past is fictionalized in the title story of *The Woman Who Had Imagination*; in it, a local chorus of tradespeople is transported to the neighboring manor house to give a lawn concert for the resident aristocrats. Bates describes the long ride to the manor house, the fields, woods, and park, the sights and scents of the country, from the point of view of the small, meticulous choir director. Since the son himself does not sing, he is free to wander the house and grounds, and he sees a lovely girl reading to a senile, demanding man. Later he again meets the girl on the shore of the park lake she had suggested he explore. She seems inviting, though mysterious, imaginative and unpredictable, and he is fascinated even after he discovers she is married to the old man he had seen her reading to.

Another story, "Millenium Also Ran," depicts a bleaker and more contemporary Evensford. The young newspaper reporter, usually bored and responsible only for getting the racing results into the "stop press" column, is told by his querulous and drunken editor to find out why a nineteen-year-old newsboy has not appeared for several days. The reporter goes through the crumbling and fetid slums to find the dirty house and to learn that the boy has died of galloping consumption. The reporter returns to the paper, too overwhelmed by the conditions he has seen to write the obituary he planned, and bets five shillings on a horse, intending to give his winnings to the boy's mother and young wife. The horse loses.

One of Bates's longest and most thorough social treatments of Rushden appears in "The Bride Comes to Evensford," separately published in 1943. The action spans more than thirty years, beginning about 1909, when a young woman who had worked in a London draper's shop comes to Evensford to work for its largest draper. Ample in its description of the town, the people, and the shop, initially almost as descriptively extensive as an Arnold Bennett novel, the story chronicles the girl's rise. She is calculating and cold as she marries the draper and gradually replaces his old mother as the controlling force in the shop. His mother dead, the draper volunteers during World War I and is killed. Now entirely in charge, the girl modernizes the shop, fires old employees, and invests her profits in slum property. Nearing fifty, she meets a young schoolmaster indifferent to her success and is fascinated by his independence and lack of apparent seriousness. But he retreats when she tries to fix his tie, a metaphor for ordering his experience. She later hears he is marrying and, going to observe his wife arriving in town, recognizes how envious, lonely, and desolate her own life is. She has become a local butt, an object for small boys to throw snowballs at. The story begins brilliantly with the prolific description of locale, but it narrows rather than deepens as it focuses relentlessly on the woman's lonely, loveless life.

Bates gradually worked the country characters around Rushden into his well-known Uncle Silas stories. Uncle Silas, a fictional character he called "Rabelaisian" or "Chaucerian," was a rural rapscallion modeled on an elderly kinsman. The first Uncle Silas story, "The Lily," appeared in *The Woman Who Had Imagination*. The story describes the sights and smells around Silas's cottage as the narrator, his grandnephew, comes to visit the lively, weathered man of ninety-three and his crabbed, carbolic housekeeper with whom he communicates by insult. Only toward the end does the story veer into anecdote as Silas tells the narrator how he stole the lily in his garden from the garden of a beautiful young married woman he wanted.

Bates did not originally plan a series of Uncle Silas stories, but wrote a few more, published in subsequent volumes, and then the character interested him enough to provide material for *My Uncle Silas* (1939). Most of the stories are anecdotal and farcical. Often, Silas is caught in a situation that might embarrass others; his clothes are stolen while he is swimming, or hidden in the closet or the cellar or the linen basket when a woman's husband or boss suddenly appears (in one of these the woman forgets she has locked him in the cellar, and he survives by stewing and eating snails, the only things he can find), but he always extricates himself and is usually rewarded with the woman's devotion. Other stories are rural tall tales, anecdotes recounting Silas's triumph over stronger men, braggarts or bullies, as in "Silas and Goliath" or "The Race." A number, too, depend on Silas's drinking or iconoclasm or raunchiness, all the lovable defiance of convention that keeps him living to the age of ninety-five.

Bates wrote no more Uncle Silas stories after 1939. But, nearly twenty years later, another version of Silas surfaced in the Larkin family in the novel *The Darling Buds of May* (1958). It became a best-seller and was quickly followed by *When the Green Woods Laugh* and *Oh! To Be in England*, novels recounting further comic adventures of the expanding family and becoming fantasies that praise the lively, anarchic spirit of old England against the drab, legalistic austerity of the welfare state. The novels were staged and televised in the early 1970s. The comic jollity of the Larkins, however, wears off even more quickly than does that of Uncle Silas, the Larkin novels revealing the curmudgeonly side of Bates complaining about trivia and the decline of British life. Although simple, the Uncle Silas stories are the purer form of farce.

World War II marked a significant change in Bates's life. In 1939 he took a job as literary editor of the *Spectator* in order to be in London daily. As an editor, he felt inadequate, but the job brought him into contact with the remarkably talented and erudite public relations division of the R.A.F., a unit that included writers such as R. F. Delderfield, John Pudney, Dudley Barker, Eric Partridge, John Strachey, and Philip Guedalla. Bates was sent through the R.A.F. Officers Training Course, then posted to various bases to write fiction about the men in the R.A.F. The stories were initially published in the *News Chronicle* under the pseudonym, created by the Air Ministry, of "Flying Officer X." An immediate success, they were reissued in two volumes that became best-sellers in England and America. The stories, crisp and understated, detail the heroism of the fliers during the first years of the war. Some are little more than sketches, such as "No Trouble at All," recounting the return of a bomber crew from a difficult mission over Occupied France, whose talk is confined to casual chatter. Others show the heroism of severely injured men, like "Sergeant Carmichael," in which a crew has to ditch its crippled plane in the English channel, or "The Beginning of Things," in which a pilot, shot down over Malta and parachuting to safety, loses an arm but is soon back flying. The heroic, as in "The Sun Rises Twice," in which a consistently "lucky" pilot does three near-Kamikaze runs at a German tanker in the channel, hits it, and brings his plane safely home, yields "no medals."

"How Sleep the Brave," the brilliant title story of one of the volumes, sensitively depicts the experience of men in a plane ditched in the North Sea. "There's No Future in It" concentrates on the pain and terror that a young girl, who must hide her concern from her narrow respectable family, feels when her lover, a bomber pilot, flies night after night. A number of the stories extensively detail the motives of those who fight. In "The Greatest People in the World," for example, a young pilot is grounded by mechanical failures, scrubbed missions, and his own incompetence. After hearing that his parents have been killed in a bombing raid, he becomes a shrewd and successful pilot on particularly difficult missions. Similarly, "The Bell" and "Yours Is the Earth" depend on the casually revealed intensity of pilots "who have lost countries or limbs or families or perhaps both." The stories also display a deliberate internationalism, containing tributes to bomber crews of diverse social classes or to fliers who are naive Australians, phlegmatically efficient Czechs, daring Texans, simple Lithuanians, or members of the Free French. Unlike some of the fiction about existential pilots, men without identity apart from their machines, by writers like St. Exupéry or Richard Hilary, Bates's stories concentrate more often on the bomber crews than on the isolated fighter pilots. In part, he values the unity, the necessary amalgamation of diversity and the dependence on each other; in part, too, as he explained in his autobiography, he had a particular appreciation of the more intricate machinery and a sympathy for those dependent on planes like the B-17, a slow, disastrous "ponderous duck" (*VW*, 22).

In his later work, in a variety of lengths and forms, Bates often returned to the setting and the issues of World War II, as in one of his best novels, *A Moment in Time* (1964), which brilliantly evokes a sheltered young girl's growing understanding of class and sexuality in the midst of the warm and frightening spring and summer of 1940, that moment when the British were "sanguine," the one word that "like Churchill, fit both optimistic and bloody at the same time." One of his most searching later stories, "Colonel Julian," the title story of a 1951 volume, describes a retired colonel who enjoys drinks with the young men on an R.A.F. base in 1944, particularly with an offhand and sophisticated pilot who had been injured and rehabilitated through extensive skin grafts. When the colonel learns that his favorite pilot, flying again, has been killed, he meditates on parallels from his service in India, from British history, medicine, and human emotions. Something of national experience, without triteness or sentimentality, is revealed.

Bates came to use the novella more and more in later life, crafting psychological depictions of characters or relationships in evocatively described social or natural settings without much attention to plot. He wrote, for example, a novella with a Madame Bovary theme, set in the Midlands town in the 1920s, called *The Sleepless Moon* (1956) and another, entitled *The Golden Oriole* (1962), concerning the hiding and the masquerades of a playful young woman torn between her attractions to a protective husband and a more exciting younger man.

No other Bates novella, however, is as psychologically probing and as resonant as *The Triple Echo*. Bates later claimed that he wrote it in 1968 but had been thinking of the fiction, wondering in what form to cast it, since 1943 and that he regarded it as "unremitting tragedy" (*WR*, 109). Set in 1942, *The Triple Echo* depicts a young woman single-handedly running an isolated farm in the Midlands while her husband is a P.O.W. held by the Japanese. A young soldier, from a farm in another part of the country but stationed near by, walks on to the farm while on leave. Bates is skillful and certain in describing the chores and the food and the gradually growing attraction that leads the soldier to desert and stay on the farm. As time passes, the relationship becomes more complicated,

the woman more possessive and rooted to her isolation, the soldier taking un-
necessary risks and, in disguise as the woman's "sister," flirting with other soldiers who have ostensibly come to use the woods nearby for training in tank
warfare. The intensity builds carefully, Bates showing considerable sympathy for
both the possessive woman and her lover, the cheerful deserter who shows little
self-awareness or anticipation of consequences. When the deserter is finally cap-
tured by another soldier, the woman shoots both her lover and his captor from
the window of her farmhouse. Whether concentrating on those who could survive the war or on those who, by accident or character, could not, Bates's fiction
achieved a particular coherence, both artistically and in popular terms, through
the experience and the issues of World War II. The early 1940s were Bates's
own "moment in time."

Toward the end of the war, in 1945, Dudley Barker, who had become the
head of the public relations unit, sent Bates to India and Burma to write fiction
concerning the war there. Bates was apparently so appalled by the plague and
filth of Calcutta and the primitive life in rural India and the jungles of Burma
that he noticed little else. He was also extremely distressed by what he saw of
the British serving there, later writing, without explaining the circumstances,
that he had heard British officers in Burma "openly talking what I could only
tell myself was pure sedition . . . luridly blasphemous" (WR, 99). After the war,
he published two novels, The Purple Plain and The Jacaranda Tree, dealing with the
forced march of the retreating English after the Japanese invasion of Burma.
Although subject matter and Bates's reputation insured a moderate popularity,
these novels were not critically successful and do not seem to duplicate as authentically the sense of time, place, and perspective, as did the earlier fiction
about the air war in Europe.

Later, Bates took a long voyage to the South Seas, at the suggestion of the
film producer David Lean, in another try at converting journalistic observation
into fiction. Bates reported finding Tahiti filthy, physically and morally, and the
smaller islands little prisons. He did write a number of stories using the islands
as settings and showing sympathy for the embattled British imprisoned there by
occupation, drink, or social dislocation. Yet, apart from the meticulously careful
physical description and the interest in anomalies such as black sand, the stories,
as evoking people or situations, might just as well have been written in English
settings. Bates's few attempts at international themes are not among his most
interesting stories.

During the 1930s he set several in Germany in which a detached English
narrator is taken on a walking tour by a friend named Karl, a remarkably energetic German who has migrated to England. The stories begin with vivid particular description of German flora and fauna, and then move to scenes of happy

and tumultuous welcome as Karl brings his English friend (in one story, friends) home to his native village. The stories are full of agreement about the need to repair the unfortunate divisions of World War I and of a standard heavy "*gemütlichkeit.*" In "A German Idyll" the narrator is enchanted by the innkeeper's lovely daughter, a rather rural and sexy version of an Aryan princess he retains as a distant vision; in "The Bath," which becomes anecdotal in the way the Uncle Silas stories do, the group of visiting Englishmen find the hospitable welcome incomplete until they are able to have steaming baths in the new house of the richest man in the village.

Bates away from England seems somewhat shallow and out of place, observing details and wanting to be fair-minded, yet uneasy, removed, often grumbling about conditions and projecting his uneasiness into standard fantasy or farce. Increasingly, he was also uneasy and petulant within the England that emerged gradually after 1945, a combination of the welfare state and the intellectual climate of a more uncertain, generous, guilty, quietly self-lacerating interest in international and class issues. His only coherent English fantasy was the jolly, rollicking Larkin family, a shallow conception that did little justice to his probity or sensitivity.

Despite the fact that Bates's "moment" had passed, that an England he could both depict and represent with significance changed gradually after 1945, Bates continued to write short stories, novellas, and novels through the early 1970s. It would, however, be a critical mistake to appraise Bates solely in terms of time and place, to stigmatize him with a "moment" positively and negatively. He did, after all, over many years, demonstrate a considerable range in subject matter and descriptive power in a variety of fictional forms, making little technical or thematic distinction between his uses of the various forms. It is, perhaps, most convenient to summarize the characteristic strengths and weaknesses of his fairly constant fictional perspective through a single example, a novel that he regarded as his most ambitious and autobiographical, *Love for Lydia* (1952). In his autobiography, Bates explained that he was describing the shoe-manufacturing town and surrounding countryside between 1929 and 1932 as he recalled them, and that the social and economic details are also as he remembered them. He also noted that the character and circumstances of Lydia, the niece who moves into the declining local manor, are fiction, derived from a single interview he had in a local Great Hall in his newspaper days and his glimpse of an aloof beauty passing through the railroad station. The central character in the novel, told in the first person, is Richardson, the young newspaper reporter who is trying to become a writer. The novel begins with effectively detailed scenes of Lydia's arrival in Evensford, watched by Richardson through the fogged and dirty glass of the newspaper office on a cold and desolate day, of their meeting, of his teaching her to ice skate on frozen streams and marshes in the surrounding countryside, his growing obsession with her, and her sybaritic, emotional, unpredictable, yet imperious and demanding nature. Fascinated by the Lydia he can only partially understand, Richardson is often jealous and likely to wander off in surly silence, especially at the provincial dances that they and their friends frequently attend. The friends, rural and urban, provincial and sophisticated, are dramatized skillfully to represent a range of class issues and conflicts in the Evensford world of 1929. Events originating in the conflicts of emotion and class, but also in some part encouraged by Richardson's retreats, lead to disaster, the suicide of one friend and the accidental death of another. Richardson wonders about his own responsibility, a question about possible complicity in disaster generated by his self-protective detachment, which he avoids answering by going to London to follow his career. A few years later, he returns to an Evensford mired in the economic slump, the great house lost, to find Lydia, having exhausted herself at a series of increasingly pointless dances, in a sanitorium and described as neurasthenic and desolate. Again, Richardson thinks of his own responsibility, wondering if his self-protective failure to give her again a love she needs and can find only in the unsatisfyingly silent adoration of the former hired chauffeur impedes her recovery. On the final page, Richardson abandons his detachment and accepts his responsibility and his love for Lydia. Yet there is a sudden, unearned quality about the conclusion, a sense of being pasted on, rather like the cryptically melodramatic foreshadowings of disaster that end some of the earlier chapters. Certainly, the reader is grateful to be spared long passages of elaborately simple self-discovery, grateful for the concluding understatement. At the same time, something is missing in the depiction of Richardson. Just as the reader never learns Richardson's first name, the reader never sees Richardson's feelings worked out, never knows whether he accepts Lydia out of love or desperation, or a particular kind of self-knowledge or self-punishment, or out of charity, never sees the development of the particular configurations of Richardson's acceptance. It matters little that the reader never fully understands Lydia, for she is always partly enigma and partly a social phenomenon. But it matters considerably more that one never fully understands Richardson, the protagonist narrator. Understatement, dramatically effective as it is, can also be evasion or an indication of insufficient development in fiction. In most of his fiction, whatever the length, Bates seems either to superimpose a mechanism of understatement or to retreat from the kind of full and penetrating treatment that a character like Richardson, given his function in the novel, requires. This ultimate incompleteness is a magnification of a similar incompleteness in some of the longer and more potentially interesting stories, as well as in some of the novellas based on psychological characterization. Bates's reticence can be con-

vincing and attractive, suggesting a possible skepticism about resolutions for-
mulated too easily and a sensible refusal to proclaim what might be taken too
insistently or simplistically. Yet in Bates this reticence can also be considered a
flaw, an incapacity or unwillingness to reveal as much about a character or a
relationship as they seem aesthetically to demand. Often, the authorial attitude
is a gentlemanly hesitation to probe difficult matters further. And Bates's skill in
and veneration for the shorter forms of fiction is, perhaps, at all stages of his
career, less a reflection of his ease in using a particular form than of the fact that
the shorter the piece the less visible is the possible incompleteness, the reticence
of the narrator himself.

For Coppard, as for Bates, working in the shorter forms of fiction was more
comfortable. In his autobiography, a form he said he disliked because it was so
sprawling, Coppard wrote that he liked to see "all round and over and under
my tale before putting a line of it down on paper" (*IM*, 33). For him, the writing
of fiction was less a form of self-examination or self-discovery than an exercise
of control. This severe control enabled Coppard to write effective vignettes,
skillfully turned ironic anecdotes, charming arguments for a particular way of
life or freedom from convention, and to do so with a sharply compressed verbal
acuity. Although Bates's work demonstrates greater range of subject matter, variety of perspectives and tones, more precise description and a more continu-
ously productive industry, he, too, was most comfortable within the cultivation
of reticence, his own version of severe and compressed control. He could, at
times, for example, show understanding of the phenomenon of the English
male, inhibited and detached; but more often such revelation was truncated by
the security of his narrator's detachment. In the work of both Coppard and
Bates, the control and understatement often produce engaging and effective
fiction; both merit respect and appreciation for what they achieved. Neither can
be charged with intellectual or emotional pretense. Yet the risk of being pretentious, in fiction, may sometimes be worth taking, may reveal discoveries about
both the self and the exterior world that carefully self-imposed reticence helps
to block off. To some extent, the limitation visible in the work of Coppard and
Bates is a limitation in the form of the short story itself, the concomitant of its
length, simultaneously its virtue and its flaw. Yet it is also a limitation that the
greatest of the short story writers, Joyce, Lawrence, Chekhov, and Mansfield, in
their capacity to reveal fully both their worlds and their perspectives, have managed to transcend. Coppard and Bates can well be appreciated both within and
despite the comfortable limitations they seldom transcend.

James Gindin

University of Michigan

V. S. PRITCHETT

At the age of twenty, V[ictor] S[awdon] Pritchett left home, vowing never to return to England. He had been born in Ipswich in 1900; had early dreams of becoming a poet despite the objections of his father, a fanatical believer in Christian Science; worked in the leather trade; and finally, after much soul-searching, left home for Paris, vowing to be a writer. "My ear was good," he wrote many years later, even "if my grammar was bad."

Pritchett's "literary" career began modestly enough, with a joke published in the *Paris Tribune*. It was followed by three essays in the *Christian Science Monitor*, and by extensive travel in Spain, in the United States, in Ireland (where he met William Butler Yeats, married, and began writing his first stories), back to Paris, and, eventually, England, where he dedicated himself to writing. I was "fanatical about writing," he stated; "the word and the sentence were my religion."

"Rain in the Sierra,"[1] Pritchett's first published story, came out in the *New Statesman*. "Tragedy in a Greek Theatre," his second, had been immediately accepted by the *Cornhill*. He was paid well for the story; more important, it was anthologized in Edward J. O'Brien's prestigious annual collection, *Best British Short Stories* (1927), and in 1930 his first collection of short fiction, *The Spanish Virgin and Other Stories*,[2] was in print.

Few of these early stories bear favorable comparison with the best of Pritchett's later work. The collection is interesting primarily for its range and variety, though it hardly suggests the directions his talent and dedication would take him and where they would continue to lead him until he had earned the reputation of being the "greatest living English short story writer."[3]

"The Corsican Inn" is early Pritchett at his best. The story opens conventionally: "I had walked . . . twenty miles out of Ajaccio and climbed into the ranges of the interior." The narrator, with his guide, stops at an inn; on the wall is a portrait of a "glum young soldier with frightened sheepish eyes," signed by the president of the republic and inscribed "Mort pour la France." A loud-mouthed drunken youth staggers into the inn, knocks over a bottle of wine, and finally "with a snigger, and a gesture indicating . . . the photograph . . . and the pool of

red wine ... shouted in mock heroic tones: 'Mort pour la France!' and spat."
The owner of the inn, the mother of the dead soldier, turns upon the blasphem-
er; her eyes, "like knives, cut through the awful silence, to the ... bone."

And here the story ends, but the reader, like the narrator, knows that all will
be changed by the incident, and we share with him the truth of his final words
concerning the blaspheming intruder: "There was no safe place for his gaze to
hide in."

"Tragedy in a Greek Theatre" begins equally conventionally, almost a parody
of the traditional story-within-a-story: "Those who used to go to Sicily for the
winter will remember old William Bantock, the artist, who had such a delightful
studio on the cliff at A——." Following the painter's death, the first-person
narrator and the proprietor of the hotel who had been old Bantock's landlord
open the "mystery room" that had been the artist's studio; the disclosure is
predictable and less important than the characterization of Bantock, overwhelmed by his first experience in Etna and the grandeur of the Greeks. As was
to be the case throughout his career, Pritchett's major preoccupation is with the
revelation of character.

In marked contrast, "The White Rabbit" and "The Cuckoo Clock" are bizarre tours de force, the first centering upon an apparently "normal" and successful young executive, his two young children, a malignant governess, a pet
rabbit and a "devilish" cat—a story with a chilling open-ended climax with
reverberations as disturbing as those in James's *The Turn of the Screw*; the second,
similarly impressive, is a mélange of fantasy, melodrama, illusion-versus-reality
about a young boy who goes "alone ... to spend the holidays" with aged relatives, a visit that glides brilliantly from realism to the macabre, a domain that
Pritchett would seldom explore in his later stories.[4]

"Fishy" and "The Sack of Life," on the other hand, are effective single-episode
stories, a form in which Pritchett was to write with great effectiveness throughout his long career. The first concerns the return to Ireland of a man, penniless,
after an absence of many years, and his reception in a local "fish dive"; the
second, slight but equally memorable, is an expert characterization, completely
devoid of plot per se, of an insane London charwoman.

Almost a decade was to elapse between *The Spanish Virgin* and *You Make Your
Own Life* (1938; as had been the case with its predecessor, there was no United
States edition). Pritchett's disastrous early marriage was behind him; he had
recovered from "one nervous illness after another"; his family had "gone up in
the world"; and most important of all he had remarried, a marriage that was to
be as complete and meaningful as its predecessor had been a failure. He became,
for the first time, whole, complete, assured, both as a man and a writer: "What
cured me," he would write years later in the first volume of his autobiography,

Midnight Oil, "was success in love, and in my work. . . . There is, I am sure, a direct connection between passionate love and the firing of the creative power. . . ."

The fourteen stories of *You Make Your Own Life* are highlighted by what was to become one of Pritchett's best-known and most frequently anthologized pieces, "Sense of Humour." The story had had its origins years before, in Ireland, its central character a lower-middle-class commercial traveler Pritchett had met when he was a reporter for the *Christian Science Monitor*. Characteristically, Pritchett worked and reworked the story before finally being satisfied with it: "that particular story presented many problems. . . . I had it on my hands for many years." Eventually revised and narrated in the first person largely through dialogue, it was rejected by many editors in England and the United States until, in 1937, John Lehmann accepted it for *New Writing*. It was a turning point in Pritchett's career, the first of his stories to "make a stir and give me what reputation I have as a writer of short stories. . . . [It] woke me up . . . and led me on to 'The Sailor,' 'The Saint,' and 'Many Are Disappointed' "; with it "I had become real at last."

Like most of Pritchett's best stories, "Sense of Humour" is a series of character revelations, relatively simple in narrative, decidedly complex in its implications. The real drama lies in the revelation of the reality beneath the exterior of three main characters, a lower-middle-class English commercial traveler, an attractive Irish girl with a "sense of humour" who clerks in the hotel where the salesman takes lodgings, and her "boy friend," a garage mechanic ("that half-wit at the garage," the traveler dubs him). Around this trio, one of whom dies a violent death, the author creates a mixture of revelations of sex-death-love-banality that leaves a stir of echoes likely to reverberate long in the reader's mind.

"Handsome Is As Handsome Does," the longest and perhaps the most ambitious story in the collection, presents an equally complex series of character revelations and reversals. Set in a French coastal pension, and built around an unattractive English couple in their forties, the story presents a tangled skein of human relations, climaxed by a near-drowning and a complicated love-revulsion relationship that ends with "two ugly people cut off from all others . . . helpless, halted, tangled people, outcasts in everything they did." Like so many of Pritchett's characters, the Corans are what the psychiatrist Edmund Bergler has termed "injustice collectors," neurotics who "suffer from a hidden need to feel that the world has wronged them."

Other notable stories range from the serious to the comic. Perhaps the most powerful—and certainly the most melodramatic—work in the entire collection is "Miss Baker," somewhat heavy-handed, perhaps, but unforgettable in its depiction of a young woman gone berserk in her search for the Lord. From its opening sentence—"When Easter came she knew that her time of fasting was drawing to a close"—to the acrid climax when she mistakes a drunken derelict for the Savior, Miss Baker is a grotesque in Sherwood Anderson's definition of the term, and her story is perhaps the angriest and harshest of Pritchett's satires against fundamentalist Christianity.

"Main Road," on the other hand, is a naturalistic study of the effect of poverty on the human spirit. As much sociological tract as conventional fiction, it presents a situation that would be quite at home in *The Grapes of Wrath* or any of the militantly Marxist stories of the American depression.

Pritchett is equally effective in some of his briefer pieces. "You Make Your Own Life," for example, illustrates what he must have had in mind when he referred to the short story as a "flash that suddenly illumines, then passes." This account of a small-town barber, his wife, and a homicidal customer who seeks a most bizarre revenge is reminiscent of Hemingway[5] in its economy and dialogue, together with an ending not unreminiscent of O. Henry—without in any way being derivative of either.

In marked contrast are pieces like "The Aristocrat" and "Eleven O'Clock," the first an amusing characterization of an old man who enters a pub, does a conjuring trick or two, and trudges back into the snow—but only after having filched the watch of one of the spectators. "Eleven O'Clock" is a pure delight, about a milkman and a very good-natured—and concupiscent—Yorkshirewoman (a contemporary Wife of Bath whose "body seemed to be laughing at her fatness") who have their sport indoors while outside the milkman's mare is indulging *her* desires by nibbling almost to extinction the hedge coming into leaf outside the fat woman's house: "'Been getting your greens, haven't you?' the milkman asks as he leaves the house. He stared at the mare and, bright under their blinkers, he saw the eyes of that cynical animal, secretive and glistening, gazing back at him."

"The Evils of Spain" is similarly unplotted, a series of conversations in a Madrid tavern, based on Pritchett's experience with the famous bullfighter Belmonte (whom he had met on a train to Spain, along with Arnold Bennett, Lord Beaverbrook, and Healy, the destroyer of Parnell and "the wickedest tongue in Ireland"). The now-familiar "Hemingway sound" permeates the story, and is particularly evident in the final paragraph: "'No,' we said, 'Leave it [the soup]. We want it.' And then we said the soup was bad, and the wine was bad and everything he [the waiter] brought was bad, but the proprietor said the soup was good and the wine was good and we said in the end it was good. We told the proprietor the restaurant was good, but he said not very good, indeed bad."

"A Spring Morning" is a delight, a briskly narrated, warmhearted tale of a brief encounter between a working-class youth and two lively young shopgirls, a thoroughly pleasant single-episode piece that might very well have been written by H. E. Bates—and it is not presumptuous to assume that Bates would have liked it immensely.

It May Never Happen, Pritchett's third collection, was published in 1945; the American edition, the first volume of his short stories to be published in the United States, came out two years later. It is highlighted, perhaps, by "The Sailor," which, like many of his stories, is based on fact or, more accurately, can be said *to grow out* of actual people and incidents, and had been conceived years before it was completed, when Pritchett, living alone in a cottage near Marlow, was aided by a "down and out sailor . . . who came down to look" after him. Like many of his stories, "The Sailor" was frequently revised before it was completed; it was to become his most-often anthologized story, though personally Pritchett "was not too keen on it."[6]

The story begins simply enough: the narrator, in London for the day, meets a sailor with a penchant for getting lost, "hopelessly, blindly lost." Living alone in the country, the narrator takes the sailor home to be his manservant. "He lives in two worlds at once," the narrator tells the third major character, an alcoholic youngish woman known locally only as the "Colonel's daughter" who, like the sailor, lives a double life. To the world of the local inhabitants, she is loud-mouthed, coarse, obscene; in reality she is sensitive, not unintelligent, honest in her own way, and more than willing to have an affair with the narrator. He too is a split personality, living in two worlds, in one of which he is self-assured and slightly contemptuous; in the other withdrawn, uncertain, and unable to give or share sexually, emotionally, intellectually. In these terms, the drama is played out, partly comic, partly sick, a curious kind of life-death, attraction-repulsion drama not infrequent in Pritchett's works, and permeated with an odor of decay as palpable as the "sour smell at the edge of the wood, where, no doubt, a dead rabbit or pigeon was rotting."

"When I was seventeen years old I lost my religious faith. It had been unsteady for some time and then, very suddenly, it went as the result of an incident in a punt on the river outside the town where we lived." So begins "The Saint," one of Pritchett's best and best-known stories—"a little masterpiece," H. E. Bates called it—at once serious and comic and without the sickly odor of decay that hovers over "The Sailor." The seventeen-year-old's uncle and aunt, not unlike Pritchett's unyielding Christian Science father, are members of a religious sect, the Purifiers; the narrative begins when the family is visited by a leader of the sect, Mr. Timberlake, "a man who had . . . performed many miracles—even, it was said . . . having twice raised the dead." The boy is taunted by his class-mates and their Irish schoolmaster, and questions the validity of the Purifiers' belief that Error and Evil are illusory ("since God could not have made them," the Believers insist, "they therefore did not exist").

The boy's uncle talks to Mr. Timberlake about his nephew's doubts, and lead-er and boy go to the river to have a good talk while punting. In a scene at once hilarious and serious, the leader turns out to be inadequate both as punter and converter; almost decapitated by the overhanging branch of a willow tree, he desperately reaches for a stronger and higher branch. The result is disaster: "there he hung . . . above the water. . . . Too late with the paddle, ... I could not save him, . . . I did not believe what I saw; indeed, our religion taught us never to believe what we saw . . . only a miracle, I found myself saying, could save him."

Silently, Mr. Timberlake is suspended between tree and water. Was he, the boy, thinks, "about to re-enact a well-known miracle? I hoped with all my will Mr. Timberlake would not walk upon the water. It was my prayer and not his that was answered."

Sixteen years pass. The narrator hears of Mr. Timberlake's death: he recalls that long-ago afternoon on the river, and "I understood why," he reflects, "though I had feared it all the time we were on the river—I understood why he did not talk to me about the origin of evil. He was honest. The ape was with us. The ape that merely followed me was already inside Mr. Timberlake eating out his heart."

"You Make Your Own Life," like "The Saint," is apparently based on Pritch-ett's recollections of past experiences, in this case those of a youth working in the small-time upholstery business owned by his uncle and a Mr. Phillimore. Each partner is out to swindle the other, and the somewhat tedious story ends after the breakup of the firm and the narrator's last, and genuinely moving, sight of Mr. Phillimore:

He was standing on London Bridge looking up at a high building where a man was cleaning windows.

"I should die," I heard him say to someone in the crowd. Then he saw me. He bared his teeth as if he were going to spit, but changed his mind. His look suggested that I was the most ridiculous thing on earth. . . .

Much more amusing and lighthearted, "The Chestnut Tree," is Pritchett's account of an apprentice of a London leather merchants' firm who is soon de-moralized by a voluptuous but heavy-footed bookkeeper ("She was curving . . .

with the swell of long breasts [and] . . . moved swan-like to her desk. But not like a swan in the water; like a swan on land. She waddled").

Then there is "Pocock Passes," the remarkable story of a relationship between two very different kinds of men drawn together by fate and the fact that each is in his fifties, enormously fat, and a dedicated drinker. Utterly different, and one of Pritchett's favorites, "Many Are Disappointed" is a small gem, overwhelming in its simplicity, unerring in its selectivity: a story of isolation and simple goodness narrated in terms of the contrast between four young cyclists and the lonely owner of a rundown public house and her young daughter. Equally effective is a very good story of wartime England, "The Voice," centering upon a Welsh clergyman buried beneath the debris of a bombed church. He is heard singing, and a member of the rescue party, a priest who regards the buried man as the "nearest thing to the devil himself," tumbles into the wreckage. "You were a fool to come down here after me. I wouldn't have done the same for you [the old man tells him]. . . . When you start feeling shaky . . . you'd better sing . . . the whiskey's gone. Sing, Lewis. Even if they don't hear, it does you good. Take the tenor, Lewis."

"The Ape" is atypical Pritchett, a blend of allegory and fantasy, with a cast including a talking pterodactyl and bands of apes interested in metaphysics, philosophy, and evolution. The fable ends with a revelation: one of the apes, who fought "like a god . . . with a science and ferocity such as we had never seen before," is finally subdued. The oldest ape examines the "panting creature" and finds the sight overwhelming: his backside is "bare and hairless—he had no tail. . . . 'It is man!' we cried. And our stomachs turned" (153).

The remaining stories include "The Lion's Den," another story of wartime England, centering upon a middle-aged father unworried by airraids. " 'He has faith,' his wife tells their son. 'He trusts in God. . . . he always did things in a big way' " (28); "The Oedipus Complex," a good-natured burlesque of a most-amusing dentist; and several brief pieces of childhood, youth, and family relations ("The Clerk's Tale," "Aunt Gertrude," and "The Fly and the Ointment")—slight, perhaps, in comparison with stories like "The Saint," "The Sailor," and "Pocock Passes," but all characterized by admirable economy and balance, and Pritchett's quiet mastery of technique.

Pritchett's continuing preoccupation, from *The Spanish Virgin* through his most recent collection of short fiction,[7] has been the revelation of character: individual human beings reacting with or against other individuals; with their own personal problems, dilemmas, and egos; with their environment; with things as they are. He has put the matter simply, succinctly, and effectively in his preface to *The Sailor, Sense of Humour, and Other Stories*: "It is difficult for a writer to define his own interest, but I think that I find the drama in human personality, in character rather than in events. . . . The drama has lain in the portrait, in the unconscious self-revelation of people. . . . It strikes me that the story lies in their double lives. . . . They dwell . . . in a solitude which they alone can populate. . . . for me the drama, the event, the plot, is the person; and the more fantastic, the more certain to be true."

Regardless of subject or setting, character or idea, Pritchett's best stories are *happenings*: they are trips, in a sense comparable to hallucinagenic trips. Something *happens*, revelations realized or unrealized, trivial or of vital importance to the individual even if, like the commercial traveler of "Sense of Humour," he himself is unaware of their significance. Something happens, and having happened, the character has been changed, if ever so slightly. His process of moral vision, his essential identity, have been temporarily or permanently altered. This lifelong concern with individual human beings—occasionally unusual or odd or even at times bizarre although Pritchett emphatically denied that he was interested in eccentrics as such—is Pritchett's hallmark.

Equally important, perhaps, is that from his beginnings, despite his early acknowledged indebtedness to Hemingway and others, Pritchett was his own man, finding his own way, his own material, his own forms, and could say quite simply and honestly: "I do not write for the reader, for people, for society. I write for myself, for my own self-regarding pleasure, trying to excel and always failing on the excellence I desire." In these terms he has created a world authentically and convincingly his own, that of the English lower-middle to middle class, a world he knew "like the palm of [his] hand," a world of individuals whose small defeats, stalemates, or victories he depicts with calm but not disinterested detachment, a world viewed for the most part with a tempered skepticism and enlivened by his presentation of the strange, the bizarre, or the grotesque that exists in the ordinary, and the ordinary that is usually inherent in the unusual. It is not, for the most part, a happy world, though at times it is alive with gaiety and humor that can range from the very funny to the macabre. It is a world that has frequently been likened to that of Dickens—a concept Pritchett vigorously rejects—but which is more Thackerayan than Dickensian; Pritchett's Vanity Fair, like Thackeray's, is "not a moral place, certainly; nor a merry one, though very noisy" and one usually "more melancholy than mirthful."

Pritchett's people, like their counterparts in real life, are troubled by the awareness of their own failures and shortcomings or elated at their small victories. They are disturbed by the recognition of their inadequacy or foolishness; more often than not they are lonely, sad, or disappointed. But they not only *endure*, as Faulkner's Negroes endured; they can be victors rather than victims, and their victories—small though they may be—are a tribute, perhaps, as a recent English critic has commented, to something inherent in the English character: "resilience, jauntiness, verve, inventiveness, courage, or downright cheek and the refusal to recognize or admit defeat."

William Peden

University of Missouri-Columbia

Notes and References

INTRODUCTION

1. Helmut E. Gerber, Introduction to *The English Short Story in Transition 1880–1920* (New York: Pegasus, 1967), xi.
2. William Dean Howells, *Criticism and Fiction and Other Essays*, ed. Clara Marburg Kirk and Rudolf Kirk (New York: New York University Press, 1959), sec. 16, p. 63.

THE EXOTIC SHORT STORY: KIPLING AND OTHERS

1. See Stephen Fender, *Plotting the Golden West: American Literature and the Rhetoric of the California Trail* (London: Cambridge University Press, 1981).
2. Ian Watt, *Conrad in the Nineteenth Century* (Berkeley: University of California Press, 1979), 43.
3. Ibid., 43.
4. W. Somerset Maugham, *Tellers of Tales* (New York: Doubleday, Doran, 1939), xxxiii–xxxiv.
5. Jeffrey Meyers, *Fiction and the Colonial Experience* (Totowa, N.J.: Rowman & Littlefield), vii.
6. Ibid., vii.
7. Ibid., viii.
8. Ibid., viii–ix.
9. Ibid., x.
10. Wendell V. Harris, "Beginnings of and for the True Short Story in England," *English Literature in Transition* 15, no. 4 (1972):276.
11. Perhaps no writer, certainly no British writer of fiction, has said more about the theory of the short story than Maugham, who in his long career as playwright, novelist, and short fictionist spanned Victorian, Edwardian-Georgian, and contemporary eras. His introductions to various collections of short stories and particularly that to his own two-volume edition of complete short stories provide a convenient starting point in tracing the tradition of exoticism in the modern British short story. See Maugham, *Tellers of Tales*, xiii–xxxix; *The Complete Short Stories of W.*

Somerset Maugham, 2 vols. (New York: Doubleday, 1931–52), 1:v–xx, 2:v–xii—hereafter cited in the text as *SM*.; "The Short Story," *Points of View* (Garden City, N.Y.: Doubleday, 1959), 163–212; introduction to *Maugham's Choice of Kipling's Best* (Garden City, N.Y.: Doubleday, 1953), vii–xxviii. Having spent his early childhood in France and his young adulthood in England, Maugham emphasizes Maupassant and Chekhov—the continental tradition in relation to the British.

Maupassant's skill and success depend on what amounts to Maugham's paraphrase of Poe's definition of the short story: "the representation of an action, complete in itself and of a certain limited length" (*The Complete Short Stories of W. Somerset Maugham*, 1:ix). Chekhov's way with a story, according to Maugham, although more subtle and moving than Maupassant's, his tendency to relegate plot to the telling of it, leaves something to be desired if the definition of story is equated with "representing" an action. What Chekhov lacked in plot, however, he made up for in atmosphere: "no one had a greater gift than he for giving you the intimate feeling of a place, a landscape, a conversation or . . . a character" (ibid., 1:xiii). Even more important to Maugham, Chekhov succeeded in "surrounding people with air so that . . . they live with a strange and unearthly life. . . . Strange, futile creatures, with descriptions of their outward seeming tacked on them like a card on an exhibit in a museum, they move as mysteriously as the tortured souls who crowded about Dante when he walked in Hell. You have the feeling of a vast, gray, lost throng wandering aimless in some dim underworld" (ibid., 1:xiii.) If Maupassant favored the anecdote (as did Maugham), if he portrayed flesh and blood people in his stories, Chekhov represented "spirit communing with spirit" (ibid., 1:xiv.); and together, one a nineteenth-century master of plot, the other of atmosphere, they set standards that have prevailed beyond France and Russia by which—Maugham believes—modern British writers of short stories must be judged.

12. Angus Wilson, *The Strange Ride of Rudyard Kipling* (New York: Viking Press, 1978), 342.

13. Ibid., 280.

14. Bonamy Dobrée, *Rudyard Kipling: Realist and Fabulist* (New York: Oxford University Press, 1967), 167.

15. Randall Jarrell, "On Preparing to Read Kipling," in *The Best Short Stories of Rudyard Kipling* (Garden City, N.Y.: Hanover House, 1961), xi; hereafter cited in the text as *RK*.

16. Rudyard Kipling, "Thrown Away," in *Plain Tales From the Hills* (New York: Charles Scribner's Sons, 1909), 18.

17. Andrew Rutherford, Preface to *Rudyard Kipling, Short Stories*, vol. 1, *"A Sahibs' War" and Other Stories* (New York: Penguin Books, 1971), 42; hereafter cited in the text as *RKS*.

18. Aldous Huxley, "Wordsworth in the Tropics," in *Do What You Will* (Doubleday, Doran, 1930), 128.

19. Lawrence Graver, *Conrad's Short Fiction* (Berkeley: University of California Press, 1969), 10–15. See also Elliot L. Gilbert, *The Good Kipling* (Oberlin: Ohio Uni-

versity Press, 1979), 190. Gilbert lists many similarities between Kipling and Conrad—not the least of which is that they were both "foreigners" to England. Gilbert also regards "The Man Who Would be King" as "extremely Conradian."

20. Graver, *Conrad's Short Fiction*, 12.

21. Ibid., 13.

22. Ibid., 13.

23. Joseph Conrad, "An Outpost of Progress," in *Tales of Unrest* (New York: Penguin Books, 1977), 85; hereafter cited in the text as *TU*.

24. Bernard C. Meyer, *Joseph Conrad: A Psychoanalytical Biography* (Princeton: Princeton University Press, 1967), 123.

25. Anthony Curtis, *Somerset Maugham* (New York: Macmillan, 1977), 142.

26. Ibid., 157.

27. Graham Greene, "Some Notes on Somerset Maugham," in *Collected Essays* (New York: Viking Press, 1969), 196; hereafter cited in the text as *GCE*.

28. Richard A. Cordell, *Somerset Maugham: A Writer for All Seasons* (Bloomington: Indiana University Press, 1969), 160.

29. Ted Morgan, *Maugham: A Biography* (New York: Simon & Schuster, 1980), 71.

30. Somerset Maugham, Preface to *Collected Short Stories*, (New York: Penguin Books, 1978), 4:8.

31. E. M. Forster, *Aspects of the Novel* (London: Edward Arnold, 1974), 78.

32. Oliver Stallybras, Introduction to *The Life to Come and Other Stories* (London: Edward Arnold, 1972), vii.

33. Frederick P. W. McDowell, *E. M. Forster* (New York: Twayne, 1969), 59.

34. George H. Thomson, "Symbolism, in E. M. Forster's Earlier Fiction," *Criticism* 3, no. 4 (Fall 1961): 304.

35. Lionel Trilling, *E. M. Forster* (New York: New Directions, 1964), 56. See also Wilfred Stone, *The Cave and the Mountain* (Stanford: Stanford University Press, 1966), 161; Stone holds that Forster grew out of the "puerility implicit in the form [of fantasy]" and moved on to the novel.

36. E. M. Forster, *The Life to Come and Other Stories*, ed. Oliver Stallybras (London: Edward Arnold, 1972), 65–82, 166–97; hereafter cited in the text as *LC*.

37. See Glen Vavaliero, *A Reading of E. M. Forster* (Totowa, N.J.: Rowman & Littlefield, 1979), 140: "read sympathetically, they [Forster's later stories] are not pornographic, though one or two are decidedly and cheerfully erotic. All are filled with a vigour and intention lacking in the weaker of his earlier tales." John Colmer, *E. M. Forster: The Personal Voice* (London: Routledge & Kegan Paul, 1975), 135, says that "of all the short stories, 'The Other Boat' points toward the work Forster might have written after *A Passage To India*, had the private censor . . . and the public censor permitted." See also John Sayre Martin, *E. M. Forster: The Endless Journey* (London: Cambridge University Press, 1976), 83; Martin calls "The Other Boat" the best of Forster's posthumous short stories.

38. David Shusterman, *The Quest for Certitude in E. M. Forster's Fiction* (Bloomington: Indiana University Press, 1965), 37.

39. Jean Rhys, *Smile Please: An Unfinished Autobiography* (New York: Harper & Row, 1979); *The Left Bank & Other Stories*, preface by Ford Madox Ford, (Freeport, N.Y.: Books for Libraries Press, 1970)—hereafter cited in the text as *LB*; *Tigers Are Better Looking* (London: Andre Deutsch, 1968); *Sleep It Off, Lady* (New York: Harper & Row, 1976).

40. Rhys, *Smile Please*, 7.

41. V. S. Pritchett, *New York Review of Books* 27 no. 13 (14 August 1980):10.

42. Arthur Mizener, *The Saddest Story* (New York: World Publishing Co., 1971), 345.

43. Thomas F. Staley, *Jean Rhys* (Austin: University of Texas Press, 1979), 23. See also Kinley E. Roby, *Jean Rhys* (Boston: G. K. Hall & Co., 1900), 32–66, A. C. Morrell, "The World of Jean Rhys's Short Stories," *World Literature Written in English* 18 (1979):235–44; Nancy J. Casey "The 'Liberated' Woman in Jean Rhys's Later Short Fiction," *Revista/Review Interamericana* 4, no. 2 (Summer 1974):264–72; and Harriet Blodgett, "Tigers Are Better Looking to Jean Rhys," *Arizona Quarterly* 32, no. 3 (Autumn 1976):227–44.

44. David Lodge, *Graham Greene* (New York: Columbia University Press, 1966), 3.

45. Graham Greene, *A Sort of Life* (New York: Simon & Schuster, 1971), 133.

46. Graham Greene, Introduction to *Collected Stories* (New York: Viking Press, 1973), viii–ix.

47. Graham Greene, *Twenty-One Stories* (New York: Penguin Books, 1980), 142, 144; hereafter cited in the text as *TOS*.

48. See Alison Lurie, "Fairy Tale Liberation," *New York Review of Books* 15, no. 11 (17 December 1970): 42–44; and Mary Rohrberger, "Walter De La Mare," in *Critical Survey of Short Fiction*, ed. Frank N. Magill (Englewood Cliffs, N.J.: Salem Press, 1981), 1250–54.

49. Edward Wagenknecht, Introduction to *The Collected Tales of Walter de la Mare* (New York: Alfred A. Knopf, 1950), vii–xxi; hereafter cited in the text as *CTM*.

50. Doris Ross McCrosson, *Walter de la Mare* (New York: Twayne, 1966), 46.

51. See Michael William Murphy, "The British Tale in the Early Twentieth Century: Walter De La Mare, A. E. Coppard, and T. F. Powys," (Ph.D. diss., University of Wisconsin, 1971), *Dissertation Abstracts International*, 32:2098A–99A. Murphy argues that de la Mare is a writer of "tales" rather than "short stories," but contributed to the demise of the tale through stylistic and generic "refinements" in narration and sophistication in language.

52. William Sansom, *Fireman Flower* (New York: Vanguard Press, 1945); hereafter cited in the text as *FF*.

53. Richard Church, *The Growth of the English Novel* (London: Methuen & Co., 1968), 2.

54. George Steiner, "An Old Man and the Sea," *New Yorker*, 23 April 1979, 145.

D. H. LAWRENCE

1. F. R. Leavis suggests the same idea when he says that the "firsthandedness" of Lawrence's presentation makes demands that most critics are not prepared to meet and has prevented his stories from being appropriately acclaimed (*D. H. Lawrence: Novelist* [New York: Alfred A. Knopf, 1956], 371–73).

2. See, for example, Keith Cushman's essay on *England, My England and Other Stories*, in *D. H. Lawrence: The Man Who Lived*, ed. Robert B. Partlow and Harry T. Moore (Carbondale: Southern Illinois University Press, 1980), 27–38.

3. *The Lonely Voice* (Cleveland: World Publishing Co., 1963), 16. O'Connor also quotes Turgenev's statement that "We all came out from under Gogol's 'Overcoat' " (14).

4. Walter Allen, *The Short Story in English* (Oxford: Oxford University Press, 1981), 99.

5. T. O. Beachcroft, *The Modest Art: A Survey of the Short Story in English* (Oxford: Oxford University Press, 1968), 209.

6. The fullest account of Lawrence's reading is Rose Marie Burwell's "A Checklist of Lawrence's Reading," in *A D. H. Lawrence Handbook*, ed. Keith Sagar (New York: Barnes & Noble, 1982), 59–125.

7. Keith Cushman, "The Young D. H. Lawrence and the Short Story," *Modern British Literature* 3 (1978):101–2.

8. *Letters of D. H. Lawrence*, vol. 1, *September 1901–May 1913*, ed. James T. Boulton (Cambridge: Cambridge University Press, 1979), 139–40.

9. Cushman, "The Young D. H. Lawrence and the Short Story," 108.

10. J. A. Hobson, "The Task of Realism," *English Review*, October 1909, 543–54.

11. Cushman, "The Young D. H. Lawrence," 109.

12. A. E. Coppard, *Collected Tales* (New York: Alfred A. Knopf, 1948), vii–viii.

13. One good discussion of Lawrence's exploratory mode is Mark Kinkead-Weekes, "The Marble and the Statue: The Exploratory Imagination of D. H. Lawrence," in *Imagined Worlds: Essays on Some English Novels and Novelists in Honour of John Butt*, ed. Maynard Mack and Ian Gregor (London: Methuen & Co. Ltd, 1968), 371–418.

14. *Letters of D. H. Lawrence*, vol. 2, *June 1913–October 1916*, ed. George J. Zytaruk and James T. Boulton (Cambridge: Cambridge University Press, 1981), 90.

15. Ibid., 544.

16. *Phoenix: The Posthumous Papers of D. H. Lawrence*, ed. Edward McDonald (London: William Heinemann, 1936), 528.

17. "Why the Novel Matters," in *Phoenix*, 535.

18. "German Books: Thomas Mann," in *Phoenix*, 308.

19. *Letters of D. H. Lawrence*, 1:491, 492. For other relevant letters see *Letters*, 1:330, 455, 470, 477. The letter to Edward Garnett of 19 November 1912 is particularly important. It contains Lawrence's defense of the form of *Sons and Lovers*, and Frieda's postscript defending Lawrence against the charge of formlessness: "really he

is the only revolutionary worthy of the name . . . any new thing must find a new shape, then afterwards one can call it 'art' " (1:479). For a similar but much later statement on form, see Lawrence's letter to Carlo Linati of 27 January 1925 (*Collected Letters*, ed. H. T. Moore [New York: Viking Press, 1962] 2:826–27).

20. Lawrence's growth during this period has been the subject of several critical discussions. See, for example, Keith Cushman, *D. H. Lawrence at Work: The Emergence of The Prussian Officer Stories* (Charlottesville: University of Virginia Press, 1978); Brian H. Finney, "D. H. Lawrence's Progress to Maturity: From Holograph Manuscript to Final Publication of *The Prussian Officer and Other Stories*," *Studies in Bibliography* 28 (1975):321–32; Janice Harris, "Insight and Experiment in D. H. Lawrence's Early Short Fiction," *Philological Quarterly* 55 (1976):418–35; Mara Kalnins, "D. H. Lawrence's 'Two Marriages' and 'Daughters of the Vicar,' " *Ariel* 7 (1976):32–49; J. C. F. Littlewood, "D. H. Lawrence's Early Tales," *Cambridge Quarterly* 1 (1966):107–24; John S. Poynter, "The Early Short Stories of D. H. Lawrence," in *D. H. Lawrence: The Man Who Lived*, 39–41; and the essay by Mark Kinkead-Weekes cited in note 13.

21. The influence of Balzac, for instance, is more substantial and lasting than that of Maupassant because it involves not simply technical facility but an attitude of sympathy toward a wide range of persons. Consider Lawrence's comment in a letter to Blanche Jennings of 11 November 1908: "Balzac can lay bare the living body of the great Life better than anybody in the world. He doesn't hesitate at the last covering; he doesn't point out all the absurdities of the intricate innumerable wrappings and accessories of the body of Life; he goes straight to the flesh; and, unlike de Maupassant or Zola, he doesn't inevitably light on a wound, or a festering sore" (*Letters of D. H. Lawrence*, 1:91–92).

22. Hardy's influence and the importance to Lawrence's development of his "Study of Thomas Hardy" have been discussed by several critics; see, for example, Roger Ebbatson, *Lawrence and the Nature Tradition: A Theme in English Fiction 1859–1914* (Atlantic Highlands, N.J.: Humanities Press, 1980); Ross C. Murfin, *Swinburne, Hardy, Lawrence and the Burden of Belief* (Chicago: University of Chicago Press, 1978); Michael Squires, *The Pastoral Novel: Studies in George Eliot, Thomas Hardy, and D. H. Lawrence* (Charlottesville: University of Virginia Press, 1974); Mark Kinkead-Weekes, "Lawrence on Hardy," in *Thomas Hardy After Fifty Years*, ed. Lance St. John Butler (Totowa, N.J.: Rowman & Littlefield, 1977) 90–103; Michael Squires, "Scenic Construction and Rhetorical Signals in Hardy and Lawrence," *D. H. Lawrence Review* 8 (1975):125–46; Richard D. Beard, "D. H. Lawrence and the *Study of Thomas Hardy*, His Victorian Predecessor," *D. H. Lawrence Review* 2 (1969):210–19; and the essay by Mark Kinkead-Weekes cited in footnote 13.

23. H. E. Bates, *The Modern Short Story* (London: Nelson & Sons, 1943), 203.

24. Philip Hobsbaum, *A Reader's Guide to D. H. Lawrence* (London: Thames & Hudson, 1981), 29–30.

25. One writer deserves fuller notice. Aldous Huxley, friend and admirer of Lawrence, wrote some thirty-five stories, most of them published in five volumes—*Limbo* (1920), *Mortal Coils* (1922), *Little Mexican* (1924), *Two or Three Graces* (1926), and *Brief Candles* (1930)—and the best gathered into the *Collected Short Stories* (1957). (For fuller information, see Claire John Eschelbach and Joyce Lee Shober, *Aldous Huxley: A Bibliog-*

raphy, 1916–1959 [Berkeley: University of California Press, 1961], and Claire John Es-chelbach and Joyce S. Marthaler, "Aldous Huxley: A Bibliography, 1914–1964 [A Supplementary Listing]," *Bulletin of Bibliography* 28 [1971]:114–17.) Because of similarities of theme, situation, and character, many of Huxley's stories invite comparison with Lawrence's—"Hubert and Minnie," for example, recalls Lawrence's stories about tem-peramentally mismatched lovers, and "The Claxtons" clearly derives from "England, My England." But scrutiny of how Huxley handles these similar elements results in unflat-tering comparisons. While Huxley's situations are sometimes highly fanciful (e.g., "Cyn-thia" or "Sir Hercules") and his wit urbane, his characters are thin when compared to Lawrence's. In effect, Huxley's pale, one-dimensional presentation of his characters heightens the achievement of Lawrence's rich, multidimensional explorations of his characters, showing that Lawrence's distinctive mode of psychological presentation was not a common achievement of his time. Further, Huxley's stories often have a brittleness arising from his writing too simply to illustrate some preconceived idea, in contrast to Lawrence's more energetic, exploratory fiction. And Huxley's satire often has an astrin-gent tone stemming from his regarding his characters as representatives of some social or intellectual type or some mode of failure to be exposed (e.g., Mr. Hutton in "The Gioconda Smile"); Lawrence's satire, while it may be equally fervent, never falls into mere vilification, mainly because his characters are never simply emblems and always seem in some way valued by their creator. Huxley is at his best in a vein that Lawrence seems scarcely capable of mining—wittier and more deftly satirical stories such as "The Tillotson Banquet," where the reader's pleasure in how he displays his characters and tricks out his situations is not troubled by profundities running beneath the surface.

26. Hobsbaum, *A Reader's Guide to D. H. Lawrence*, 120.

27. Mark Schorer, "Technique as Discovery," *Hudson Review* 1 (1948):67–87. The essay has been reprinted frequently.

28. Ibid., 76–77.

29. Ibid., 77.

30. James Joyce, *A Portrait of the Artist as a Young Man* (New York: Viking Press, 1964), 215. Stephen's phrase adapts ideas expressed by Flaubert in his letters: see, for example, the letters reprinted in *The Workshop of Daedalus: James Joyce and the Raw Materials for "A Portrait of the Artist as a Young Man,"* ed. Robert Scholes and Richard M. Kain (Evanston, Ill.: Northwestern University Press, 1965), 247–48.

31. D. H. Lawrence, *The Complete Short Stories* (New York: Viking Press, 1961), 2:303; hereafter cited in the text as *CSS*.

32. The device of illustrating the subtleties of attributed narration by restate-ment in the first person is borrowed from Donald Ross, Jr., "Who's Talking? How Characters Become Narrators in Fiction," *Modern Language Notes* 91 (1976):1222–42.

33. "*A Propos* of *Lady Chatterley's Lover*," in *Sex, Literature and Censorship*, ed. Harry T. Moore (New York: Viking Press, 1959), 96–97.

34. Donald Ross, "Who's Talking?" 1229. Ross cites the paragraph in *Complete Short Stories* (1:225) beginning "She went forward. . . ."

35. Lawrence's exploration of inherently vague regions of the psyche has parallels in the thought of A. N. Whitehead and Michael Polanyi. Compare Whitehead's chal-

lenge to Hume's presupposition that what is clearest and most distinct in our thought is therefore most important ("Objects and Subjects," in *Adventures in Ideas* [New York: Macmillan, 1933]), and Polanyi's discussion of "subsidiary awareness" in *Personal Knowledge: Towards a Post-Critical Philosophy* (Chicago: University of Chicago Press, 1958; rev. ed. 1962).

36. Virginia Woolf, "Modern Fiction," *Collected Essays*, vol. 2 (New York: Harcourt, Brace & World, 1967), 106.

37. *Letters of D. H. Lawrence*, 2:182–84.

38. For a fuller discussion of this topic see Thomas H. McCabe, "Rhythm as Form in Lawrence: 'The Horse-Dealer's Daughter,' " *PMLA* 87 (1972):65–68.

39. Aldous Huxley is indicating this same quality when he refers to landscape as the "background and the principal personage" of all Lawrence's novels (Introduction to *The Letters of D. H. Lawrence* [New York: Viking Press, 1932], xxx). To turn to Hardy for a prototypical passage, consider the "psychic milieu" evoked by the several paragraphs in section 20 of *Tess of the D'Urbervilles* describing Tess and Angel's early mornings together, beginning "At these non-human hours they could get quite close to the waterfowl."

40. Lawrence speaks directly to this point in "The Novel" when he says, "And this is the beauty of the novel; everything is true in its own relationship, and no further. . . . So, if a character in a novel wants two wives—or three—or thirty: well, that is true of that man, at that time, in that circumstance. It may be true of other men, elsewhere or elsewhen. But to infer that all men at all times want two, three, or thirty wives; or that the novelist himself is advocating furious polygamy; is just imbecility" (*Phoenix II* [New York: Viking Press, 1970], 422).

VIRGINIA WOOLF AND
KATHERINE MANSFIELD

1. Twenty-one are available in *The Haunted House and Other Short Stories* (New York: Harcourt, Brace & World, 1944); and *Mrs. Dalloway's Party: A Short Story Sequence*, ed. Stella McNichol (London: Hogarth Press, 1973).

2. Frank O'Connor, *The Lonely Voice: A Study of the Short Story* (Cleveland: World Publishing Co., 1965), 21–23.

3. For the reader who seeks a similar salvation and has not the short story in hand, let it be known that the mark turns out to be a snail.

4. O'Connor, *The Lonely Voice*, 16.

5. Introduction to *Anti-Story*, ed. Philip Stevick (New York: Free Press, 1971), xx.

6. *The Stories of Katherine Mansfield*, ed. John Middleton Murry (New York: Alfred A. Knopf, 1937).

7. "Prelude" is a masterpiece, a landmark in the history of the modern short story. Its continuation, "At the Bay," written four years later and conceived as the

second part of a book, is even finer. Gone is the dramatic, but somewhat forced, symbolism of the Aloe plant; in its place is simply the presence of the sea.

8. Anthony Alpers, *The Life of Katherine Mansfield* (New York: Viking Press, 1980), 126, 238.

9. Mansfield's are available in three places: *The Letters of Katherine Mansfield*, ed. John Middleton Murry (1 vol. ed.: New York: Alfred A. Knopf, 1932), hereafter cited in the text as *LKM*; "Fifteen Letters from Katherine Mansfield to Virginia Woolf," *Adam International Review*, nos. 370–75 (1972–75):19–24; and *Letters to John Middleton Murry*, ed. John Middleton Murry (New York: Alfred A. Knopf, 1951), hereafter cited in the text as *LJM*; Margaret Scott of the Trumbull Library in Wellington is editing a complete collection of the letters. Woolf's complete letters are published in six volumes as *The Letters of Virginia Woolf*, ed. Nigel Nicolson and Joanne Trautmann (New York: Harcourt, Brace, Jovanovich, 1975–80), hereafter cited in the text as *LVW*. Apparently only two letters from Woolf to Mansfield have survived, and only one is printed, which doubtless has contributed to the undervaluing of the friendship despite the strong emphasis placed upon it by Woolf's biographer, Quentin Bell, in *Virginia Woolf*, 2 vols. (London: Hogarth Press, 1972). Ann L. McLaughlin has made the relationship her special subject. See, for instance, "The Same Job: The Shared Writing Aims of Katherine Mansfield and Virginia Woolf," *Modern Fiction Studies*, Autumn 1978, 369–82.

10. Woolf, "Modern Fiction," *The Common Reader* (New York: Harcourt, Brace & World, 1925), 154.

11. Alpers, *The Life of Katherine Mansfield*, 249–52.

12. "Modern Fiction," 157.

13. *The Diary of Virginia Woolf*, vol. 2, ed. Anne Olivier Bell (London: Hogarth Press, 1978), 14.

SAKI AND WODEHOUSE

1. Quotations from Saki's stories are drawn from the one-volume *Complete Works of Saki / H. H. Munro* (Garden City, N.Y.: Doubleday, 1976). The Saki canon is readily available. American readers are much indebted to Viking Press for its handsome individual volumes of the stories and novels, commencing in 1927 and running into the 1930s, and there are other omnibus editions: see A. J. Langguth, *Saki: A Life of Hector Hugh Munro* (New York: Simon & Schuster, 1981), 318–19, and Charles H. Gillen, *H. H. Munro* (New York: Twayne, 1969).

I have also resorted to omnibus volumes of Wodehouse when possible; in particular, *The World of Jeeves* (London: Barrie & Jenkins, 1971), and *The World of Mr. Mulliner* (London: Barrie & Jenkins, 1972). My account of his "school stories" employs his own collection *Tales of St. Austin's* (London: Black, 1903), and *The Uncollected Wodehouse* (New York: Seabury Press, 1976), edited by David A. Jasen, who has assiduously unearthed neglected short fiction of the Master. Other story-volumes mentioned are the English editions of Barrie and Jenkins, except for *Eggs, Beans, and Crumpets* (London: Herbert Jenkins, 1940). Eileen McIlvaine's massive bibliography in *P. G. Wodehouse: A Centenary Celebration, 1881–1981*, ed. J. H. Heineman and D. R. Bensen (New York: Oxford University Press, 1981) is helpful in its short-story listings. For Wodehouse's autobiographical comments on fiction writing I have used the American version of *Author! Author!* (New York: Simon & Schuster, 1962), a revision of the earlier English *Performing Flea* (London: Herbert Jenkins, 1953). The three full-scale biographies of Wodehouse are marginal to my purposes, but provided helpful background. David A. Jasen's *P. G. Wodehouse: A Portrait of a Master*, rev. ed. (New York: Mason & Lipscomb, 1981) is especially strong on W.'s American theatrical career, which he has also discussed elsewhere. Benny Green's *P. G. Wodehouse: A Literary Biography* (London: Rutledge Press, 1981) is lively and thoroughly researched, and Frances Donaldson's *P. G. Wodehouse: A Biography* (New York: Knopf, 1982) contains incisive criticism, though its primary claim to attention is the special knowledge of a long-time family friend.

Langguth's *Saki* reprints a number of hitherto unnoticed short stories, published but uncollected. His literary judgment is generally shrewd. Otherwise the most searching evaluations are probably to be found in fugitive book reviews. The more extensive Wodehouse literature is pervasively affectionate, witty, and modish, with a tendency toward the Baker Street Irregular prankishness that characterizes Conan Doyle studies. Wodehousians usually treat his fictional characters as real people with recorded histories. R. B. D. French's brief *P. G. Wodehouse* (Edinburgh: Oliver & Boyd, 1966) is unusual in remembering that they were created rather than born. Richard Usborne (*Wodehouse at Work to the End* [London: Barrie & Jenkins, 1976]) is probably the most important as well as the earliest serious Wodehouse student, and I have leaned on his work for help, as my references to him indicate. As far as I know, however, no one has dealt extensively with the later short stories as such.

A. E. COPPARD AND
H. E. BATES

1. H. E. Bates, *Autobiography*, vol. 2, *The Blossoming World* (London: Michael Joseph, 1971), 81–82; hereafter cited in the text as *BW*.

2. H. E. Bates, *Autobiography*, vol. 1, *The Vanished World* (London: Michael Joseph, 1969), 159–60; hereafter cited in the text as *VW*.

3. A. E. Coppard, *It's Me, O Lord!* (London: Methuen, 1957), 215–16; hereafter cited in the text as *IM*.

4. H. E. Bates, *Autobiography*, vol. 3, *The World in Ripeness* (London: Michael Joseph, 1972), 124–25; hereafter cited in the text as *WR*.

5. Quoted in entry on Coppard by Bert Bender in *Critical Survey of Short Fiction*, ed. Frank Magill (Englewood Cliffs, N.J.: Salem Press, 1981), 3:1194.

6. Frank O'Connor, *The Lonely Voice: A Study of the Short Story* (Cleveland: World Publishing Company, 1963), 171.

7. Ford Madox Ford, *New York Herald Tribune*, 27 March 1927.

8. Dennis Vannatta, *H. E. Bates* (Boston: Twayne, 1983), 32.

9. Henry Miller, Preface to The Best of *H. E. Bates* (Boston: Little, Brown, 1963).

V. S. PRITCHETT

1. In the first volume of his memoirs, *Midnight Oil* ([New York: Penguin, 1974], 164–47), Pritchett comments on the origins of the story: "My trouble was that I had no story to write. I was full of stories without knowing it. The difficulty of the young writer is that he does not recognize what is inside him. My mind really evaded any story I knew. . . . But I sat down to try because I was tiring of my life as a newspaper correspondent. . . . I remembered all that rain and . . . those gipsies in Granada. I found in the newspaper some account of a gipsy quarrel. Somewhere in this . . . lay the most alarming thing in the world: a subject. I called the story 'Rain in the Sierra.' It was very short, but it took weeks to get it into shape. A good three years passed before it was published. . . . I have not read it since for I dread the prose I shall find there and I am rather ashamed of having written on the Spanish gipsy, the corniest of subjects. Still, I had begun."

2. *The Spanish Virgin and Other Stories* (London: Benn, 1930). It had been preceded by *Marching Spain* (1928), the outgrowth of Pritchett's walking across Spain; and by his first novel, *Claire Drummer* (1929). Because of its length, one hundred and sixty pages, I have not discussed the title novella.

3. On the dust jacket to *Selected Stories* (London: Chatto & Windus, 1978) in the American edition Pritchett is labeled "one of the foremost storytellers of our time"; and on the dust jacket to *On the Edge of the Cliff* (London: Chatto & Windus, 1979) no less an authority than Frank Kermode calls him "the finest English writer alive."

4. A notable exception is the unforgettable "A Story of Don Juan," from *Collected Stories* (London: Chatto & Windus, 1956).

5. Early in his career Pritchett learned a great deal from Hemingway and from Dorothy Edwards, a now almost-forgotten Welsh writer who "had written a story, in the first person, in which a character unconsciously reveals his obtuseness by assuming an air of reasonableness and virtue; and, in Hemingway, I found the vernacular put to similar use. . . . In . . . [my] writing, American influence—particularly that of Hemingway—is clear" (*Midnight Oil*, 189–90).

6. William Peden, interview with V. S. Pritchett, London, 18 September 1968.

7. Post-1945 collections of Pritchett's stories include *Collected Stories; The Sailor, Sense of Humour and Other Stories* (New York: Knopf, 1956). The London edition contains the twenty-eight stories originally contained in *You Make Your Own Life* and *It May Never*

Happen, and nine previously uncollected stories: "The Collection," "Double Divan," "The Ladder," "The Landlord," "Passing the Ball," "The Satisfactory," "The Sniff," "A Story of Don Juan," and "Things as They Are." The American edition contains twenty-five stories, seven from *You Make Your Own Life*, thirteen from *It May Never Happen*, and five previously uncollected pieces: "The Landlord," "Passing the Ball," "The Satisfactory," "The Sniff," and "Things As They Are" (a subsequent anthology, *The Saint and Other Stories* [New York: Penguin, 1966], contains twenty-one selections from the 1956 edition); *When My Girl Comes Home* (New York: Knopf, 1961); *The Key to My Heart: A Comedy in Three Parts* (London: Chatto & Windus, 1963; New York, 1964); *Blind Love and Other Stories* (London: Chatto & Windus, 1969); *The Camberwell Beauty and Other Stories* (New York: Random House, 1974); *Selected Stories* (London: Chatto & Windus); *On the Edge of the Cliff* (London: Chatto & Windus); *More Collected Stories* (London: Chatto & Windus, 1983).

Bibliography

Selected Bibliography of English Short Story Collections

Peter Henry Abrahams
Dark Testament. London: G. Allen & Unwin, 1942.

Richard Aldington
At All Costs. London: William Heinemann, 1930.
Last Straws. Paris: Hours Press, 1930.
Roads to Glory. London: Chatto & Windus, 1930.
Soft Answers. London: Chatto & Windus, 1932.

Michael Arlen
The Romantic Lady and Other Stories. London: W. Collins Sons & Co., 1921.
These Charming People. London: W. Collins Sons & Co., 1923. Selections as *The Man with the Broken Nose and Other Stories* (1927).
May Fair, In Which Are Told the Last Adventures of These Charming People. London: W. Collins Sons & Co., 1925. Selections as *The Ace of Cads*.
Ghost Stories. London: W. Collins Sons & Co., 1927.
Babes in the Woods. London: Hutchinson & Co., 1929.
The Ancient Sin and Other Stories, Selected from These Charming People, May Fair, and *The Romantic Lady*. London: W. Collins Sons & Co., 1930.
The Short Stories of Michael Arlen, Containing Confessions of a Naturalised Englishman, Portrait of a Lady on Park Avenue, These Charming People, The Romantic Lady, Transatlantic, May Fair. London: W. Collins Sons & Co., 1933.
The Crooked Coronet and Other Misrepresentations of the Real Facts of Life. London, Toronto: William Heinemann, 1937.

Maurice Baring
Orpheus in Mayfair and Other Stories. London: William Heinemann, 1925.
The Glass Mender and Other Stories. London: J. Nisbet & Co., 1910. Reprinted as *The Blue Rose Fairy Book* (1911).
Half a Minute's Silence and Other Stories. London: William Heinemann, 1925.

165

Sabine Baring-Gould
Dartmoor Idylls. London: Methuen & Co., 1896.
Furze Bloom: Tales of the Western Moors. London: Methuen & Co., 1899.
Jacquetta and Other Stories. London: Methuen & Co., 1890.
Margery of Quether and Other Stories. London: Methuen & Co., 1891.
In a Quiet Village. London: Isbister & Co., 1900.
Monsieur Pichelmère and Other Stories. London: Digby, Long & Co., 1905.

H. E. Bates
The Seekers. London: John & Edward Bumpus, 1926.
The Spring Song and In View of the Fact That . . . : Two Stories. London: E. Archer, 1927.
Day's End, and Other Stories. London: Jonathan Cape, 1928.
Seven Tales and Alexander. London: Scholartis Press, 1929.
The Black Boxer: Tales. London: Pharos, 1932.
The House with the Apricot and Two Other Tales. London: Golden Cockerel Press, 1933.
Thirty Tales. London: Jonathan Cape, 1934.
The Woman Who Had Imagination and Other Stories. London & Toronto: Jonathan Cape, 1934.
Cut and Come Again: Fourteen Stories. London: Jonathan Cape, 1935.
Something Short and Sweet: Stories. London: Jonathan Cape, 1937.
Country Tales: Collected Short Stories. London: Reader's Union, 1938. Reprint. London: Jonathan Cape, 1940.
The Flying Goat: Stories. London: Jonathan Cape, 1939.
My Uncle Silas: Stories. London: Jonathan Cape, 1939.
The Beauty of the Dead and Other Stories. London: Jonathan Cape, 1940.
The Greatest People in the World and Other Stories by Flying Officer "X." London: Jonathan Cape, 1942. Reprinted in *Something in the Air* (1944).
How Sleep the Brave and Other Stories by Flying Officer "X." London: Jonathan Cape, 1943. Reprinted in *Something in the Air* (1944).
Something in the Air: Comprising the Greatest People in the World and How Sleep the Brave: Stories by Flying Officer "X." London: Jonathan Cape, 1944.
Thirty-One Selected Tales. London: Jonathan Cape, 1947.
Colonel Julian. London: Michael Joseph; Boston: Little Brown, 1951.
The Stories of Flying Officer "X". London: Jonathan Cape, 1952.
The Nature of Love: Three Short Novels. London: Michael Joseph, 1953; Boston: Little Brown, 1954.
The Daffodil Sky. London: Michael Joseph, 1955; Boston: Little Brown, 1956.
The Sleepless Moon. London: Michael Joseph; Boston: Little Brown, 1956.
Death of a Huntsman. London: Michael Joseph, 1957. Reprinted as *Summer in Salander* (Boston: Little Brown, 1957).
Sugar for the Horse. London: Michael Joseph, 1957.
The Watercress Girl. London: Michael Joseph, 1959; Boston: Little Brown, 1960.
An Aspidistra in Babylon. London: Michael Joseph, 1960. Reprinted as *The Grapes of Paradise* (Boston: Little Brown, 1960).

Now Sleeps the Crimson Petal. London: Michael Joseph, 1961. Reprinted as *The Enchantress and Other Stories* (Boston: Little Brown, 1961).

The Golden Oriole. London: Michael Joseph; Boston: Little Brown, 1962.

Seven by Five: Stories 1926–1961. London: Michael Joseph, 1963. Reprinted as *Best of Bates* (1963).

The Four Beauties. London: Michael Joseph, 1968.

The Triple Echo. London: Michael Joseph, 1970.

The Fountain of Flowers. London: Michael Joseph, 1974.

The Yellow Meads of Asphodel. London: Michael Joseph, 1976.

Barbara Baynton

Bush Studies. London: Duckworth, 1902.

Cobbers. London: Duckworth, 1917. Contains *Bush Studies* plus two stories.

Max Beerbohm

The Happy Hypocrite. London: John Lane, 1897.

A Christmas Garland. London: William Heinemann, 1912. Rev. ed., 1950.

Arnold Bennett

Tales of the Five Towns. London: Chatto & Windus, 1905.

The Loot of Cities: Being the Adventures of a Millionaire in Search of Joy, a Fantasia. London: Alston Rivers, 1905. Rev. ed., 1917.

The Grim Smile of the Five Towns. London: Chapman & Hall, 1907.

The Matador of the Five Towns and Other Stories. London: Methuen & Co., 1912.

Elsie and the Child: A Tale of Riceyman Steps and Other Stories. London: Cassell & Co., 1924.

The Woman Who Stole Everything and Other Stories. London: Cassell & Co., 1927.

E. F. Benson

A Double Overture. Chicago: C. H. Sergel Co., 1894.

The Room in the Tower and Other Stories. London: Mills & Boon, 1912.

The Countess of Lowndes Square and Other Stories. London: Cassell & Co., 1920.

Visible and Invisible. London: Hutchinson & Co., 1923.

Spook Stories. London: Hutchinson & Co., 1928.

More Spook Stories. London: Hutchinson & Co., 1934.

Stella Benson

Twenty. London: Macmillan & Co , 1918.

Hope Against Hope and Other Stories. London: Macmillan & Co., 1931.

Christmas Formula and Other Stories. London: Joiner & Steele, 1932.

Pull Devil, Pull Baker. New York: Harper & Brothers, 1933.

Collected Short Stories. London: Macmillan & Co., 1936.

Sir Walter Besant

The Case of Mr. Lucraft and Other Stories. 2 vols. London: Chatto & Windus, 1876. With James Rice.

'Twas in Trafalgar's Bay and Other Stories. London: Chatto & Windus, 1879. With James Rice.

The Ten Years' Tenant and Other Stories. London: Chatto & Windus, 1881. With James Rice.

Uncle Jack. London: Chatto & Windus, 1885.

Verbena Camillia Stephanotis. London: Chatto & Windus, 1892.

In Deacon's Orders. London: Chatto & Windus, 1895.

A Five Years' Tryst and Other Stories. London: Methuen & Co., 1902.

Rolf Boldrewood (T. A. Browne)

A Romance of Canvas Town and Other Stories. London: Macmillan & Co., 1898.

In Bad Company and Other Stories. London: Macmillan & Co., 1901.

Mary Elizabeth Braddon

All Along the River. London: Simpkin & Marshall, 1893.

Mary Chavelita Bright ("George Egerton")

Keynotes. London: John Lane, 1893.

Discords. London: John Lane, 1894.

Symphonies. London: John Lane, 1897.

Fantasias. London: John Lane, 1898.

Flies in Amber. London: Hutchinson & Co., 1905.

John Buchan

Grey Weather: Moorland Tales of My Own People. London: John Lane, 1895.

The Moon Endureth: Tales and Fancies. London: W. Blackwood & Sons, 1902. 2d ed., 1918.

G. K. Chesterton

The Club of Queer Trades. London: Harper & Bros., 1905.

The Innocence of Father Brown. London: Cassell & Co., 1911.

The Wisdom of Father Brown. London: Cassell & Co., 1914.

The Man Who Knew Too Much and Other Stories. London: Cassell & Co., 1922.

Tales of the Long Bow. London: Cassell & Co., 1925.

The Incredulity of Father Brown. London: Cassell & Co., 1926.

The Secret of Father Brown. London: Cassell & Co., 1927.

The Poet and the Lunatics: Episodes in the Life of Gabriel Gale. London: Cassell & Co., 1929.

Four Faultless Felons. London: Cassell & Co., 1930.

The Scandal of Father Brown. London: Cassell & Co., 1935.

Stories, Essays and Poems. London: J. M. Dent & Sons, 1935. Reprint, 1953.

The Paradoxes of Mr. Pond. London: Cassell & Co., 1936.
The Coloured Lands. London: Sheed & Ward, 1938.

Agatha Christie

Poirot Investigates. London: John Lane, 1924.
The Under Dog and Other Stories. New York: Dodd, Mead & Co., 1926.
Partners in Crime. London: W. Collins Sons & Co., 1929.
The Thirteen Problems. London: W. Collins Sons & Co., 1932. Reprinted as *The Tuesday Club Murders* (1933).
The Hound of Death and Other Stories. London: Odhams Press, 1933.
The Listerdale Mystery and Other Stories. London: Collins, 1934.
Parker Pyne Investigates. London: Collins, 1934. Reprinted as *Mr. Parker Pyne, Detective* (1934).
Murder in the Mews and Other Stories. London: Collins, 1937. Reprinted as *Dead Man's Mirror and Other Stories* (1937).
The Regatta Mystery and Other Stories. New York: Dodd, Mead & Co., 1939. Reprinted as *Poirot and the Regatta Mystery* (London: Todd Publishing Co., 1943).

Joseph Conrad

Tales of Unrest. London: T. Fisher Unwin, 1898.
Youth: A Narrative, with Two Other Stories. Edinburgh: William Blackwood & Sons, 1902.
Typhoon and Other Stories. London: William Heinemann, 1903.
A Set of Six. London: Methuen & Co., 1908.
'Twixt Land and Sea. London: J. M. Dent & Sons, 1912.
Within the Tides: Tales. London: J. M. Dent & Sons, 1915.
Complete Short Stories. London: Hutchinson & Co., 1933.

A. E. Coppard

Adam and Eve and Pinch Me: Tales. Waltham St. Lawrence: Golden Cockerel Press, 1921.
Clorinda Walks in Heaven: Tales. Waltham St. Lawrence: Golden Cockerel Press, 1922.
The Black Dog and Other Stories. London: Jonathan Cape, 1923.
Fishmonger's Fiddle: Tales. London: Jonathan Cape, 1925.
The Field of Mustard: Tales. London: Jonathan Cape, 1926.
Silver Circus: Tales. London: Jonathan Cape, 1928.
Pink Furniture. London: Jonathan Cape, 1930.
Nixey's Harlequin: Tales. London: Jonathan Cape, 1931.
Fares Please. London: Jonathan Cape, 1932.
Dunky Fitlow: Tales. London: Jonathan Cape, 1933.
Polly Oliver: Tales. London: Jonathan Cape, 1935.
The Ninepenny Flute: Twenty-one Tales. London: Macmillan & Co., 1937.
You Never Know, Do You? and Other Tales. London: Methuen & Co., 1939.
Ugly Anna. London: Macmillan & Co., 1944.

Selected Tales. London: Macmillan & Co., 1946.
Dark-eyed Lady. London: Methuen & Co., 1947.
Collected Tales. New York: Alfred A. Knopf, 1948.
Fearful Pleasures. London: Methuen, 1951.
Lucy in her Pink Jacket. London: Peter Nevill, 1954.

Hubert Crackanthorpe
Wreckage, Seven Studies. London: William Heinemann, 1893.
Village Tales. London: William Heinemann, 1895.
Sentimental Studies and a Set of Village Tales. London: William Heinemann, 1895.
Vignettes: A Miniature Journal of Whim and Sentiment. London: John Lane, 1896.
Last Stories. London: William Heinemann, 1897.
Collected Stories, 1893–1897. Edited by William Peden. Gainesville, Fla.: Scholars Facsimiles and Reprints, 1969.

Rhys Davies
The Song of Songs and Other Stories. London: E. Archer, 1927.
The Stars, the World, and the Women. London: William Jackson, 1930.
A Pig in a Poke. London: Joiner & Steele, 1931.
Daisy Matthews and Three Other Tales. Waltham St. Lawrence: Golden Cockerel Press, 1932.
Love Provoked. London: Putnam, 1933.
The Things Men Do: Short Stories. London: William Heinemann, 1936.
Selected Stories. London: Maurice Fridbert, 1945.
The Trip to London: Stories. London: William Heinemann, 1946.

Walter de la Mare
Story and Rhyme. New York: E. P. Dutton, 1900.
The Riddle and Other Stories. London: Selwyn & Blount, 1923.
Ding Dong Bell. London: Selwyn & Blount, 1924.
Broomsticks and Other Tales. London: Constable, 1925.
The Connoisseur and Other Stories. London: Collins, 1926.
Told Again: Traditional Tales. Oxford: Blackwell, 1927.
Stories from the Bible. London: Faber & Gwyer, 1929; Faber & Faber, 1933.
On The Edge. London: Faber & Faber, 1930.
The Lord Fish. London: Faber & Faber, 1933.
The Wind Blows Over. London: Faber & Faber, 1936.
The Best Stories of Walter de la Mare. London: Faber & Faber, 1942.
The Magic Jacket and Other Stories. London: Faber & Faber, 1943.
The Scarecrow and Other Stories. London: Faber & Faber, 1945.
The Dutch Cheese and Other Stories. London: Faber & Faber, 1946.
Collected Stories for Children. London: Faber & Faber, 1947.
The Collected Tales of Walter de la Mare. New York: Alfred A. Knopf, 1950.
A Beginning and Other Stories. London: Faber & Faber, 1955.

Mazo de la Roche
Explorers of the Dawn. London: Cassell & Co., 1922.
The Scared Bullock and Other Stories of Animals. London: Macmillan & Co., 1939.

Norman Douglas
Unprofessional Tales. London: T. F. Unwin, 1901. With Elsa Douglas.

Ernest Dowson
Dilemmas: Stories and Studies in Sentiment. London: Elkin Mathews, 1895.
Poems and Prose. New York: Boni & Liveright, 1919.
Stories. Edited by M. Longaker. Philadelphia: University of Pennsylvania Press, 1947.

Arthur Conan Doyle
Mysteries and Adventures. London: W. Scott, 1889. Reprinted as *The Gully of Bluemans-dyke and Other Stories* (1893).
The Captain of the Polestar and Other Tales. London: Longmans & Co., 1890.
The Adventures of Sherlock Holmes. London: George Newnes, 1892.
The Memoirs of Sherlock Holmes. London: George Newnes, 1893.
The Green Flag and Other Stories of War and Sport. London: Smith, Elder & Co., 1900.
Adventures of Gerard. London: George Newnes, 1903.
The Return of Sherlock Holmes. London: George Newnes, 1905.
Round the Fire Stories. London: Smith, Elder & Co., 1908.
The Last Galley: Impressions and Tales. London: Smith, Elder & Co., 1911.
His Last Bow: Some Reminiscences of Sherlock Holmes. London: John Murray, 1917.
Danger! and Other Stories. London: John Murray, 1918.
The Empty House and Other Tales. London: George Newnes, 1921.
The Man With the Twisted Lip and Other Tales. London: George Newnes, 1921.
The Case-Book of Sherlock Holmes. London: John Murray, 1927.
The Maracot Deep and Other Stories. London: John Murray, 1929.

Daphne du Maurier
Come Wind, Come Weather. London: William Heinemann, 1940.
Consider the Lilies. London: Todd Publishing Co., 1943.
Nothing Hurts for Long and Escort. London: Todd Publishing Co., 1943.

Roderick Finlayson
Brown Man's Burden. Auckland: Unicorn Press, 1938.
Sweet Beulah Land. Auckland: Griffin Press, 1942.
Brown Man's Burden and Later Stories. Edited by Bill Pearson. Auckland: Auckland University Press, 1973.

E. M. Forster
The Celestial Omnibus and Other Stories. London: Sidgwick & Jackson, 1911.
The Eternal Moment and Other Stories. London: Sidgwick & Jackson, 1928.

The Collected Tales. New York: Alfred A. Knopf, 1947. Reprinted as *The Collected Short Stories* (London: Sidgwick & Jackson, 1948).

Albergo Empedocle and Other Writings. Introduction by George H. Thomson. New York: Liveright, 1971.

The Life to Come and Other Stories. London: Edward Arnold, 1972.

John Galsworthy

From the Four Winds. London: T. Fisher Unwin, 1897.

Five Tales. London: William Heinemann, 1918. Reprinted as *The First and the Last* and *The Stoic* (1920) and as *The Apple Tree and Other Tales* (1965).

Tatterdemalion. London: William Heinemann, 1920.

Captures. London: William Heinemann, 1923.

Caravan: The Assembled Tales. London: William Heinemann, 1925.

David Garnett

The Old Dovecote and Other Stories. London: E. Mathews & Marrot, 1928.

William Gerhardie

Pretty Creatures. London: Ernest Benn, 1927.

Lewis Grassic Gibbon (Leslie Mitchell)

Persian Dawns, Egyptian Nights: Two Story-Cycles. London: Jarrolds, 1933.

Henry Franklin Belknap Gilbert

Of Necessity. London: John Lane, 1898.

George Gissing

Human Odds and Ends: Stories and Sketches. London: Lawrence & Bullen, 1898.

The House of Cobwebs and Other Stories. London: Archibald Constable & Co., 1906.

Sins of the Fathers and Other Tales. Edited by Vincent Starrett. Chicago: Pascal Covici, 1924.

A Victim of Circumstance and Other Stories. London: Constable & Co., 1927.

Stories and Sketches. Edited by A. C. Gissing. London: Michael Joseph, 1938.

R. B. Cunninghame Graham

Thirteen Stories. London: William Heinemann, 1900.

Success. London: Duckworth & Co., 1902.

Faith. London: Duckworth & Co., 1909.

Hope. London: Duckworth & Co., 1910.

Charity. London: Duckworth & Co., 1912.

El Rio de la Plata. London: Lea y cia, 1914.

Scottish Stories. London: Duckworth & Co., 1914.

Thirty Tales and Sketches. Edited by Edward Garnett. London: Duckworth & Co., 1929.

Kenneth Grahame
The Headswoman. New York: John Lane, 1898.

Graham Greene
The Basement Room and Other Stories. London: Cresset Press, 1935.
Twenty-Four Stories. London: Cresset Press, 1939. With James Laver and Sylvia Town-
send Warner.
Nineteen Stories. New York: Viking Press, 1947.
Collected Stories. New York: Viking Press, 1973.
Twenty-One Stories. New York: Penguin Books, 1980.

Frederick Phillip Grove
Tales from the Margin: The Selected Short Stories of Frederick Philip Grove. Edited by Desmond Pacey. Toronto: Ryerson Press, 1971.

Neal M. Gunn
Hidden Doors. Edinburgh: Porpoise Press, 1929.

Rider Haggard
Allan's Wife and Other Tales. London: Spencer Blackett, 1889.
Black Heart and White Heart and Other Stories. London: Longmans & Co., 1900.
Smith and the Pharaohs and Other Tales. Bristol: J. W. Arrowsmith, 1920.

Thomas Hardy
Wessex Tales: Strange, Lively and Commonplace. London: Macmillan & Co., 1888.
A Group of Noble Dames. London: Osgood, McIlvaine & Co.; New York: Harper &
Bros., 1891.
Life's Little Ironies: A Set of Tales. London: Osgood, McIlvaine & Co., 1894. Reprint,
1896, 1912.
A Changed Man, The Waiting Supper, and Other Tales. London: Osgood, McIlvaine & Co.,
1913. Vol. 18 of Hardy's *Works.*
Stories and Poems of Thomas Hardy. Edited by N. V. Meeres. London: Macmillan & Co.,
1934.

Henry Harland
A Latin-Quarter Courtship and Other Stories. London: Cassell & Co., 1890.
Mademoiselle Miss and Other Stories. London: William Heinemann, 1893.
Grey Roses. London: John Lane, 1895.
Comedies and Errors. London: John Lane, 1898.

L. P. Hartley
Night Fears and Other Stories. London: Putnam, 1924.
The Killing Bottle. London: Putnam, 1932.

G. A. Henty

In Battle and Breeze: Sea Stories. London: Partridge & Co., 1896. With George Manville
    Fenn and W. Clark Russell.
Bears and Decoits and Other Stories. London: Blackie & Son, 1901.
In the Hands of the Malays and Other Stories. London: Blackie & Son, 1905.
A Soldier's Daughter and Other Stories. London: Blackie & Son, 1906.

Anthony Hope

Sport Royal and Other Stories. London: Innes & Co., 1893.
The Heart of Princess Osva and Other Stories. London: Longmans & Co., 1896.

Richard Hughes

A Moment of Time, London: Chatto & Windus, 1926.
Burial, and The Dark Child. London: Privately printed, 1930.
The Spider's Palace and Other Stories. London: Chatto & Windus, 1931.
Don't Blame Me! and Other Stories. London: Chatto & Windus, 1940.

Aldous Huxley

Limbo. London: Chatto & Windus, 1920.
Mortal Coils. London: Chatto & Windus, 1922.
Little Mexican and Other Stories. London: Chatto & Windus, 1924.
Two or Three Graces and Other Stories. London: Chatto & Windus, 1926.
Brief Candles: Stories. New York: Fountain Press; London: Chatto & Windus, 1930.
Stories, Essays and Poems. London: J. M. Dent & Sons, 1937.
Twice Seven: Fourteen Selected Stories. London: Reprint Society, 1944.

W. W. Jacobs

Many Cargoes. London: Lawrence & Bullen, 1896.
Sea Urchins. London: Lawrence & Bullen, 1898. Reprinted as *More Cargoes* (1899).
Light Freights. London: Methuen & Co., 1901.
Odd Craft. London: George Newnes, 1903.
Captains All. London: Hodder & Stoughton, 1905.
Short Cruises. London: Hurst & Blackett, 1907.
Sailor's Knots. London: Methuen & Co., 1909.
Ship's Company. London: Hodder & Stoughton, 1911.
Night Watches. London: Hodder & Stoughton, 1914.
Deep Waters. London: Hodder & Stoughton, 1919.
Fifteen Stories. London: Methuen's Modern Classics, 1926.
Sea Whisper. London: Hodder & Stoughton, 1926.
Selected Tales. London: G. G. Harrap & Co., 1928.
Snug Harbour: Collected Stories. New York: Scribner's Sons, 1931.
Selected Short Stories. Edited by Hugh Greene. London: Bodley Head, 1975.

Montague Rhodes James

Ghost-Stories of an Antiquary. London: Edward Arnold, 1904.
More Ghost Stories of an Antiquary. London: Edward Arnold, 1911.
A Thin Ghost and Others. London: Edward Arnold, 1919.
A Warning to the Curious and Other Ghost Stories. London: Edward Arnold, 1925.

Jerome K. Jerome

The Observations of Henry. Bristol: J. W. Arrowsmith, 1884.
John Ingerfield and Other Stories. London: McClure & Co., 1894.
The Passing of the Third Floor Back and Other Stories. London: Hurst & Blackett, 1907.

Anna Kavan

Asylum Piece and Other Stories. London: Jonathan Cape, 1940.
I Am Lazarus: Short Stories. London: Jonathan Cape, 1941.

Rudyard Kipling

In Black and White. Allahabad, India: A. H. Wheeler & Co., 1888.
The Phantom 'Rickshaw and Other Tales. Allahabad, India: A. H. Wheeler & Co., 1888. Rev. ed., 1890.
Plain Tales for the Hills. Calcutta: Thacker, Spink & Co., 1888.
Soldiers Three: A Collection of Stories. Allahabad, India: A. H. Wheeler & Co., 1888.
The Story of the Gadsbys, A Tale Without a Plot. Allahabad, India: A. H. Wheeler & Co., 1888.
Under the Deodars, Allahabad, India: A. H. Wheeler & Co., 1888. Rev. ed., 1890.
Wee Willie Winkie and Other Child Stories. Allahabad, India: A. H. Wheeler & Co., 1888. Rev. ed., 1890.
The Courting of Dinah Shadd and Other Stories. New York: Harper & Bros., 1890.
Indian Tales. New York: United States Book Co., 1890. Contains *In Black and White, The Phantom 'Rickshaw, Plain Tales from the Hills,* and *Soldiers Three*.
Mine Own People. New York: United States Book Co., 1891.
Many Inventions. London: Macmillan & Co., 1893.
The Jungle Book. London: Macmillan & Co.; New York: Century Co., 1894.
The Second Jungle Book. London: Macmillan & Co., 1895.
Soldier Tales. London: Macmillan & Co., 1896. Reprinted as *Soldier Stories* (1896).
The Day's Work. New York: Doubleday & McClure Co., 1898.
The Kipling Reader. London: Macmillan & Co., 1900. Reprinted as *Selected Stories* (1925).
Just So Stories. London: Macmillan & Co., 1902.
Traffics and Discoveries. London: Macmillan & Co., 1904.
Abaft the Funnel. New York: Doubleday, Page & Co., 1909.
Actions and Reactions. London: Macmillan & Co., 1917.
The Writings in Prose and Verse of Rudyard Kipling. New York: Charles Scribner's Sons, 1909.

A Diversity of Creatures. London: Macmillan & Co., 1917.
Selected Stories. Edited by William Lyon Phelps. Garden City, N.Y.: Doubleday, Page
     & Co., 1921.
Debits and Credits. Garden City, N.Y.: Doubleday, Doran & Co., 1926.
Selected Stories. Edited by J. Macfarlan. London: Macmillan & Co., 1929.
Thy Servant a Dog, Told by Boots. London: Macmillan & Co., 1930. Revised as *Thy
     Servant a Dog and Other Dog Stories* (1938).
Humorous Tales. London: Macmillan & Co., 1931.
Animal Stories. London: Macmillan & Co., 1932.
Limits and Renewals. New York: Doubleday, Doran & Co., 1932.
All the Mowgli Stories. London: Macmillan & Co., 1933.
Collected Dog Stories. Garden City, N.Y.: Doubleday, Doran & Co., 1934.
The Collected Works of Rudyard Kipling. Burwash Edition. New York: Doubleday, Doran
     & Co., Inc., 1941.
The Best Short Stories of Rudyard Kipling. Edited by Randall Jarrell. Garden City, N.Y.:
     Hanover House, 1961.
Short Stories. Vol. 1. "A Sahib's War" and Other Stories. Edited by Andrew Rutherford.
     New York: Penguin Books, 1971.
The Portable Kipling. Edited by Irving Howe. New York: Penguin Books, 1982.

D. H. Lawrence

The Prussian Officer and Other Stories. London: Duckworth & Co., 1914.
England, My England and Other Stories. New York: T. Seltzer, 1922.
The Woman Who Rode Away and Other Stories. London: Martin Secker, 1928.
Love Among the Haystacks and Other Pieces. London: Nonesuch Press, 1930.
The Lovely Lady. London: Martin Secker, 1932.
A Modern Lover. London: Martin Secker, 1934.
The Tales of D. H. Lawrence. London: Martin Secker, 1934.
Stories, Essays and Poems. London: J. M. Dent & Sons, 1939.
The Complete Short Stories. 3 vols. New York: Viking, 1962.
Phoenix II: Uncollected, Unpublished, and Other Prose Writings by D. H. Lawrence. Edited by
     Warren Roberts and Harry T. Moore. London: Heinemann, 1968.
The Princess and Other Stories. Edited by Keith Sagar. 2 vols. Harmondsworth: Penguin,
     1971.

Henry Lawson

Short Stories in Prose and Verse. Sydney: L. Lawson, 1894.
While the Billy Boils. Sydney: Angus & Robertson, 1896.
On the Track and Over the Sliprails. Sydney: Angus & Robertson, 1900.
The Country I Come From. Edinburgh: W. Blackwood & Sons, 1901.
Joe Wilson and His Mates. Edinburgh: William Blackwood & Sons, 1901.
Children of the Bush. London: Methuen & Co., 1902. Reprinted as *Send Round the Hat*
     and *The Romance of the Swat* (1907).

Triangles of Life and Other Stories. Melbourne: Standard Publishing Co., 1913.
Prose Works. 2 vols. Sydney: Home Entertainment Library, 1935. Reprint. Sydney: Angus & Robertson, 1937.
Three Stories. Melbourne: Lothian Publishing Co., 1944.
Stories. Edited by Cecil Mann. Sydney: Angus & Robertson, 1964.
Short Stories and Sketches 1888–1922. Edited by Colin Roderick. Sydney: Angus & Robertson, 1972. Vol. 1 of *Collected Prose*.

Stephen Leacock
Sunshine Sketches of a Little Town. New York: John Lane Co., 1912.
Arcadian Adventures with the Idle Rich. New York: John Lane Co., 1914.
Winsome Winnie and Other New Nonsense Novels. New York: John Lane Co., 1920.

John Alexander Lee
Shining with the Shiner. Hamilton, New Zealand: F. W. Mead, 1944.

Rosamond Lehmann
The Gypsy's Baby and Other Stories. London: Collins, 1946.

Wyndham Lewis
The Wild Body, A Soldier of Humour, and Other Stories. London: Chatto & Windus, 1927.

Jack Lindsay
Come Home at Last and Other Stories. London: I. Nicholson & Watson, 1936.

Eric Linklater
The Revolution. London: White Owl Press, 1934.
God Likes Them Plain: Short Stories. London: Jonathan Cape, 1935.

Henry Dawson Lowry
Wreckers and Methodists and Other Stories. London: William Heinemann, 1893.

George MacDonald
The Gifts of the Child Christ and Other Tales. 2 vols. London: Sampson Low & Co., 1882. Reprinted as *Stephen Archer and Other Tales* (1883).
The Light Princess and Other Fairy Tales. London: Blackie & Son, 1893.
The Fairy Tales. Edited by Greville MacDonald. 5 vols. London: G. Allen & Unwin, 1904.

Arthur Machen
The Chronicle of Clemendy; or, The History of IX Joyous Journeys. Carbonnek: Privately printed, 1888.
The Three Imposters; or, The Transmutations. London: John Lane, 1895.

The House of Souls. London: E. Grant Richards, 1906.
The Angel of Mons: The Bowmen and Other Legends of the War. London: Simpkin, Marshall &
   Co., 1915.
The Shining Pyramid. London: Martin Secker, 1923.
The Glorious Mystery. Edited by Vincent Starrett. Chicago: Covici-McGee Co., 1924.
Ornaments in Jade. New York: A. A. Knopf, 1924.
The Children of the Pool and Other Stories. London: Hutchinson & Co., 1936.
The Cosy Room and Other Stories. London: Rich & Cowan, 1936.

Roger Mais
And Most of All Man. Kingston, Jamaica: City Printery, 1939.
Face and Other Stories. Kingston, Jamaica: The Universal Printery, 1942.

H. A. Manhood
Nightseed. London: Jonathan Cape, 1928.
Apples of the Night. London: Jonathan Cape, 1932.
Crack of Whips. London: Jonathan Cape, 1934.
Fierce and Gentle. London: Jonathan Cape, 1935.
Sunday Bugles. London: Jonathan Cape, 1939.
Lunatic Broth, and Other Stories. London: Jonathan Cape, 1944.
Selected Stories, 1928–1944. London: Jonathan Cape, 1947.

Katherine Mansfield
In a German Pension. London: Stephen Swift & Co., 1911.
Prelude. Richmond, Surrey: Hogarth Press, 1918.
Bliss and Other Stories. London: Constable & Co., 1920.
The Garden Party and Other Stories. London: Constable & Co., 1922.
The Dove's Nest and Other Stories. London: Constable & Co., 1923.
Something Childish and Other Stories. London: Constable & Co., 1924. Reprinted as *The
   Little Girl and Other Stories* (1924).
The Aloe. London: Constable & Co., 1930. Reprinted as "Prelude" in *Bliss*.
The Short Stories of Katherine Mansfield. New York: Alfred A. Knopf, 1937.
Collected Stories. London: Constable & Co., 1945.
Undiscovered Country: The New Zealand Stories. Edited by Ian A. Gordon. London: Long-
   man & Co., 1974.

A. E. W. Mason
Ensign Knightley and Other Stories. London: F. A. Stokes Co., 1901.
The Four Corners of the World. New York: Scribner's Sons, 1917.
Dilemmas. London: Hodder & Stoughton, 1934.

W. Somerset Maugham
Orientations. London: T. F. Unwin, 1899.

The Trembling Leaf: Little Stories of the South Sea Islands. London: William Heinemann, 1921. Reprinted as *Sadie Thompson and Other Stories* (1928) and *Rain and Other Stories* (1933).

The Casuarina Tree: Six Stories. London: Woods & Sons, 1926. Reprinted as *The Letter: Stories of Crime* (1930).

Six Stories Written in the First Person Singular. London: William Heinemann, 1931.

Ah King: Six Stories. London: William Heinemann, 1933.

East and West: The Collected Short Stories. Garden City, N.Y.: Doubleday, Doran & Co., 1934. Reprinted as *Altogether* (1934).

Favorite Short Stories. Garden City, N.Y.: Doubleday, Doran & Co., 1934.

Cosmopolitans: Very Short Stories. London: William Heinemann, 1936.

The Round Dozen. London: World Books, n.d. Reprint. London: Reprint Society, 1939.

The Mixture as Before: Short Stories. London: William Heinemann, 1940. Reprinted as *Great Stories of Love and Intrigue* (1947).

The Complete Short Stories of Somerset Maugham. New York: Garden City, 1952.

The World Over: Stories of Manifold Places and People. Garden City, N.Y.: Doubleday, 1952.

Seventeen Lost Stories. Edited by Craig V. Showalter. Garden City, N.Y.: Doubleday, 1969.

Collected Short Stories. New York: Penguin Books, 1980.

George Meredith

The Tale of Chloe. New York: J. W. Lovell Co., 1890.

The Tale of Chloe and Other Stories. New York: C. Scribner's Sons, 1894.

Short Stories. New York: C. Scribner's Sons, 1898.

A. A. Milne

The Secret and Other Stories. London: Methuen & Co., 1929.

Arthur Morrison

The Shadows Around Us: Authentic Tales of the Supernatural. London: Simpkin, 1891.

Martin Hewitt, Investigator. London: Ward, Lock & Bowden, 1894.

Tales of Mean Streets. London: Methuen & Co., 1894.

Chronicles of Martin Hewitt. London: Ward, Lock & Bowden, 1895.

Adventures of Martin Hewitt: Third Series. London: Ward, Lock & Co., 1896.

The Dorrington Deed-Box. London: Ward, Lock & Co., 1897.

The Red Triangle: Being Some Further Chronicles of Martin Hewitt. London: E. Nash, 1903.

The Green Eye of Goona: Stories of a Case of Tokay. London: E. Nash, 1904. Reprinted as *The Green Diamond* (1904).

Divers Vanities. London: Methuen & Co., 1905.

Green Ginger. London: Hutchinson & Co., 1909.

Arthur Morrison in Short Stories of Today and Yesterday. London: G. G. Harrap, 1929.
Fiddle O' Dreams. London: Hutchinson & Co., 1933.

H. H. Munro ("Saki")
Reginald. London: Methuen, 1904.
Reginald in Russia and Other Sketches. London: Methuen, 1910.
The Chronicle of Clovis. London: John Lane, 1911.
Beasts and Super-Beasts. London: John Lane, 1914.
The Toys of Peace and Other Papers. London: John Lane, 1919.
The Square Egg and Other Sketches, with Three Plays. London: John Lane, 1924.
The Short Stories of Saki. Edited by Christopher Morley. New York: The Viking Press, 1930.
Complete Works of Saki/H. H. Munro. Garden City, N.Y.: Doubleday, 1976.

R. K. Narayan
Dodu and Other Stories. Mysore: Indian Thought Publications, 1943.
Malgudi Days. Mysore: Indian Thought Publications, 1943.

Margaret Oliphant
Neighbours on the Green: A Collection of Stories. London: Macmillan & Co., 1889.
The Two Marys. London: Methuen & Co., 1896.
The Lady's Walk. London: Methuen, 1897.
The Ways of Life: Two Stories. London: Smith, Elder, 1897.
That Little Cutty and Two Other Stories. London: Macmillan & Co., 1898.
A Widow's Tale and Other Stories. Edinburgh: William Blackwood & Sons, 1898.

Ouida (Marie Louise de la Ramée)
Le Selve and Other Tales. London: T. Fisher Unwin, 1896.
La Strega and Other Stories. London: Sampson Low, Marston & Co., Ltd., 1899.
Street Dust and Other Stories. London: F. V. White & Co., 1901.

Vance Palmer
The World of Men. London: Euston Press, 1915.
Separate Lives. London: S. Paul & Co., 1931.
Sea and Spinifex. Sydney: Shakespeare Head Press, 1934.

William Plomer
I Speak of Africa. London: Hogarth Press, 1927.
Paper Houses. London: L. & V. Woolf, 1929.
The Child of Queen Victoria and Other Stories. London: Jonathan Cape, 1933.
Curious Relations. London: Jonathan Cape, 1945. Under pseudonym William D'Arfey, with Anthony Butts.

Hal Porter
Short Stories. Adelaide, Australia: Advertiser, 1942.

Llewelyn Powys
Ebony and Ivory. London: Grant Richards, Ltd., 1923.

T. F. Powys
The Left Leg. London: Chatto & Windus, 1923.
A Strong Girl, and The Bride: Two Stories. London: E. Archer, 1926.
The House with the Echo: Twenty-Six Stories. London: Chatto & Windus, 1928.
Fables. London: Chatto & Windus, 1929. Reprinted as *No Painted Plumage* (1934).
The White Paternoster and Other Stories. London: Chatto & Windus, 1930.
The Tithe Barn, and The Dove and the Eagle. London: K. S. Bhat, 1932.
Captain Patch: Twenty-one Stories. London: Chatto & Windus, 1935.
Bottle's Path and Other Stories. London: Chatto & Windus, 1946.
God's Eyes A-Twinkle. London: Chatto & Windus, 1947.
Rosie Plum and Other Stories. Edited by Francis Powys. London: Chatto & Windus, 1966.

Katharine Susannah Prichard
Kiss on the Lips and Other Stories. London: Jonathan Cape, 1932.
Potch and Colour. Sydney: Angus & Robertson, 1944.

V. S. Pritchett
The Spanish Virgin and Other Stories. London: E. Benn, Ltd., 1930.
You Make Your Own Life. London: Chatto & Windus, 1938.
It May Never Happen and Other Stories. London: Chatto & Windus, 1945.
The Sailor, Sense of Humor, and Other Stories. New York: Knopf, 1956.
Collected Stories. London: Chatto & Windus, 1956.
When My Girl Comes Home. New York: Knopf, 1961.
Blind Love and Other Stories. London: Chatto & Windus, 1969.
The Camberwell Beauty and Other Stories. New York: Random House, 1974.
Selected Stories. London: Chatto & Windus, 1978.
On the Edge of the Cliff. London: Chatto & Windus, 1979.

Arthur Quiller-Couch ("Q")
Noughts and Crosses: Stories, Studies, Sketches. London: Cassell & Co., 1891.
I Saw Three Ships and Other Winter's Tales. London: Cassell & Co., 1892.
The Delectable Duchy: Stories, Studies, Sketches. London: Cassell & Co., 1893.
Fairy Tales, Far and Near Re-Told by Q. London: Cassell & Co., 1895.
Wandering Heath: Stories, Studies and Sketches. London: Cassell & Co., 1895.
Old Fires and Profitable Ghosts. London: Cassell & Co., 1900.
The Laird's Luck and Other Fireside Tales. London: Cassell & Co., 1901.

The White Wolf and Other Fireside Tales. New York: C. Scribner's Sons, 1901.
Two Sides of the Face: Midwinter Tales. New York: C. Scribner's Sons, 1903.
Shakespeare's Christmas and Other Stories. London: Smith, Elder & Co., 1904.
Merry-Garden and Other Stories. London: Methuen, 1907.
Corporal Sam and Other Stories by "Q." London: Smith, Elder & Co., 1910.
My Best Book. London: Fowey Cottage Hospital Bazaar, 1912.
News from the Duchy. Bristol: J. W. Arrowsmith, 1913.
Mortallone and Aunt Trinidad: Tales of the Spanish Main. Bristol: J. W. Arrowsmith, 1917.
Selected Stories. London: J. M. Dent & Sons, 1921.
Tales and Romances. 30 vols. London: J. M. Dent & Sons, 1928.
Q's Mystery Stories. London: J. M. Dent & Sons, 1937.
Shorter Stories. London: J. M. Dent & Sons, 1946.

Jean Rhys

The Left Bank and Other Stories. New York: Harper, 1927. Reprint. Freeport, N.Y.: Books for Libraries Press, 1970.
Tigers Are Better-Looking. London: Andre Deutsch, 1968.
Sleep It Off, Lady. New York: Harper & Row, 1976.

Henry Handel Richardson (Ethel Robertson)

The End of a Childhood and Other Stories. London: William Heinemann, 1934.

Frederick Rolfe ("Baron Corvo")

Stories Toto Told Me. London: John Lane, 1898.
In His Own Image. London: John Lane, 1901.
Three Tales of Venice. Thames Ditton, Surrey: Corrine Press, 1913.
The Cardinal Prefect of Propaganda and Other Stories. London: N. Vane, 1957.

Steele Rudd (Arthur Hoey Davis)

Dad in Politics and Other Stories. Sydney: N.S.W. Bookstall, 1908. Reprinted as *For Life and Other Stories* (1908).

William Sansom

Fireman Flower and Other Stories. London: Hogarth Press, 1944.
Three Stories by William Sansom. London: Hogarth, 1946.
Westminster in War. London: Faber & Faber, 1947.
South: Aspects and Images from Corsica, Italy, and Southern France. London: Holder & Stoughton, 1948.
A Touch of Sun. London: Hogarth, 1952.
A Contest of Ladies. London: Reynal & Hitchcock, 1956.
Among the Dahlias and Other Stories. London: Hogarth, 1957.
Selected Short Stories, Chosen by the Author. Baltimore: Penguin, 1960.

The Stories of William Sansom. Introduction by Elizabeth Bowen. Boston: Little, Brown
    & Co., 1963.
The Ulcerated Milkman. London: Hogarth, 1966.

Frank Sargeson
Conversation with My Uncle and Other Stories. Auckland, New Zealand: Unicorn Press,
    1936.
A Man and His Wife. Christchurch, New Zealand: Caxton Press, 1940.
Collected Stories 1935–1963. Edited by Bill Pearson. Auckland, New Zealand: Long-
    man Paul, 1964.

Dorothy Sayers
Lord Peter Views the Body. London: V. Gollancz, 1928.
Hangman's Holiday. London: V. Gollancz, 1933.
In the Teeth of Evidence and Other Stories. London: V. Gollancz, 1939.

Olive Schreiner
Dreams. London: T. F. Unwin, 1891.
Dream Life and Real Life. Boston: Roberts Bros.; London: Unwin, 1893.
Stories, Dreams and Allegories. Edited by S. C. Cronwright-Schreier. London: T. F. Un-
    win, 1923.

William Sharp ("Fiona Macleod")
The Sin-Eater and Other Tales. Chicago: Stone & Kimball, 1895.
Madge o' the Pool, The Gypsy Christ, and Other Tales. London: A. Constable & Co., 1896.
The Washer of the Ford and Other Legendary Moralities. Chicago: Stone & Kimball, 1896.

May Sinclair
Two Sides of a Question. New York: Taylor, 1901.
The Judgment of Eve and Other Stories. London: Hutchinson & Co., 1914. Reprinted as
    Return of the Prodigal (New York: Macmillan, 1914).
Uncanny Stories. London: Hutchinson & Co., 1923.

Christina Stead
The Salzburg Tales. London: P. Davies, 1934.

Robert Louis Stevenson
New Arabian Nights. London: Chatto & Windus, 1882.
The Dynamiter: More New Arabian Nights. London: Longmans, Green, 1885. With Fan-
    ny Stevenson.
The Merry Men and Other Tales and Fables. London: Chatto & Windus, 1887.
The Bottle Imp. New York: G. Munro's Son, 1893.
Island Night's Entertainments. London: Cassell & Co., 1893.

The Ebb Tide: A Trio and Quartette. London: William Heinemann, 1894. With Lloyd
   Osbourne.
The Amateur Emigrant from the Clyde to Sandy Hook. Chicago: Stone & Kimball, 1895.
The Body-Snatcher. New York: Merriam Co., 1895.
Fables. London: Longmans, Green, 1896.
The Strange Case of Dr. Jekyll and Mr. Hyde, with Other Fables. London: Longmans, Green,
   1896.
The Suicide Club. New York: Scribner, 1896.
The Waif Woman. London: Chatto & Windus, 1916.
When the Devil Was Well. Boston: Bibliophile Society, 1921.

George Slythe Street
Episodes. London: William Heinemann, 1895.
A Book of Stories. Westminster: Archibald Constable & Co., 1902.

Edgar Wallace
Smithy Abroad: Barrack Room Sketches. London: E. Hulton, 1909.
Sanders of the River. London: Ward, Lock & Co., 1911.
The People of the River. London: Ward, Lock & Co., 1912.
The Admirable Carfew. London: Ward, Lock & Co., 1914.
Bones of the River. London: Ward, Lock & Co., 1914.
Bosambo of the River. London: Ward, Lock & Co., 1914.
Bones, Being Further Adventures in Mr. Commissioner Sanders Country. London: Ward, Lock
   & Co., 1915.
The Keepers of the King's Peace. London: Ward, Lock & Co., 1915.
Smithy and the Hun. London: C. A. Pearson, 1915.
Lieutenant Bones. London: Ward, Lock & Co., 1918.
The Adventures of Heine. London: Ward, Lock & Co., 1919.
Bones in London. London: Ward, Lock & Co., 1921.
The Law of the Four Just Men. London: Hodder & Stoughton, 1921.
Chick. London: Ward, Lock & Co., 1923.
Educated Evans. London: Webster's Publications, 1924.
The Mind of Mr. J. G. Reeder. London: Hodder & Stoughton, 1925. Reprinted as *The Murder
   Book of J. G. Reeder*.
More Educated Evans. London: Webster's Publications, 1926.
Sanders. London: Hodder & Stoughton, 1926. Reprinted as *Mr. Commissioner Sanders*
   (Garden City, N.Y.: Doubleday, Doran & Co., 1930).
The Brigand. London: Hodder & Stoughton, 1927.
Good Evans! London: Webster's Publications, 1927.
The Mixer. London: John Long, 1927.
Again Sanders. London: Hodder & Stoughton, 1928.
Again the Three Just Men. London: Hodder & Stoughton, 1928. Reprinted as *The Law
   of the Three Just Men* (1931).

Elegant Edward. London: Readers Library Publishing Co., 1928.

The Orator. London: Hutchinson & Co., 1928.

The Thief in the Night. London: Readers Library Publishing Co.; New York: World Wide Publishing Co., 1928.

Again the Ringer. London: Hodder & Stoughton, 1929. Reprinted as *The Ringer Returns* (Garden City, N.Y.: Doubleday, Doran & Co., 1931).

The Big Four. London: Readers Library Publishing Co., 1929.

The Black. London: Readers Library Publishing Co., 1929.

Circumstantial Evidence. London: George Newnes, 1929.

Fighting Snub Reilly. London: George Newnes, 1929.

For Information Received. London: George Newnes, 1929.

Forty-eight Short Stories. London: George Newnes, 1929.

The Ghost of Down Hill, and The Queen of Sheba's Belt. London: Readers Library Publishing Co., 1929.

The Governor of Chi-Foo. London: George Newnes, 1929.

The Lady of Little Hell. London: George Newnes, 1929.

The Little Green Man. London: George Newnes, 1929.

The Lone House Mystery. London: W. Collins & Co., 1929.

Planetoid 127, and The Sweizer Pump. London: Readers Library Publishing Co., 1929.

The Prison-Breakers. London: George Newnes, 1929.

Red Aces, Being Three Cases of Mr. Reeder. London: Hodder & Stoughton, 1929.

The Reporter. London: Readers Library Publications, 1929.

The Iron Grip. London: Readers Library Publishing Co., 1930.

Killer Kay. London: George Newnes, 1930.

The Lady Called Nita. London: George Newnes, 1929.

Mrs. William Jones and Bill. London: George Newnes, 1930.

The Stretelli Case and Other Mystery Stories. New York: International Fiction Library, 1930.

The Law of the Three Just Men. Garden City, N.Y.: Doubleday, Doran & Co., 1931.

The Guv'nor and Other Stories. London: W. Collins Sons & Co., 1932. Reprinted as *Mr. Reeder Returns*. (Garden City, N.Y.: Doubleday, Doran & Co., 1932).

Sergeant Sir Peter. London: Chapman & Hall, 1932. Reprinted as *Sergeant Dunn, C.I.D.* (1962).

The Steward. London: W. Collins Sons & Co., 1932.

The Last Adventure. London: Hutchinson & Co., 1934.

The Woman from the East and Other Stories. London: Hutchinson & Co., 1934.

The Undisclosed Client. London: Digit Books, 1963.

Hugh Walpole

The Thirteen Travellers. London: Hutchinson & Co., 1921.

The Silver Thorn. London: Macmillan & Co., 1928.

All Souls' Night. London: Macmillan & Co., 1933.

Head in Green Bronze and Other Stories. London: Macmillan & Co., 1938.

Sylvia Townsend Warner

Some World Far from Ours, and Stay, Corydon, Thou. London: E. Mathews & Marrot, 1929.

Elinor Barley. London: Cresset Press, 1930.

A Moral Ending and Other Stories. London: William Jackson, Ltd., 1931.

The Salutation. London: Chatto & Windus, 1932.

More Joy in Heaven and Other Stories. London: Cresset Press, 1935.

The Cat's Cradle Book. New York: Viking Press, 1940.

A Garland of Straw and Other Stories. London: Chatto & Windus, 1943.

The Museum of Cheats and Other Stories. London: Chatto & Windus, 1947.

Winter in the Air and Other Stories. London: Chatto & Windus, 1955.

The Cat's Cradle. London: Chatto & Windus, 1960.

A Stranger with a Bag, and Other Stories. London: Chatto & Windus, 1966.

Swans on the River. New York: Viking Press, 1966.

The Innocent and the Guilty. London: Chatto & Windus, 1971.

Scenes of Childhood and Other Stories. London: Chatto & Windus, 1981.

Price Warung (William Astley)

Tales of the Convict System. Sydney: Bulletin Newspaper Co., 1892.

Tales of the Early Days. London: G. Robertson, 1894.

Tales of the Old Regime, and The Bullet of the Fated Ten. Melbourne: G. Robertson, 1897.

Half-Crown Bob and Tales of the Riverine. Melbourne: G. Robertson, 1898.

Tales of the Isle of Death (Norfolk Island). Melbourne: G. Robertson, 1898.

Evelyn Waugh

Mr. Loveday's Little Outing and Other Sad Stories. London: Chapman & Hall, 1936.

Work Suspended and Other Stories Written Before the Second World War. London: Chapman & Hall, 1949.

Frederick Wedmore

Renunciations. London: Elkin Mathews & John Lane, 1893.

English Episodes. London: Elkin Mathews, 1894.

H. G. Wells

Select Conversations with an Uncle, Now Extinct, and Two Other Reminiscences. London: John Lane; New York: Merriam, 1895.

The Stolen Bacillus and Other Incidents. London: Methuen, 1895.

The Plattner Story and Others. London: Methuen, 1897.

Thirty Strange Stories. New York: E. Arnold, 1897.

Tales of Space and Time. New York: Doubleday & McClure, 1899.

Twelve Stories and a Dream. London: Macmillan & Co., 1903.

The Country of the Blind and Other Stories. London: T. Nelson & Sons, 1911. Rev. ed. London: Golden Cockerel Press, 1939.

The Door in the Wall and Other Stories. London: G. Richards, 1911.

Tales of Life and Adventure. London: W. Collins, 1923.

Short Stories. London: E. Benn, Ltd., 1927. Reprinted as *Complete Short Stories* (1966).

Henry Williamson

The Peregrine's Saga and Other Stories of the Country Green. London: W. Collins Sons & Co., 1923. Reprinted as *Sun Brothers* (New York: E. P. Dutton, 1925).

The Old Stag: Stories. London: G. P. Putnam's Sons, 1926.

The Village Book. London: Jonathan Cape, 1930.

The Labouring Life. London: Jonathan Cape, 1932. Reprinted as *As the Sun Shines* (New York: E. P. Dutton, 1933).

The Linhay on the Downs and Other Adventures in the Old and New World. London: Jonathan Cape, 1934.

Life in a Devon Village. London: Faber & Faber, 1945.

Tales of a Devon Village. London: Faber & Faber, 1945.

P. G. Wodehouse

Tales of St. Austin's. London: A. & C. Black, 1903.

The Man Upstairs. London: Methuen, 1914.

The Man With Two Left Feet. London: Methuen, 1917.

My Man Jeeves. London: George Newnes, 1919. Incorporated with revisions in *Carry On, Jeeves*.

The Clicking of Cuthbert. London: Herbert Jenkins, 1922. Reprinted as *Golf Without Tears* (New York: George H. Doran, 1924).

The Inimitable Jeeves. London: Herbert Jenkins, 1923. Reprinted as *Jeeves* (New York: George H. Doran, 1923).

Ukridge. London: Herbert Jenkins, 1924. Reprinted as *He Rather Enjoyed It* (New York: George H. Doran, 1926).

Carry On, Jeeves. London: Herbert Jenkins, 1925.

The Heart of a Goof. London: Herbert Jenkins, 1926. Reprinted as *Divots* (New York: George H. Doran, 1927).

Meet Mr. Mulliner. London: Herbert Jenkins, 1927.

Mr. Mulliner Speaking. London: Herbert Jenkins, 1929.

Very Good, Jeeves. London: Herbert Jenkins, 1930.

The Jeeves Omnibus. London: Herbert Jenkins, 1931.

Mulliner Nights. London: Herbert Jenkins, 1933.

Blandings Castle. London: Herbert Jenkins, 1935.

Mulliner Omnibus. London: Herbert Jenkins, 1935.

Young Men in Spats. London: Herbert Jenkins, 1936.

Lord Emsworth and Others. London: Herbert Jenkins, 1937. Reprinted as *Crime Wave at Blandings* (New York: Doubleday Doran, 1937).

Weekend Wodehouse. London: Herbert Jenkins, 1939.

Eggs, Beans and Crumpets. London: Herbert Jenkins, 1940.

The World of Jeeves. London: Barrie & Jenkins, 1971.
The World of Mr. Mulliner. London: Barrie & Jenkins, 1972.
The Uncollected Wodehouse. New York: Seabury Press, 1976.

Virginia Woolf
Two Stories. London: Hogarth Press, 1917. With Leonard Woolf.
Monday or Tuesday. London: Hogarth Press, 1921.
A Haunted House and Other Stories. London: Hogarth Press, 1943.
Nurse Lugton's Golden Thimble. London: Hogarth Press, 1966.
Mrs. Dalloway's Party: A Short Story Sequence. Edited by Stella McNichol. London: Hogarth Press, 1973.

Israel Zangwill
Ghetto Tragedies. London: McClure & Co., 1893.
The King of the Schnorrers: Grotesques and Fantasies. London: William Heinemann, 1894.
They That Walk in Darkness. London: William Heinemann, 1899.
The Grey Wig: Stories and Novelettes. London: William Heinemann, 1903.
Ghetto Comedies. London: William Heinemann, 1907.

Selected Bibliography of Books
and Articles of General Interest

Allen, Walter. *The Short Story in English*. Oxford: Clarendon Press; New York: Oxford University Press, 1981.

Bates, H. E. *The Modern Short Story*. London: Thomas Nelson & Sons, 1941. Reprint. Michael Joseph, 1972.

Beachcroft, T. O. *The Modest Art, A Survey of the Short Story in English*. London: Oxford University Press, 1968.

Bennett, Bruce. "Australian Experiments in Short Fiction." *World Literature Written in English* 15 (1976):359–66.

———. "The Short Story." In *The Literature of Western Australia*, 105–46. Nedlands: University of West Australia Press, 1979.

Canby, Henry Seidel. *The Short Story in English*. New York: H. Holt & Co., 1909.

Fonlon, Bernard. "The Philosophy, the Science and the Art of the Short Story." *Abbia* 34–37 (1979):427–38.

Harland, Henry. "Concerning the Short Story." *Academy and Literature* 51 (5 June 1895), fiction supp.

Harris, Wendell. *British Short Fiction in the Nineteenth Century: A Literary and Bibliographic Guide*. Detroit: Wayne State University Press, 1979.

———. "English Short Fiction in the Nineteenth Century." *Studies in Short Fiction* 6 (1968):1–93.

Hedberg, Johannes. "What Is a 'Short Story'? And What Is an 'Essay'?" *Moderna Språk* 74 (1980):113–20.

Ingram, Forrest L., S.J. "The Dynamics of Short Story Cycles." *New Orleans Review* 2 (1979):7–12.

Jessup, Alexander, and Canby, Henry Seidel, eds. *The Book of the Short Story*. New York. Appleton, 1903.

Lohafer, Susan. *Coming to Terms with the Short Story*. Baton Rouge: Louisiana State University Press, 1983.

Magill, Frank N., ed. *Critical Survey of Short Fiction*. 7 Vols. Englewood Cliffs, N.J.: Salem Press, 1981.

Martin, Peter. "The Short Story in England: 1930s Fiction Magazines." *Studies in Short Fiction* 14 (1977):233–40.

Matthews, Brander. *The Philosophy of the Short Story*. New York: Longmans & Green, 1901.

Maugham, W. Somerset. "The Short Story." In *Essays by Divers Hands, Being the Transactions of the Royal Society of Literature of the United Kingdom*. N.S., vol. 25, edited by Sir Edward Marsh, 120–34. London: Oxford University Press, 1950.

Mertner, Edgar, "Zur Theorie der Short Story in England und Amerika." *Anglia* 64, no. 2 (1940):188–205.

Moorhouse, Frank. "What Happened to the Short Story?" *Australian Literary Studies* 8 (1977):179–82.

O'Connor, Frank. *The Lonely Voice: A Study of the Short Story*. Cleveland: World Publishing Co., 1963.

O'Faoláin, Seán. *The Short Story*. London: Collins, 1948.

Pain, Barry. *The Short Story*. New York: G. H. Doran Co., 1916.

Walker, Warren S., comp. *Twentieth-Century Short Story Explication*. Hamden, Conn.: Shoe String Press, 1980.

Ward, A. C. *Aspects of the Modern Short Story: English and American*. London: University of London Press, 1924.

Wedmore, Frederic. "The Short Story." *Nineteenth Century* 43 (March 1898).

Welty, Eudora. *Short Stories*. New York: Harcourt, Brace, 1950.

Articles and Books Devoted to Specific Authors

Peter Abrahams
Ogungbesan, Kolawole. *The Writing of Peter Abrahams*. London: Hodder & Stoughton, 1979.
Wade, Michael. *Peter Abrahams*. London: Evans Bros., 1972.

Richard Aldington
Smith, Richard Eugene. *Richard Aldington*. Boston: Twayne, 1977.

Michael Arlen
Keyisbian, Harry. *Michael Arlen*. Boston: Twayne, 1975.

Barbara Baynton
Krimmer, Sally. "New Light on Barbara Baynton." *Australian Literary Studies* 7 (1976):425–33.

H. E. Bates
Vanatta, Dennis Paul. *H. E. Bates*. Boston: Twayne, 1983.

Max Beerbohm
Lynch, [John Gilbert] Bohun. *Max in Perspective*. London: William Heinemann, 1922.
McElderry, Bruce, Jr. *Max Beerbohm*. New York: Twayne, 1972.

Stella Benson
Bedell, R. Meredith. *Stella Benson*. Boston: Twayne, 1983.
Roberts, R. Ellis. *Portrait of Stella Benson*. London: Macmillan Co., 1939.

G. K. Chesterton
Robson, W. W. "Chesterton's Father Brown Stories." *Southern Review*, n.s. 5 (1969):611–29.
Scheick, William J. "The Twilight Harlequinade of Chesterton's Father Brown Stories." *Chesterton Review* 4 (1977–78):104–14.

Agatha Christie

Bargainnier, Earl F. *The Gentle Art of Murder: The Detective Fiction of Agatha Christie.* Bowling Green: Popular, 1980.

Fitzgibbon, Russell H. *The Agatha Christie Companion.* Bowling Green: Popular, 1980.

Joseph Conrad

Birrell, T. A. "The Simplicity of *Typhoon*: Conrad, Flaubert and Others." *Dutch Quarterly Review of Anglo-American Letters* 10 (1980):272–95.

Bruss, Paul S. " 'The End of the Tether': Teleological Diminishing in Conrad's Early Metaphor of Navigation." *Studies in Short Fiction* 13 (1976):311–20.

Burjorjee, Dinshaw M. "Comic Elements in Conrad's 'The Secret Sharer.' " *Conradiana* 7 (1975):51–61.

Culbertson, Diana. " 'The Informer' as Conrad's Little Joke." *Studies in Short Fiction* 11 (1974):430–33.

Curley, Daniel. "The Writer and His Use of Material: The Case of 'The Secret Sharer.' " *Modern Fiction Studies* 13 (1967):179–94.

Daleski, H. M. " 'The Secret Sharer': Questions of Command." *Critical Quarterly* 17 (1975):268–79.

David, Deirdre. "Selfhood and Language in 'The Return' and 'Falk.' " *Conradiana* 8 (1976):137–47.

Dussinger, G. R. " 'The Secret Sharer': Conrad's Psychological Study." *Texas Studies in Literature and Language* 10 (1969):599–608.

Gilley, L. "Conrad's 'Secret Sharer.' " *Midwest Quarterly* 8 (1967):319–30.

Glassman, Peter J. *Language and Being: Joseph Conrad and the Literature of Personality.* New York: Columbia University Press, 1976.

Graver, Lawrence. *Conrad's Short Fiction.* Berkeley: University of California Press, 1969.

Hagopian, J. V. "The Pathos of 'Il Conde.' " *Studies in Short Fiction* 3 (1965):31–8. Reprint, with changes, from *Insight II: Analyses of Modern British Literature*, edited by J. V. Hagopian and Martin Dolch, 62–70. Frankfurt Am Main: Hirschgraben, 1964.

Harkness, Bruce, ed. *Conrad's "Secret Sharer" and the Critics.* Belmont, Calif.: Wadsworth, 1962.

———. "The Secret of 'The Secret Sharer' Bared." *College English* 27 (1965):55–61.

Henig, Suzanne, and Talamantes, Florence W. "Conrad and Balzac: A Trio of Balzacian Interrelationships: 'The Sisters,' 'The Tremolino,' and 'The Arrow of Gold.' " *Polish Review* 20, no. 2–3 (1975):58–70.

Hughes, Douglas A. "Conrad's 'Il Conde': 'A Deucedly Queer Story.' " *Conradiana* 7 (1975):17–25.

Johnson, B. M. "Conrad's 'Falk': Manuscript and Meaning." *Modern Language Quarterly* 26 (1965):267–84.

Kirschner, P. "Conrad and Maupassant." *Review of English Literature* 6 (1965):37–51.

———. "Conrad and Maupassant: Moral Solitude and 'A Smile of Fortune.' " *Review of English Literature* 7 (1966):66–77.

Leiter, L. H. "Echo Structures: Conrad's 'The Secret Sharer.' " *Twentieth Century Literature* 5 (1960):159–75.

Meyer, Bernard C. *Joseph Conrad: A Psychoanalytic Biography*. Princeton: Princeton University Press, 1967.

Murdrick, M., ed. *Conrad: A Collection of Critical Essays*. Englewood Cliffs, N.J.: Prentice-Hall, 1966.

O'Hara, J. D. "Unlearned Lessons in 'The Secret Sharer.' " *College English* 26 (1965):444–50.

Otten, Terry. "The Fall and After in 'The Secret Sharer.' " *Southern Humanities Review* 12 (1978):221–30.

Pinsker, Sanford. " 'Amy Foster': A Reconsideration." *Conradiana* 9 (1977):179–86.

Rice, Thomas Jackson. "Conrad's 'The Lagoon': Malay and Pharisee." *Christianity and Literature* 25, no. 4 (1976):25–33.

———. "*Typhoon*: Conrad's Christmas Story." *Cithara* 14, no. 2 (1975):19–35.

Schwarz, D. R. " 'A Lonely Figure Walking Purposefully': The Significance of Captain Whalley in Conrad's 'The End of the Tether.' " *Conradiana* 7 (1975):165–73.

———. "The Self-Deceiving Narrator of Conrad's 'Il Conde.' " *Studies in Short Fiction* 6 (1969):187–93.

Simmons, J. L. "The Dual Morality in Conrad's 'Secret Sharer.' " *Studies in Short Fiction* 2 (1965):209–20.

Stallman, R. W. *The Art of Conrad: A Critical Symposium*. East Lansing: Michigan State University Press, 1960.

Steiner, Joan E. "Conrad's 'The Secret Sharer': Complexities of the Doubling Relationship." *Conradiana* 12 (1980):173–86.

Tolley, A. T. "Conrad's Favorite Story." *Studies in Short Fiction* 3 (1966):314–20.

Walton, J. H. "Mr. X's 'Little Joke': The Design of Conrad's 'Informer.' " *Studies in Short Fiction* 4 (1967):322–33.

Watt, Ian. *Conrad in the Nineteenth Century*. Berkeley: University of California Press, 1981.

Watts, Cedric. "The Mirror-Tale: An Ethico-Structural Analysis of Conrad's *The Secret Sharer*." *Critical Quarterly* 19, no. 3 (1977):25–37.

Weston, John Howard. " 'Youth': Conrad's Irony and Time's Darkness." *Studies in Short Fiction* 11 (1974):399–407.

Whiting, G. W. "Conrad's Revisions of Six of His Short Stories." *PMLA* 48 (1933):552–57.

Williams, Porter, Jr. "The Brand of Cain in 'The Secret Sharer.' " *Modern Fiction Studies* 10 (1964):27–30.

———. "The Matter of Conscience in Conrad's 'Secret Sharer.' " *PMLA* 79 (1964):626–30.

Wills, J. H. "Conrad's 'The Secret Sharer.' " *University of Kansas City Review* 28 (1961):115–26.

———. "A Neglected Masterpiece: Conrad's 'Youth.' " *Texas Studies in Literature and Language* 4 (1962):591–601.

Willy, Todd G. "The Call to Imperialism in Conrad's 'Youth': A Historical Reconstruction." *Journal of Modern Literature* 8 (1980):39–50.

Young, Gloria L. "Chance and the Absurd in Conrad's 'The End of the Tether' and 'Freya of the Seven Isles.'" *Conradiana* 7 (1975):253–61.

A. E. Coppard

O'Connor, Frank. *The Lonely Voice: A Study of the Short Story*. Cleveland: World Publishing Co., 1963, 170–86.

Hubert Crackanthorpe

Crackanthorpe, David. *Hubert Crackanthorpe and English Realism in the 1890s*. Columbia: University of Missouri Press, 1977.

Harris, Wendell. "Hubert Crackanthorpe as Realist." *English Literature in Transition* 6 (1963):76–84.

Peden, William. "Hubert Crackanthorpe: Forgotten Pioneer." *Studies in Short Fiction* 7 (Fall 1970):539–48.

————. Introduction to *Collected Stories (1893–1897) of Hubert Crackanthorpe*. Gainesville: Scholars' Facsimiles and Reprints, 1969, vii–xxvi.

Rhys Davies

Rees, David. *Rhys Davies*. Writers of Wales Series. Cardiff: University of Wales Press 1975.

Ernest Dawson

Longaker, Mark, ed. Introduction to *The Stories of Ernest Dawson*. Philadelphia: University of Pennsylvania Press, 1947.

Walter de la Mare

Clark, Leonard. *Walter de la Mare*. New York: Henry Z. Walck, Inc., 1961.

Hopkins, Kenneth. *Walter de la Mare*. London: Longmans, Green, & Co., 1957.

McCrosson, Doris Ross. *Walter de la Mare*. New York: Twayne, 1966.

Megroz, R. L. *Walter de la Mare: A Biographical and Critical Study*. New York: George H. Doran Co., 1924.

Reid, Forrest. *Walter de la Mare: A Critical Study*. London: Faber & Faber, 1929.

Wagenknecht, Edward. Introduction to *The Collected Tales of Walter de la Mare*. New York: Alfred A. Knopf, 1950, vii–xxi.

Arthur Conan Doyle

Conroy, Peter. "The Importance of Being Watson." *Texas Quarterly* 21, no. 1 (1978):84–102.

Moorman, Charles. "The Appeal of Sherlock Holmes." *Southern Quarterly* 14 (1976):71–82.

Ousby, Ian. *Bloodhounds of Heaven: The Detective in English Fiction from Godwin to Doyle*. Cambridge: Harvard University Press, 1976.

Poston, Lawrence. "City versus Country: A Holmesian Variation on an Old Theme." *Etudes Anglaises* 33 (1980):156–70.

E. M. Forster
Bander, Laurence. *E. M. Forster: A Critical Study*. London: Rupert Har-Davis, 1968.
Bowen, Elizabeth. "A Passage to E. M. Forster." In *Aspects of E. M. Forster*, edited by Oliver Stallybrass, 1–12. London: Edward Arnold; New York: Harcourt, Brace & World, 1969.
Cavaliero, Glen. *A Reading of E. M. Forster*. Totowa, N.J.: Rowman & Littlefield, 1979.
Colmer, John. *E. M. Forster: The Personal Voice*. London: Routledge & Kegal Paul, 1975.
Confalonieri, Mariachiari Beneduce. "I Racconti di E. M. Forster." *English Miscellany* 18 (1967):163–205.
Crews, Frederick C. "E. M. Forster: The Limitations of Mythology." *Comparative Literature* 12 (Spring 1960):97–112.
Gardner, Philip. *E. M. Forster*. Essex: Longman Group Ltd., 1977.
Godfrey, Denis. *E. M. Forster's Other Kingdom*. Edinburgh: Oliver & Boyd, 1968.
Hagopian, J. V. "Eternal Moments in the Short Fiction of Forster." *College English* 27 (1965):209–15.
Herz, Judith Scherer. "From Myth to Scripture: An Approach to Forster's Later Short Fiction." *English Literature in Transition* 24 (1981):206–12.
———. "The Narrator as Hermes: A Study of the Early Short Fiction." In *E. M. Forster: A Human Exploration*, edited by G. K. Das and John Beer, 17–27. New York: New York University Press, 1979.
Irwin, W. R. "The Survival of Pan." *PMLA* 76 (June 1961):159–67.
Kelvin, Norman. *E. M. Forster*. Carbondale: Southern Illinois University Press, 1967.
Macaulay, Dame Rose. *The Writings of E. M. Forster*. London: Hogarth Press, 1938.
Malek, James S. "Persona, Shadow, and Society: A Reading of Forster's 'The Other Boat.'" *Studies in Short Fiction* 14 (1977):21–27.
Martin, John Sayre. *E. M. Forster: The Endless Journey*. London: Cambridge University Press, 1976.
McDowell, Frederick P. W. *E. M. Forster*. New York: Twayne, 1969.
Schmerl, Rudolf B. "Fantasy as Technique." *Virginia Quarterly Review* 43, no. 4 (1967):644–56.
Shahane, V. A. *E. M. Forster: A Study in Double Vision*. New Delhi: Arnold-Heinemann, 1975.
Shusterman, David. *The Quest for Certitude in E. M. Forster's Fiction*. Bloomington: Indiana University Press, 1965.
Thomson, George H. *The Fiction of E. M. Forster*. Detroit: Wayne State University Press, 1967.
Trilling, Lionel. *E. M. Forster*. Norfolk, Conn.: New Directions, 1943.

John Galsworthy
Poettgen, Heinz, and Stader, Karl Heinz. "John Galsworthy's 'The Man Who Kept his Form.'" *Die Neueren Sprachen* 4 (1956):158–70.

Reilly, Joseph P. "John Galsworthy and His Short Stories." *Catholic World* 123 (1926):754–62.

Smit, Jan Henrik. *The Short Stories of John Galsworthy*. Rotterdam: Druk D. van Sihn Y Zonen, 1947.

Zumwatt, E. E. "The Myth of the Garden in Galsworthy's 'Apple Tree.'" *Research Studies* (Washington) 27 (1959):129–34.

George Gissing

Cope, Jackson I. "Definition as Structure in Gissing's 'Ryecroft Papers.'" *Modern Fiction Studies* 3 (1957):127–40.

Coustillas, Pierre, and Partridge, Colin, eds. *Gissing: The Critical Heritage*. London: Routledge & Kegan Paul, 1972.

Harris, Wendell. "An Approach to Gissing's Short Stories." *Studies in Short Fiction* 2 (1965):138–40.

Mitchell, J. M. "Notes on George Gissing's Stories." *Studies in English Literature* (Tokyo) 38 (1962):195–205.

R. B. Cunninghame Graham

Davies, Laurence. "Cunninghame Graham's South American Sketches," *Comparative Literature Studies* 9 (1972):253–65.

Gallo, Antonio, and Arce, J. M. *Robert Cunninghame Graham: Vida y Obra*. New York: Hispanic Institute, 1947.

Kocmanová, Jessie. "R. B. Cunninghame Graham: A Little Known Master of Realist Prose." *Philologica Pragensia* 7, no. 1 (1964):14–30.

Macauley, Robie. "Stranger, Tread Light." *Kenyon Review* 17 (1955):280–90.

MacShane, Frank. "R. B. Cunninghame Graham." *South Atlantic Quarterly* 68 (1969):198–207.

Smith, James S. "R. B. Cunninghame Graham as a Writer of Short Fiction." *English Literature in Transition* 12 (1969):61–75.

Stallman, Robert Wooster. "Robert Cunninghame Graham's South American Sketches." *Hispania* 28 (1945):69–75.

Watts, Cedric, and Davies, Laurence. *Cunninghame Graham: A Critical Biography*. Cambridge: Cambridge University Press, 1979.

Graham Greene

Atkins, John. *Graham Greene*. London: Calder & Boyars, 1966.

Boardman, Gwenn R. *The Aesthetics of Exploration*. Gainesville: University of Florida Press, 1971.

Coulthard, A. R. "Graham Greene's 'The Hint of an Explanation': A Reinterpretation." *Studies in Short Fiction* 8, no. 4 (1971):601–5.

DeVitis, A. A. *Graham Greene*. New York: Twayne, 1964.

Evans, Robert O. *Graham Greene: Some Critical Considerations*. Lexington: University of Kentucky Press, 1963.

Hynes, Samuel. *Graham Greene: A Collection of Critical Essays*. Englewood Cliffs, N.J.: Prentice-Hall, Inc., 1973.

Koga, Hideo. "Graham Greene as a Short Story Writer." In *Essays on Graham Greene and His Work*. Hiroshima: Hiroshima University Press, 1977.

Kunkel, Francis L. *The Labyrinthine Ways of Graham Greene*. Mamaroneck, N.Y.: Paul P. Appel Publishers, 1973.

Liberman, M. M. "The Uses of Anti-Fiction: Greene's 'Across the Bridge.' " *Georgia Review* 27 (1973):321–28.

Lodge, David. *Graham Greene*. New York: Columbia University Press, 1966.

McCartney, Jesse F. "Politics in Graham Greene's 'The Destructors.' " *Southern Humanities Review* 12 (1978):31–41.

Stinson, John J. "Graham Greene's 'The Destructors': Fable for a World Far East of Eden." *American Benedictine Review* 24 (1973):510–18.

Zambrano, Ana Laura. "Greene's Visions of Childhood: 'The Basement Room' and *The Fallen Idol*," *Literature/Film Quarterly*, 2, no. 4 (1974):324–31.

Frederick Philip Grove

Spettigue, Douglas O. *FPG: The European Years*. Ontario: Oberon Press, 1973.

————. *Frederick Philip Grove*. Studies in Canadian Literature Series, no. 3. Toronto: Copp Clark, 1969.

Stobie, Margaret. *Frederick Philip Grove* New York: Twayne, 1973.

Sutherland, Ronald. *Frederick Philip Grove*. Toronto: McClelland & Stewart, 1969.

Rider Haggard

Scott, J. E. "Hatchers-out of Tales." *New Colophon* 1 (1948):348–56.

Thomas Hardy

Benazon, Michael. "Dark and Fair: Character Contrast in Hardy's 'Fiddler of the Reels.' " *Ariel* 9, no. 2 (1978):75–82.

Brady, Kristin. "Conventionality as Narrative Technique in Hardy's 'On the Western Circuit.' " *Journal of the Eighteen Nineties Society* 9 (1978):22–30.

Carpenter, Richard C. *Thomas Hardy*. New York: Twayne, 1964, 69–79.

Guerard, Albert. *Thomas Hardy: The Novels and Stories*. Cambridge: Harvard University Press, 1949.

Kaneko, Masonabu. "Hardy no Tanpenshosetsu" ["Hardy's Short Stories"]. In *20 Seiki Bungaku no Senkusha Thomas Hardy* [*Thomas Hardy as a Forerunner of Twentieth-Century Literature*], edited by Mamoru Osawa, 319–47. Tokyo: Shinozaki Shorin, 1977.

O'Connor, W. V. "Cosmic Irony in Hardy's 'The Three Strangers.' " *English Journal* 47 (1958):248–54.

Quinn, Marie A. "Thomas Hardy and the Short Story." In *Budmouth Essays on Thomas Hardy*, edited by F. B. Pinion, 54–85. Dorchester: Hardy Society, 1976.

Wilson, Keith. "Hardy and the Hangman: The Dramatic Appeal of 'The Three Strangers.' " *English Literature in Transition* 24 (1981):155–60.

L. P. Hartley

Jones, Edward T. *L. P. Hartley* Boston: Twayne, 1978.

G. A. Henty

Schmidt, Nancy J. "The Writer as Teacher: A Comparison of the African Adventure Stories of G. A. Henty, René Guillot and Barbara Kimenye." *African Studies Review* 19, no. 2 (1976):69–80.

Montague Rhodes James

Butts, Mary. "The Art of Montague Rhodes James." *London Mercury* 29 (1934):306–17.

Cox, J. R. "Ghostly Antiquary; The Stories of Montague Rhodes James." *English Literature In Transition* 12 (1969):197–202.

Lloyd, L. J. "The Ghost Stories of Montague Rhodes James " *Book Handbook* 4 (1947):237–52.

Penzoldt, Peter. *The Supernatural in Fiction*. London: Peter Nevill, 1952, 191–202.

Richardson, Maurice. "The Psychoanalysis of Ghost Stories." *Twentieth Century* 166 (1959).419–31.

Russell, Samuel D. "Irony and Horror: The Art of M. R. James." *Haunted* 1 (1964):43–52; (June 1968):96–106.

Warren, Austin. "The Marvels of M. R. James, Antiquary." *Connections* (Ann Arbor, Mich.), 1970, 86–107.

Wilson, Edmund. "A Treatise of Tales of Horror," *New Yorker* 27 May 1944, 72ff.: Reprinted in *Classics and Commercials* (New York: Farrar, Strauss, 1950), 172–81.

Rudyard Kipling

Arendt, Hannah. "The Imperialist Character." *Review of Politics* 12 (1950):303–20.

Barrie, James M. "Mr. Kipling's Stories." *Contemporary Review* 59 (1891):364–72.

Belliappa, K. C. "Kipling's *The Man Who Would Be King*: A Parable of Empire Building." *Commonwealth Quarterly* 2, no. 8 (1948):27–33.

Cooper, Frederic Taber. *Some English Story Tellers*. New York: Holt, 1912, 122–47.

Cornell, Louis L. "The Development of Kipling's Prose from 1883 *Through Plain Tales from the Hills*." *English Literature in Transition* 8, no. 4 (1964):194–206.

Croft-Cooke, Rupert. *Rudyard Kipling*. Denver: Swallow, 1948.

Dobrée, Bonamy. *Rudyard Kipling, Realist and Fabulist*. London & New York: Oxford University Press, 1967.

Falls, Cyril Bentham. *Rudyard Kipling: A Critical Study*. London: Secker, 1915.

Fussell, Paul. "Irony, Freemasonry, and Humane Ethics in Kipling's 'The Man Who Would Be King.' " *English Literary History* 25 (1958):216–33.

Gilbert, Elliot L. "The Aesthetics of Violence." *English Literature in Transition* 7, no. 4 (1964):207–17.

————. *The Good Kipling: Studies in the Short Story*. Athens: Ohio University Press, 1970.

————. *Kipling and the Critics*. New York: New York University Press, 1965.

Gosse, Edmund. "Two Pastels, 1l: Mr. Rudyard Kipling's Short Stories." In *Questions at Issue*, 255–93. London: Heinemann, 1893.

Harrison, James. "Kipling's Jungle Eden," *Mosaic*, 7, no. 2 (1974):151–64.

Hart, Walter Morris. *Kipling the Story Writer*. Berkeley: University of California Press, 1918.

Henn, T. R. *Kipling*. London: Oliver & Boyd, 1967, 19–62, 125–37.

Hicks, Granville. *Figures of Transition: A Study of British Literature at the End of the Nineteenth Century*. New York: Macmillan, 1939, 276–83, 301–11.

Hinchcliffe, Peter. "Coming to Terms with Kipling: *Puck of Pook's Hill, Rewards and Fairies*, and the Shape of Kipling's Imagination." *University of Toronto Quarterly* 45 (1975):75–90.

Hooker, William Brian. "The Later Work of Mr. Kipling." *North American Review* (Boston) 193 (1911):721–32.

James, Henry. Introduction to *Mine Own People*. New York: International Publishing, 1891. Reprinted in *Views and Reviews* (Boston: Ball Publishing, 1908), 225–41.

Jarrell, Randall. "On Preparing to Read Kipling." *American Scholar* 31 (1962):220–35. Reprinted in *A Sad Heart at the Supermarket* (New York: Atheneum, 1962), 114–39.

Kaufman, Esther. "Kipling and the Technique of Action." *Nineteenth Century Fiction* 6 (1951):107–20.

Lang, Andrew. "Mr. Kipling's Stories." In *Essays in Little*, 198–205. New York: Scribner, 1891.

Le Gallienne, Richard. *Rudyard Kipling: A Criticism*. London: John Lane, 1900.

Lyon, James K. "Kipling's 'Soldiers Three' and Brecht's *A Man's a Man*." In *Essays on Brecht: Theater and Politics*, edited by Siegfried Mews and Herbert Knust, 99–113. Chapel Hill: University of North Carolina Press, 1974.

Mason, Eugene. "On the Short Story, and Two Modern Exemplars." In *A Book of Preferences in Literature*, 41–66. London: John Wilson, 1915.

Matthews, Brander. "The Story of the Short Story from Esop to Kipling." *Munsey's Magazine* 35 (1906):539–47.

Penzoldt, Peter. *The Supernatural in Fiction*. London: Peter Nevill, 1952, 118–45.

Rao, K. Bhaskara. *Rudyard Kipling's India*. Norman: University of Oklahoma Press, 1967.

Rodway, A. E. "The Last Phase." In *From Dickens to Hardy*, edited by Boris Ford, 385–98, 401, 403. Harmondsworth: Penguin, 1958.

Routh, Harold Victor. *English Literature and Ideas in the Twentieth Century: An Inquiry into Present Difficulties and Future Prospects*. New York: Longmans, 1948, 12–19.

Rutherford, Andrew. *Kipling's Mind and Art*. Stanford: Stanford University Press, 1974.

Shahane, Vasant A. *Rudyard Kipling: Activist and Artist*. Carbondale: Southern Illinois University Press, 1973, 82–107.

Singh, Bhupal. "Rudyard Kipling." In *A Survey of Anglo-Indian Fiction*, 68–108. London: Oxford University Press, 1934.

Stewart, J. I. M. "Kipling." In *Eight Modern Writers*, 223–93. Oxford: Clarendon Press, 1963.

———. *Rudyard Kipling*. New York: Dodd, Mead & Co., 1966.

Tompkins, J. M. S. *The Art of Rudyard Kipling*. Lincoln: University of Nebraska Press, 1965.

———. "Kipling's Later Tales: The Theme of Healing." *Modern Language Review* 45 (1950):18–32.

Wilson, Angus. *The Strange Ride of Rudyard Kipling: His Life and Works*. New York: Viking Press, 1978.

Wilson, Edmund. "The Kipling that Nobody Reads." *Atlantic Monthly* 167 (February 1941):201–14; (March 1941):350–54. Reprinted in *The Wound and the Bow* (Boston: Houghton, 1941).

D. H. Lawrence

Amon, Frank. "D. H. Lawrence and the Short Story." In *The Achievement of D. H. Lawrence*, edited by Frederick J. Hoffman and Harry T. Moore, 222–34. Norman: University of Oklahoma Press, 1953.

Becker, George H. *D. H. Lawrence*. New York: Frederick Ungar Publishing Co., 1980.

Cowan, James, C. *D. H. Lawrence: An Annotated Bibliography of Writings About Him*. 2 vols. De Kalb: Northern Illinois University Press, 1982–84.

Cushman, Keith. "The Achievement of *England, My England and Other Stories*." In *D. H. Lawrence: The Man Who Lived*, edited by Robert B. Partlow and Harry T. Moore, 27–38. Carbondale: Southern Illinois University Press, 1980.

———. *D. H. Lawrence at Work: The Emergence of the "Prussian Officers" Stories*. Charlottesville: University Press of Virginia, 1978.

———. "D. H. Lawrence at Work: 'The Shadow in the Rose Garden.'" *D. H. Lawrence Review* 8 (1975):31–46.

———. "The Young D. H. Lawrence and the Short Story." *Modern British Literature* 2 (1978):101–12.

Draper, Ronald P. *D. H. Lawrence*. New York: Twayne, 1964.

Ford, George H. *Double Measure: A Study of the Novels and Stories of D. H. Lawrence*. New York: Holt, Rinehart & Winston, 1965.

Garcia, Reloy, and Karaboatsos, James, eds. *Concordance to the Short Fiction of D. H Lawrence*. Lincoln: University of Nebraska Press, 1972.

Harris, Janice. "Insight and Experiment in D. H. Lawrence's Early Short Fiction." *Philological Quarterly* 55 (1976):418–35.

Hirsch, Gordon D. "The Laurentian Double: Images of D. H. Lawrence in the Stories." *D. H. Lawrence Review* 10 (1977):270–76.

Hobsbaum, Philip. *A Reader's Guide to D. H. Lawrence*. London: Thames & Hudson, 1980.

Hough, Graham. *The Dark Sun: A Study of D. H. Lawrence*. London: Duckworth, 1956.

Kalnins, Mara. "D. H. Lawrence's 'Two Marriages' and 'Daughters of the Vicar.'" *Ariel* 7 (1976):32–49.

Kinkead-Weekes, Mark. "The Marble and the Statue: The Exploratory Imagination of D. H. Lawrence." In *Imagined Worlds: Essays on Some English Novels and Novelists in Honour of John Butt*, edited by Maynard Mack and Ian Gregor, 371–418. London: Methuen & Co. Ltd., 1968.

Krishnamurthi, M. G. *D. H. Lawrence: Tale as a Medium*. Mysore: Rao & Raghavan, 1970.

Littlewood, J. C. F. "D. H. Lawrence's Early Tales." *Cambridge Quarterly* 1 (1966):107–24.

Mackenzie, D. Kenneth. "Ennui and Energy in *England, My England*." In *D. H. Lawrence: A Critical Study of the Major Novels and Other Writings*, edited by A. H. Gomme, 120–41. New York: Barnes & Noble, 1978.

Moynahan, Julian. *The Deed of Life: The Novels and Tales of D. H. Lawrence*. Princeton: Princeton University Press, 1963.

Nehls, Edward H. *D. H. Lawrence: A Composite Biography*. 3 vols. Madison: University of Wisconsin Press, 1957–59.

Niven, Alistair. *D. H. Lawrence: The Writer and his Work*. London: Longman Group, 1980.

Piccolo, Anthony. "Ritual Strategy: Concealed Form in the Short Stories of D. H. Lawrence." *Mid-Hudson Language Studies* 2 (1979):88–99.

Pinion, F. B. *A D. H. Lawrence Companion: Life, Thought, and Works*. London: Macmillan, 1978.

Poynter, John S. "The Early Short Stories of D. H. Lawrence." In *D. H. Lawrence: The Man Who Lived*, edited by Robert B. Partlow and Harry T. Moore, 39–41. Carbondale: Southern Illinois University Press, 1980.

Pritchard, R. E. *D. H. Lawrence: Body of Darkness*. London: Hutchinson University Library, 1971.

Rose, Shirley. "Physical Trauma in D. H. Lawrence's Short Fiction." *Contemporary Literature* 16 (1975):73–83.

Ross, Donald, Jr. "Who's Talking? How Characters Become Narrators in Fiction." *Modern Language Notes* 91 (1976):1222–42.

Scott, James F. "D. H. Lawrence's Germania: Ethnic Psychology and Cultural Crisis in the Shorter Fiction." *D. H. Lawrence Review* 10 (1977):142–64.

Slade, Tony. *D. H. Lawrence*. New York: Arco Publishing Co., 1970.

Temple, J. "The Definition of Innocence: A Consideration of the Short Stories of D. H. Lawrence." *Studia Germanica Gaudensia* 20 (1979):105–18.

Vickery, John B. "Myth and Ritual in the Shorter Fiction of D. H. Lawrence." *Modern Fiction Studies* 5 (1959):65–82.

West, Anthony. *D. H. Lawrence*. London: Arthur Barker, 1950.

Widmer, Kingsley. *The Art of Perversity: D. H. Lawrence's Shorter Fictions*. Seattle: University of Washington Press, 1962.

Henry Lawson

Dobrez, Livio. "The Craftsmanship of Lawson Revisited." *Australian Literary Studies* 7 (1976):375–88.

Hope, A. D. *Native Companions*. Sydney: Angus & Robertson, 1974, 216–24, 262–76.

Kiernan, Brian. "Ways of Seeing: Henry Lawson's 'Going Blind.'" *Australian Literary Studies* 9 (1980):286–97.

Maddocks, John. "Narrative Technique in Lawson's Joe Wilson Stories." *Southerly* 37 (1977):97–107.

Matthews, Brian. *The Receding Wave: Henry Lawson's Prose.* Melbourne: Melbourne University Press, 1972.

Murray-Smith, Stephen. *Henry Lawson.* Melbourne: Lansdowne Press, 1962.

Phillips, A. A. *Henry Lawson.* New York: Twayne, 1970.

Roderick, Colin, ed. *Henry Lawson Criticism 1894–1971.* Sydney: Angus & Robertson, 1972.

————. *Henry Lawson: Poet and Short Story Writer.* Sydney: Angus & Robertson, 1966.

————. "Henry Lawson's Joe Wilson: Skeleton Novel or Short Story Sequence?" *Overland* 66 (1977):35–47.

Stephen Leacock

Curry, Ralph, and Lewis, Janet. "Stephen Leacock: An Early Influence on F. Scott Fitzgerald." *Canadian Review of American Studies* 7 (1976):5–14.

Ferris, Ina. "The Face in the Window: *Sunshine Sketches* Reconsidered." *Studies in Canadian Literature* 3 (1978):178–85.

Kushner, J., and MacDonald, R. D. "Leacock: Economist/Satirist in *Arcadian Adventures* and *Sunshine Sketches.*" *Dalhousie Review* 56 (1976):493–509.

Magee, William H. "Genial Humor in Stephen Leacock." *Dalhousie Review* 56 (1976):268–82.

Mantz, Douglas. "The Preposterous and the Profound: A New Look at the Envoi of *Sunshine Sketches.*" *Journal of Canadian Fiction* 19 (1977):95–105.

Zegulka, J. M. "Passionate Provincials: Imperialism, Regionalism, and Point of View." *Journal of Canadian Fiction* 22 (1978):80–92.

Wyndham Lewis

Beatty, Michael. "The Earliest Fiction on Wyndham Lewis and *The Wild Body.*" *Theoria* 48 (1977):37–45.

Lafourcade, Bernard. "The Taming of the Wild Body." In *Wyndham Lewis, a Revaluation: New Essays,* edited by Jeffrey Meyers, 68–84. Montreal: McGill-Queen's Press, 1980.

Arthur Machen

Gekle, William Francis. *Arthur Machen: Weaver of Fantasy.* Millbrook, N.Y.: Round Table Press, 1949.

Matteson, Robert S. "Arthur Machen: A Vision of an Enchanted Land." *Personalist* 46 (1965):253–68.

Tyler, Robert L. "Arthur Machen: The Minor Writer and His Function." *Approach: A Literary Quarterly,* 1960, 21–26.

Roger Mais

Ogunyemi, Chikwenye Okonjo. "From a Goat Path in Africa: Roger Mais and Jean Toomer." *Obsidian* 5, no. 3 (1979):7–21.

Katherine Mansfield

Alpers, Antony. *The Life of Katherine Mansfield.* New York: Viking Press, 1980.

Berkman, Sylvia. *Katherine Mansfield: A Critical Study.* New Haven: Yale University Press, 1951.

Bowen, Elizabeth. Introduction to *Stories by Katherine Mansfield.* New York: Vintage, 1956.

Daly, Saralyn. *Katherine Mansfield.* New York: Twayne, 1965.

Gordon, Ian A. *Katherine Mansfield.* London: Longmans, Green, & Co., 1963.

L. M. [Ida Baker]. *Katherine Mansfield: The Memories of L. M.* London: Michael Joseph, 1971.

McLaughlin, Ann L. "The Same Job: The Shared Writing Aims of Katherine Mansfield and Virginia Woolf." *Modern Fiction Studies* 24, no. 3 (1978):369–82.

Magalaner, Marvin. *The Fiction of Katherine Mansfield.* Carbondale: Southern Illinois University Press, 1971.

Meyers, Jeffrey. "Katherine Mansfield: A Bibliography of International Criticism, 1921–1977." *Bulletin of Bibliography and Magazine Notes* 34 (1977):53–67.

———. *Katherine Mansfield: A Biography.* London: Hamish Hamilton, 1978.

Murry, John Middleton. *Katherine Mansfield and Other Literary Studies.* London: Constable, 1959.

Sutherland, Ronald. "Katherine Mansfield: Plagiarist, Disciple, or Ardent Admirer." *Critique* 5, no. 2 (1962):58–76.

W. Somerset Maugham

Cordell, Richard A. *Somerset Maugham: A Writer for All Seasons.* Bloomington: Indiana University Press, 1969.

Curtis, Anthony. *Somerset Maugham.* New York: Macmillan, 1977.

Gordon, Caroline. "Notes on Chekhov and Maugham." *Sewanee Review* 57, no. 3 (1949):401–10.

Huxley, Aldous. "Wordsworth in the Tropics." In *Do What You Will*, 123–39. Garden City, N.Y.: Doubleday, Doran & Co., 1929.

Morgan, Ted. *Maugham: A Biography.* New York: Simon & Schuster, 1980.

George Meredith

Ketcham, Carl H. "Meredith at Work: 'The Tale of Chloe.'" *Nineteenth Century Fiction* 21 (1966):235–48.

Arthur Morrison

Bell, Jocelyn. "A Study of Arthur Morrison." *Essays and Studies*, 1952, 77–89.

Findlater, Jane Helen. "The Slum Movement in Fiction." *National Review* 35 (1900):447–54. Reprinted in *Stones from a Glass House* (London: James Nisbet, 1904), 65–88.

Hector Hugh Munro ("Saki")

Cheikin, Miriam Quen. "Saki: Practical Jokes as a Clue to Comedy." *English Literature in Transition* 21 (1978):121–33.

Gillen, Charles H. *H. H. Munro*. New York: Twayne, 1969.

Langguth, A. J. *Saki: A Life of Hector Hugh Munro*. New York: Simon & Schuster, 1981.

Mais, S. P. B. "The Humour of Saki." In *Books and Their Writers*, 311–30. London: Grant Richards, 1920.

Orel, Harold. "H. H. Munro and the Sense of a Failed Community." *Modern British Literature* 4 (1979):87–96.

Porterfield, Alexander. "Saki." *London Mercury* 12 (1925):385–94.

Spear, G. J. *The Satire of Saki*. New York: Exposition Press, 1963.

T. F. Powys

Hunter, W. *The Novels and Stories of T. F. Powys*. Cambridge: Cambridge University Press, 1930.

V. S. Pritchett

Hughes, Douglass, A. "V. S. Pritchett: An Interview." *Studies in Short Fiction* 13 (1976):423–32.

Jean Rhys

Blodgett, Harriet. "Tigers Are Better-Looking to Jean Rhys," *Arizona Quarterly* 32, no. 3 (1976):227–44.

Casey, Nancy J. "The 'Liberated' Woman in Jean Rhys's Later Short Fiction." *Revista/Review Interamericana* 4, no. 2 (1974):204–72.

Mellown, Elgin N. "A Bibliography of the Writings of Jean Rhys, With a Selected List of Reviews and Other Critical Writings." *World Literature Written in English* 16 (1977):179–202.

Mizener, Arthur. *The Saddest Story*. New York: World Publishing Co., 1971, 344–50.

Morrell, A. C. "The World of Jean Rhys's Short Stories." *World Literature Written in English* 18 (1979):235–44.

Staley, Thomas F. "The Emergence of a Form: Style and Consciousness in Jean Rhys's Quartet." *Twentieth Century Literature* 24, no. 2 (1978):202–24.

————. *Jean Rhys: A Critical Study*. Austin: University of Texas Press, 1979.

Wolfe, Peter. *Jean Rhys*. Boston: Twayne, 1980.

Henry Handel Richardson

Elliott, William D. *Henry Handel Richardson (Ethel Florence Lindesay Richardson)*. Boston: Twayne, 1975.

Steele Rudd

Hope, A. D. *Native Companions*. Sydney: Angus & Robertson, 1974, 262–76.

Ilkin, Van. "Steele Rudd as Failed Artist." *Southerly* 36 (1976):363–76.

William Sansom

Chalpin, Lila. *William Sansom*. Boston: Twayne, 1980.

Firchow, Peter. *The Writer's Place*. Minneapolis: University of Minnesota Press, 1974.

Michel-Michot, Paulette. *William Sansom: A Critical Assessment*. Paris: Société d' Edition "Les Belles Lettres," 1971.

Neumeyer, Peter F. "Franz Kafka and William Sansom." *Wisconsin Studies in Contemporary Literature* 7 (1966):76–84.

Frank Sargeson

Edmond, Lauris. "The Later Stories." *Islands* 2 (1973):415–23.

Dorothy Sayers

Durkin, Mary Brian. *Dorothy L. Sayers*. Boston: Twayne, 1980.

Hone, Ralph E. *Dorothy L. Sayers: A Literary Biography*. Kent: Kent State University Press, 1979.

Olive Schreiner

Marquard, Jean. "Olive Schreiner's 'Prelude': The Child as Artist." *English Studies in Africa* 22 (1979):1–11.

Wilhelm, Cherry. "Olive Schreiner: Child of Queen Victoria: Stories, Dreams, Allegories." *English in Africa* 6, no. 2 (1979):63–69.

May Sinclair

Zegger, Hrisey D. *May Sinclair*. Boston: Twayne, 1976.

Robert Louis Stevenson

Beach, Joseph Warren. "The Sources of Stevenson's 'Bottle Imp.' " *Modern Language Notes* 25 (1910):12–18.

Egan, J. J. " 'Markheim': A Drama of Moral Psychology." *Nineteenth Century Fiction* 20 (1966):377–84.

Paluka, F. J. "Technique in Four Stevenson Stories." *Florida State University Studies* 11 (1953):75–88.

Parsons, C. O. "Stevenson's Use of Witchcraft in 'Thrawn Janet.' " *Studies in Philology* 43 (1946):551–71.

Saposnik, I. S. " 'Markheim': A Fictional Christmas Sermon." *Nineteenth Century Fiction* 21 (1966):277–82.

Swearingen, Roger G. *The Prose Writings of Robert Louis Stevenson: A Guide*. Hamden, Conn.: Shoe String Press, 1980.

Evelyn Waugh

Blayac, Alain. " 'Bella Fleace Gave a Party' or, The Archetypal Image of Waugh's Sense of Decay." *Studies in Short Fiction* 15 (1978):69–73.

Stannard, Martin. "Work Suspended: Waugh's Climacteric." *Essays in Criticism* 28 (1978):302–20.

H. G. Wells

Bergonzi, Bernard. *The Early H. G. Wells*. Manchester: Manchester University Press, 1961.

Costa, Richard. *H. G. Wells*. New York: Twayne, 1967.

McConnell, Frank. *The Science Fiction of H. G. Wells*. New York: Oxford University Press, 1981.

Williamson, Jack. *H. G. Wells: Critic of Progress*. Baltimore, Md.: Mirage Press, 1973.

P. G. Wodehouse

Aldridge, John W. "P. G. Wodehouse: The Lesson of the Young Master." In *New World Writing No. 13*. New York: New American Library, 1958.

Donaldson, Frances. *P. G. Wodehouse: A Biography*. New York: Knopf, 1982.

French, R. B. D. *P. G. Wodehouse*. Edinburgh: Oliver & Boyd, 1966.

Green, Benny. *P. G. Wodehouse: A Literary Biography*. London: Rutledge Press, 1981.

Hall, Robert A., Jr. *The Comic Style of P. G. Wodehouse*. Hamden, Conn.: Archon, 1974.

Heineman, J. H., and Bensen, D. R., eds. *P. G. Wodehouse: A Centenary Celebration, 1881–1981*. London: Oxford University Press, 1981.

Jasen, David A. *P. G. Wodehouse: A Portrait of a Master*. New York: Mason & Lipscomb, 1974. Rev. ed., 1981.

Olney, Clarke, "Wodehouse and the Poets." *Georgia Review* 16, no. 4 (1962):392–99.

Orwell, George. "In Defense of P. G. Wodehouse." In *Dickens, Dali and Others*. New York: Reynal & Hitchcock, 1946.

Stevenson, Lionel. "The Antecedents of P. G. Wodehouse." *Arizona Quarterly* 5 (1959):226–34.

Swinnerton, Frank. *The Georgian Literary Scene*. 6th ed. New York: Farrar & Strauss, 1951.

Usborne, Richard. *Wodehouse at Work*. London: Herbert Jenkins, 1961.

———. *Wodehouse at Work to the End*. London: Barrie & Jenkins, 1976.

Voorhees, Richard J. *P. G. Wodehouse*. New York: Twayne, 1966.

West, Robert H. "The High Art of Quality Frivolity." *South Atlantic Bulletin* 37, no. 1 (1972):12–19.

Wind, Herbert W. *The World of P. G. Wodehouse*. New York: Praeger, 1972.

Virginia Woolf

Baldeshweiler, Eileen. "The Lyric Short Story: the Sketch of a History." *Studies in Modern Short Fiction* 6, no. 4 (1969):443–53.

Bell, Quentin. *Virginia Woolf*. 2 vols. London: Hogarth Press, 1972.

Blackstone, Bernard. *Virginia Woolf: A Commentary*. New York: Harcourt, Brace, Jovanovich, 1972.

Daiches, David. *Virginia Woolf*. Rev. ed. New York: New Directions, 1963.

Fleishman, Avrom. "Forms of the Woolfian Short Story." In *Virginia Woolf: Revaluation and Continuity*, edited by Ralph Freedman, 44–70. Berkeley: University of California Press, 1980.

Guiguet, Jean. *Virginia Woolf and Her Works*. New York: Harcourt, Brace & World, 1966.

Lewis, Thomas S. W. "Vision in Time: Virginia Woolf's 'An Unwritten Novel.' " in *Virginia Woolf: A Collection of Criticism*, edited by Thomas S. W. Lewis, 15–22. New York: McGraw-Hill, 1975.

Israel Zangwill

Adams, Elsie Bonita. *Israel Zangwill*. New York: Twayne, 1971.

Wohlgelernter, Maurice. *Israel Zangwill: A Study*. New York: Columbia University Press, 1964.

Index